STUDY GUIDE FOR USE WITH

Labour Market
ECONOMICS
Theory, Evidence and Policy in Canada
Fifth Edition

Dwayne Benjamin
University of Toronto

Morley Gunderson
University of Toronto

W. Craig Riddell
University of British Columbia

Prepared by
David Gray
University of Ottawa

McGraw-Hill
Ryerson

Toronto Montréal Boston Burr Ridge, IL Dubuque, IA Madison, WI New York
San Francisco St. Louis Bangkok Bogotá Caracas Kuala Lumpur Lisbon London Madrid
Mexico City Milan New Delhi Santiago Seoul Singapore Sydney Taipei

McGraw-Hill
Ryerson Limited

A Subsidiary of The **McGraw·Hill** Companies

STUDY GUIDE
for use with
Labour Market Economics
Fifth Edition

ISBN: 0-07-089155-9

1 2 3 4 5 6 7 8 9 10 CP 0 9 8 7 6 5 4 3 2

Printed and bound in Canada

Vice President and Editorial Director: Pat Ferrier
Senior Sponsoring Editor: Lynn Fisher
Developmental Editor: Daphne Scriabin
Marketing Manager: Kelly Smyth
Production Coordinator: Madeleine Harrington
Printer: Canadian Printco, Ltd.

TABLE OF CONTENTS

Chapter 1   Introduction to Labour Market Economics 1
Chapter 2   Labour Supply: Individual Attachment to the Labour Market........................ 5
Chapter 3   Labour Supply and Public Policy: Work Incentive Effects of
             Alternative Income Maintenance Schemes 17
Chapter 4   Labour Supply Over the Life Cycle 26
Chapter 5   Demand for Labour in Competitive Labour Markets...................................... 35
Chapter 6   Labour Demand, Nonwage Benefits, and Quasi-Fixed Costs........................ 45
Chapter 7   Wages and Employment in a Single Labour Market 53
Chapter 8   Compensating Wage Differentials 63
Chapter 9   Human Capital Theory: Applications to Education and Training................... 72
Chapter 10   Wage Structures Across Markets 84
Chapter 11   The Economics of Immigration.. 95
Chapter 12   Discrimination and Male-Female Earnings Differentials 103
Chapter 13   Optimal Compensation Systems, Deferred Compensation, and
             Mandatory Retirement.. 113
Chapter 14   Union Grown and Incidence 123
Chapter 15   Wage and Employment Determination Under Collective Bargaining............. 130
Chapter 16   Union Impact on Wage and Nonwage Outcomes 141
Chapter 17   Unemployment: Meaning and Measurement 151
Chapter 18   Unemployment: Causes and Consequences.. 160
Chapter 19   Wage Changes, Price Inflation, and Unemployment 172

PREFACE

Although this well-known textbook dates back many years to the first edition of Gunderson and Riddell, there has never been a study guide for Canada's premier labour economics textbook until now. Although there always existed problems and questions at the end of each chapter, I suspect that almost all students, including my own, totally ignored them unless the professor assigned them. Even in that case, unless the solutions are provided, the students approach end-of-chapter questions and problems with great trepidation, as they have no idea what type of answer is expected from them. As a result, end-of-chapter exercises in most textbooks are seldom utilized by the students. Four years ago, McGraw-Hill Ryerson requested that I author a solutions manual for all of the hundreds of end-of-chapter exercises in the Benjamin, Gunderson, and Riddell textbook. That manual also contained hundreds of multiple choice questions that were designed primarily for testing purposes. The distribution of that manual was limited to instructors, however, who could release only the solutions to selected problems by the cumbersome process of photocopying. In response to the request by some instructors for a study guide that could be distributed directly to students, as exists for any introductory text, McGraw-Hill Ryerson has published this work.

The purpose of this study guide is straightforward. As I perceptually tell my students in my school-marmish demeanour, they grossly overestimate their grasp and retention of the material that I present during my lectures. I often say that after having delivered any lecture, while about 75% of the points go over their heads, the students perceive that only 25% of the material remains to be learned. One of the keys to academic success is to "know when you do not know," and hence, further study, review, and exercise are required. The study guide is thus designed to provide students with practice opportunities, illustrations of the major points, models, and concepts, and many samples of potential examination material. That final feature, of course, is the ultimate motivator. Overall, it is designed to be a one-stop-shop as far as studying activities are concerned, which should facilitate these activities.

Each chapter of the study guide is divided into six parts. First, there are the "Chapter Highlights," which are organized according to the same scheme as each chapter. These chapter summaries are more involved than the ones that appear at the end of each chapter in the textbook, but not too lengthy so that they lose their original purpose as an outline of the major points and concepts. This feature was not contained in the solution's manual that accompanied the fourth edition. The next part of each chapter of the study guide is the "Helpful Hints" section, which is also a novel feature. In developing this brief section, I relied on my memory, trying to recall the specific points of confusion that my own students revealed to me as we covered the material. I also added tips that I think most experienced teachers of economics know, such as the adage that one should draw the budget lines first and then draw the indifference curves with the points of tangency. The "Helpful Hints" section lists some common mistakes and perils to which I have been sensitized due to my teaching experience. In particular, the most common error is confusing one element of a course — often presented in another chapter — with another.

The third and the fourth sections consist of the solutions to the end-of-chapter questions and the end-of-chapter problems, respectively. The fifth edition of the textbook contains many totally new exercises, most of which I think are of high quality, substantive, and of reasonable difficulty. A good number of exercises from the prior versions of the textbook have been dropped. All of these revised exercises have been road-tested, and in my view, very few of them are of the window-dressing type. I have attempted to provide thorough pedagogical explanations to all solutions. From my undergraduate days, I recall my intimidating frustration with skimpy solutions manuals — typically authored by graduate students with zero teaching experience — that had an "emperor's new clothes" tone. For many problems, the final equation or calculation was presented, but the process was so obvious to any student of normal intelligence that no explanation of the approach and the steps taken was necessary. In this part of the study guide, I have strived to stress the lesson that is to be learned from each problem or question: That is, what point from the textbook is being evoked and illustrated?

Each multiple choice question has five responses. In my view, most of them are of intermediate-level difficulty. None of them are arduously long, and I have studiously avoided double-layered multiple choice questions that students despise.

The final section of each chapter consists of the answers to the multiple choice questions. For most questions, I have provided a brief comment on the incorrect answers as well as the correct answers, a feature that I believe is fairly rare in study guides. Since we as a profession often rely heavily on this mode of evaluation, these explanations are designed to not only assist learning and clear up confusion but also to give students more practice in taking multiple choice examinations. Hopefully, they will feel more comfortable with multiple choice questions, regardless of their content.

Acknowledgements

I should like to thank Daphne Scriabin, at McGraw-Hill Ryerson, who served as my point-person and assisted with the production stages. Thanks also go to Carrie Withers and Madeleine Harrington. My friend and colleague Dwayne Benjamin of the University of Toronto provided me with useful advice and encouragement regarding how to raise my productivity. I also am grateful to my wife, Catherine, and my two daughters, Rachel and Rebecca, who supported me in a different way.

Ottawa, Ontario
January 2002

CHAPTER 1

Chapter Highlights

1. Decisions by Individuals, Firms, and Governments

The three major types of actors in labour markets are individuals, firms, and governments. The decisions of individuals underlie the labour supply, while the decisions of firms underlie the labour demand. Governments make a range of decisions that affect the environment in which the employees and employers interact. The basis of this textbook is the analytical framework in which the labour market operates.

2. Subject Matter of Labour Market Economics

The essence of labour market economics is an analysis of the determinants of the various dimensions of labour supply and demand and their interaction in market structures, as they in turn generate wages, employment, and unemployment. The two basic elements are labour supply and labour demand. Many facets of labour supply, such as immigration, retirement activity, and the decision to work part-time, lend themselves to economic analysis. Labour supply can be examined from quality perspectives as well as quantity perspectives, such as education and training. Many facets of labour demand, such as the roles of fixed versus variable labour costs, also lend themselves to economic analysis. Once the forces of labour demand and labour supply are superimposed, the three primary outcomes that are the focus of labour market analysis are equilibrium wages, employment, and unemployment. Labour markets give rise to wage structures, which consist of a hierarchy of wage differentials across occupations, regions, industrial sectors, gender, races, and so on. They also give rise to wage differentials by education level. Another facet of labour economics is its interface with human-resource management and industrial relations. Finally, the variable of unemployment is analysed from a microeconomic and a macroeconomic perspective.

3. Preliminary Explorations of Labour Market Outcomes

This section gives a brief statistical description of activity in the Canadian labour market. Examples are listed in Table 1.1. The distribution of earnings of individual workers in the Canadian labour market is illustrated in Figure 1.1, a diagram that is called a histogram. The distribution of hours worked of individual workers in the Canadian labour market is illustrated in Figure 1.2. These two diagrams illustrate the extent of two obvious facts: Not every worker earns the same wage, and not every worker works the same number of hours. If that were so, then we probably would not have much reason to study labour economics. The incredible variation in these major labour market outcomes of wages, employment, and unemployment give richness to the field of labour economics and forms the focus of labour market analysis.

4. The Supply-and-Demand Model: The Workhorse of Labour Economics

There are two primary ingredients of the neo-classical supply-and-demand model: behavioural assumptions regarding how buyers and sellers respond to prices and other factors, as well as assumptions about how buyers and sellers interact, and how the market determines the level and terms of exchange. In the purely neo-classical model, it is assumed that there are not many impediments to rapid and costless trade.

The two forces that underlie the basic model are supply and demand. Labour supply is the relationship between the quantity supplied of labour and the wage rate, holding all other factors fixed. Labour demand is the relationship between the quantity demanded of labour and the wage rate, holding all other factors fixed. The intersection of the two curves gives the equilibrium wage and equilibrium employment level. The wage that equilibrates the labour market is called the market-clearing wage. Although this equilibrium outcome often does not occur in practice, it serves as a useful benchmark wage and employment level to which actual wages and employment levels can be compared. A basic implication is that otherwise identical workers should be paid the same wage. Another implication is the absence of involuntary unemployment, which means that all of those who are willing to work at the going wage are employed. The fact that this prediction is often not realized in practice poses a challenge for the purely neo-classical supply-and-demand model, as does the observed phenomenon of persistent wage differentials between workers that appear to be fairly homogeneous. It turns out that the model can be embellished to take account of real-world features of labour markets, such as uncertainty and imperfect information. The central tenet of the neo-classical supply-and-demand model — that the market wage adjusts to clear the labour market — remains, but in the more complicated labour market models, wages play several other roles as well.

5.   Current Policy Issues

Labour economics is rich in applications of public policy interventions. On the supply side, income maintenance, income tax, and income transfer programs, such as unemployment insurance, play an important role in affecting choices. On the demand side, some policy questions have been brought to the fore because of new competitive pressures from sources such as global competition and rapid technological change. The wage differentials between educational categories are much higher than was the case 30 years ago, and the distribution of earnings is less equal. These phenomena are related to labour demand pressures, and there is pressure for government intervention. A pertinent policy question for macroeconomic analysis is the upward trend in unemployment since the early 1970s, and the possible interventions on the part of the government that may abate that trend.

6.   Similarities and Differences between the Labour Market and Other Markets

A key issue in labour market economics is whether the labour market is so different from other markets that the basic tools of economics, especially the neo-classical supply-and-demand model, do not apply. The labour market does indeed have some particular features that distinguish it from other markets, most notably the sociological, institutional, and legislative constraints that play a major role in labour markets. There is also a high degree of market imperfections, such as imperfect information. In addition, the primary price variable in the labour market, the wage, serves a variety of functions. The price of labour services — the wage — is also part of the worker's identity in society, and this has repercussions for how labour markets operate and how they are viewed. The fact that labour markets and how they operate are very much different than other types of markets has led many analysts to adopt an interdisciplinary approach that blends labour economics with domains such as industrial relations, human-resource management, and sociology.

7. Alternative Perspectives

There is a brief mention of three paradigms that are alternatives to the neo-classical model and are mostly antitheses to the neo-classical approach. These three approaches are institutionalism, dualism, and radicalism. Institutionalism eschews theoretical models and graphical analysis in favour of methodologies of descriptive realism and case studies. Dualism is also called segmentation theory; the labour market is characterized as dichotomous. Radicalism is typically based on Marxism, which emphasizes the role of class struggle between the labourers and the capitalists in shaping economic, political, and social activity.

Helpful Hints

- This chapter deserves a careful and thoughtful reading, as it highlights a number of themes that unify this entire textbook. It outlines the central economic actors, economic forces, economic assumptions, and economic outcomes that are part and parcel of the neo-classical approach to labour economics.
- Table 1.1 displays the mean income, or the average values, received by individual Canadian workers in 1994. The only statistic describing the distribution of income is the average. Figure 1.1 consists of a histogram of the distribution of labour market earnings of individuals. A histogram diagram shows the entire distribution rather than just one descriptive feature, such as the mean. A histogram can give you an idea of the dispersion of earnings among individuals, whereas a simple mean value cannot.
- Another statistic that describes the distribution of variables such as earnings is the median, which is the 50th percentile value. Whenever one is examining the distribution of variables such as earnings, it is desirable to know the mean, the median, and the standard deviation.

Multiple Choice Questions

1. What are the three primary economic outcomes that are the focus of labour economics?
   a) Wages, employment levels, and unemployment levels
   b) Wages, profits, and utility levels
   c) The wage structure, labour demand, and labour supply
   d) Institutionalism, dualism, and radicalism
   e) None of the above

2. What are the three major economic actors that are involved in shaping labour market outcomes?
   a) Wages, employment levels, and unemployment levels
   b) Wages, profits, and utility levels
   c) The labour market equilibrium, labour demand, and labour supply
   d) Firms, workers, and governments
   e) None of the above

3. Which of the following statements concerning the market clearing wage is *false*?
   a) It is the equilibrium wage level.
   b) It typically prevails in real-world labour markets.
   c) It is the wage level at which the quantity demanded of labour equals the quantity supplied of labour.
   d) It serves as a useful benchmark for evaluating wage outcomes.
   e) All of the above statements are false.

4. Which of the following statements is *true*?
   a) Labour market imperfections, such as uncertainty and imperfect information, render neo-classical labour market theory invalid.
   b) Conventional supply-and-demand analysis takes account of labour market imperfections, such as uncertainty and imperfect information.
   c) While one can apply supply-and-demand analysis to labour markets, labour markets have attributes that distinguish them in notable fashion from other types of markets.
   d) The existence of involuntary unemployment is ruled out in the purely neo-classical approach.
   e) The existence of wage differentials between seemingly identical workers is ruled out in the purely neo-classical approach.

5. What trait do the alternative perspectives of the labour market have in common?
   a) They are based on a class struggle between labourers and owners of capital.
   b) Market forces are the primary determinants of labour market outcomes, but these outcomes are often unjust.
   c) They all hold that the conventional labour market model should take account of imperfect information, political constraints, and uncertainty.
   d) They all hold that analysis should be based on descriptive realism rather than mathematical tools and graphical analysis.
   e) None of the above.

Answers to Multiple Choice Questions

1. A   This is made explicit on page 3. Response B gives outcomes, but not the most important ones. For response C, labour demand and labour supply are not outcomes. Response D refers to three different approaches.

2. D   This is made explicit on page 1. Response A refers to the three primary outcomes, and response B refers to other labour market outcomes. For response C, labour demand and labour supply are not economic decision-makers.

3. B   On page 12, the authors indicate that often the going wage is not the market-clearing wage. Responses A, C, and D are true. See the subsection entitled "Wages and Employment in a Competitive Labour Market."

4. C   See the subsection entitled "Wages and Employment in a Competitive Labour Market." For response C, see the last paragraph of that section on page 12.

5. E   Response A is only true for the Marxist perspective. For response B, neither dualism nor institutionalism accords much of a role for market forces in shaping labour market outcomes. For response C, all of these approaches claim that the market-based model should be jettisoned, not modified. Response D applies only to the institutionalist perspective; the Marxist approach can be quite analytically rigorous.

CHAPTER 2

Chapter Highlights

1.   Quantifying Labour Market Attachment

Labour supply is always analysed in a sequential procedure. First we analyse whether the individual participates in the labour force. If he/she does participate, then we determine the length of time that he/she works. Both of these questions can be analysed within the same framework.

The labour force (LF) is comprised of all working-age persons (POP, for population) who are active in the labour market, either employed (E) or unemployed (U), that is, LF = E + U. The labour force participation rate is the fraction of the working-age population that is in the labour force (LFPR = (E + U) / POP = LF / POP). The unemployment rate (UR) is the fraction of the labour force that is unemployed (U) and actively seeking employment.

The choice of how many hours to work includes choices such as the length of the workday, the length of the workweek (full-time versus part-time), the length of the work year (including vacations, and so on), overtime work, and flex-time work.

2.   Basic Income-Leisure Model

This is the theoretical part of the chapter, which relies heavily on graphical analysis. This model of worker behaviour is based on a premise that he/she does have some degree of control over the employment situation and, therefore, has some margin to make voluntary choices.

The worker has preferences among two goods that give him/her positive marginal utility: income and leisure. Income is the good placed on the vertical axis; leisure is the good placed on the horizontal axis. The indifference curve represents the locus of all combinations of the two goods that generate an equal amount of total utility. The slope of the indifference curve is called the marginal rate of substitution (MRS) between income and leisure, and it is equal to the negative of the marginal utility of leisure divided by the marginal utility of income. The indifference curve typically is curved away from the origin, and it never is curved toward the origin. Each worker has a whole map of indifference curves, and higher indifference curves are preferred to lower ones.

The budget constraint is a linear function of the levels of the same two goods — income and leisure — and it reflects the trade-off between them. The equation of the budget line in slope intercept form is $I = w (T - l) + Y_n$, where I is the level of income earned from work, w is the wage level, T is the time endowment (that is, maximum number of hours that could be worked), l is the number of hours of leisure, and Y_n is the income that is not earned from working. The slope of the budget line is given by the negative of w. The intercept on the income axis is typically called full income, which corresponds to the maximum amount of work. There is only one budget line per individual.

There are two types of equilibria: interior solutions and corner solutions. Interior solutions involve a positive number of hours worked, yet this number is still below the maximum number of hours that could be worked. Geometrically, this equilibrium occurs at the point of tangency between the highest possible indifference curve and the budget line. At this point, the slope of the budget constraint equals the slope of the indifference curve. Mathematically, the marginal rate of substitution equals the wage rate in absolute value terms. Intuitively, the rate at which the market allows the worker to substitute between income and leisure (that is, the wage rate is the opportunity cost of one hour of leisure) is equal to the rate at which the individual is willing to substitute income for leisure. A corner solution is an "all or nothing" choice. There are only two possibilities for corner solutions: the time endowment (T) is allocated either entirely to leisure (so $l = T$ at the lower corner) or entirely to work (so $l = 0$ at the upper corner). Again, we select the point of intersection between the highest possible indifference curve and the budget line, but this point will not be a tangency. This implies that the slopes of the two curves will not be equal, and marginal rate of substitution does not equal the wage rate. If the indifference curve is steeper than the budget line, the absolute value of the MRS exceeds the absolute value of the wage, and the individual works zero hours. The reservation wage, which is the lowest wage at which the worker will supply any hours of work, is given by the slope of the indifference curve at zero hours of work, which means at point T along the horizontal axis.

3.   Comparative Statics

Comparative statics involves analysis of the impact of changes in parameters, such as wage, preferences, and Y_n, on the choice of hours worked and, hence, income earned on the labour market. An increase in Y_n has the effect of reducing (increasing) the number of hours worked if leisure is a normal (inferior) good. The budget constraint shifts outwards in parallel fashion. A decrease in Y_n has the effect of increasing (decreasing) the number of hours worked if leisure is a normal (inferior) good. The budget constraint shifts inwards in parallel fashion. A change in Y_n will bring about only income effects.

On the other hand, a change in the wage brings about both an income effect and a substitution effect. If leisure is a normal good, which is usually assumed to be the case, the two effects work in opposite directions, and the net effect of a wage change depends on their relative magnitudes. Changes in the wage cause the budget line to rotate. If wages increase (decrease), the budget line becomes steeper (flatter) and the worker is induced to take less (more) leisure according to the substitution effect. As wages increase (decrease), however, he/she also becomes better (worse) off, and that force pushes him/her to take more (less) leisure according to the income effect.

The choice to participate is tantamount to whether the individual works zero hours (non-participation) or a positive number of hours. If wages increase (decrease), the budget line becomes steeper (flatter). If the wage is still below the reservation wage, the worker still chooses to work zero hours, which corresponds to the lower right-hand corner solution. As the wage level rises, it reaches and then surpasses the reservation wage. The worker will supply some hours of work, and an interior solution to the left of the corner solution would emerge. The substitution effect induces the worker to take less leisure, as the wage, or the opportunity cost of leisure, increases. In the neighbourhood of the reservation wage, income effects from wage changes are nil because non-participants are not earning any income from working.

The labour force participation decision boils down to two variables, the market wage that the individual could (or actually does) earn on the labour market and his/her reservation wage. Any factor that raises (lowers) the former, while the latter remains fixed, makes labour force participation more (less) likely. Any factor that raises (lowers) the latter, while the former remains fixed, makes labour force participation less (more) likely.

4.   Deriving the Individual Supply Curve of Labour

The supply curve is drawn in wage-hours of workspace. It can be derived from the income-leisure choice diagram. The hypothetical wage levels are the ordinates for the supply curve of labour. As the wage rate is raised by increments, the budget line rotates clockwise. For very low wages (below the reservation wage), the choice is at the lower right-hand corner, and zero hours of labour are supplied. As the wage surpasses the reservation wage, interior solutions are attained. The amount of labour supplied is given by T, the time endowment, minus the amount of leisure that is read off of the horizontal axis of the income-leisure choice diagram. For fairly low wage levels, the positive substitution effect of the wage increases will dominate the negative income effect of them (assuming that leisure is a normal good), and thus the labour supply curve slopes upward. For fairly high wage levels, the positive substitution effect of the wage increases will be dominated by the negative income effect of them, and thus the labour supply curve slopes downward.

5.   Empirical Evidence

Some recent measures of the LFPR that are fairly consistent with the predictions of the theoretical model are presented in Table 2.3. Factors that are positively associated with the *market* wage level of the individual are supposed to raise the probability of participating in the labour market via the substitution effect. Factors that are positively associated with the *reservation* wage level of the individual, such as his/her non-labour income or preferences toward leisure versus income, lower the probability of participating in the labour market. The overall supply schedule (for men and women combined) is thought to be upward sloping over the relevant ranges of wages, although the elasticity of labour supply is quite low (inelastic). For high wage levels, the labour supply curve for men may be backwards bending. The wage elasticity of supply is generally higher for women than for men.

6.   Added and Discouraged Worker Effects

A discouraged worker is a jobless worker who has withdrawn from the labour force because he/she believes that his/her opportunities on the labour market are unfavourable. This type of behaviour is most prominent during recessions and can be interpreted as a substitution effect in response to low perceived returns from working. An added worker is an individual who has joined the labour force in response to a decline in family labour market income. This type of behaviour is also most prominent during recessions and can be interpreted as an income effect in response to a drop in family earnings.

7.   Hidden Unemployment

Discouraged workers are jobless, but they are not considered to be officially unemployed because they are not actively searching for work. To the extent that they are classified as out of the labour force (OLF) rather than U, the official level of unemployment is lowered.

8.   Moonlighting, Overtime, and Flexible Working Hours

The model of labour supply, with the income-leisure choice diagram, can be applied to several particular employment situations. In each case, a worker is not able to select his/her preferred number of hours of work. Underemployment refers to the case where the worker is prevented from working as many hours as he/she would freely choose, which means that he/she is not on his/her highest indifference curve given the income constraint. The indifference curve will cut the budget constraint in this case; there is no tangency. The worker may be interested in moonlighting under these circumstances. Overemployment refers to the case where the worker is required to work more hours than he/she would freely choose. The indifference curve will cut the budget constraint in this case; there is no tangency. An over-employed worker might be interested in working overtime at premium pay.

9.   Appendix: Consumer Choice Theory

This is a compact summary of consumer choice theory, which can be found in either the text or an appendix of any textbook of basic microeconomics. A mastery of high school algebra and the Cartesian coordinate plane is required. After a review of the two central elements of consumer choice theory, budget constraints and consumer preferences, they are superimposed on the same graph in order to generate the consumer optimum. Comparative statics involves an analysis of the change in the consumer's choice that results from changes in the relative price of the two goods and/or the level of income. This model is applied quite directly to the model of labour supply.

Helpful Hints

- It might be useful to review the concepts and the mechanics of indifference curve analysis and income effects/substitution effects. This material can be found in the appendix to Chapter 2 of this textbook. You should feel quite comfortable with the content of that section.
- Be careful not to confuse the directions along the horizontal axis of the income-leisure choice diagram. Leisure time increases as we move from left to right, and working time increases as we move from right to left. You may want to get into the habit of drawing a rightward arrow for more leisure and a leftward arrow for more work.
- The budget constraint gives only the maximum income level that could be received by working a certain number of hours. Until we superimpose the indifference curve, which gives the preference, we do not know how many hours of work or leisure will be chosen.
- There are three types of solutions, or equilibrium situations. First, there is the lower right-hand corner solution at the right edge of the diagram. In this case, work hours are zero. The indifference curve is steeper than the budget constraint, but they do share the point (T, Y_n). Second, there is the situation in which the worker cannot select his/her ideal hours due to some restriction. In this case, there is no tangency, and the indifference curve cuts the budget line at the given number of hours. Finally, there is the interior solution, at which the worker can choose his/her ideal number of hours. Only in this case is there a point of tangency between the indifference curve and the budget line at which they have equal slopes. Do not always expect there to be a smooth, interior solution.
- Always draw the budget line first and then draw indifference curves.
- The applications treated toward the end of the chapter are somewhat hard. Usually you can draw a normal indifference map, as the key is the budget line, which frequently will have kinks in mid-range. Start from the right-hand corner point described above, determine the level of non-labour income (Y_n) that is associated with the time endowment (T), and move by hourly increments to the left. Ask yourself what the wage is (that is, the hourly return from working) as the individual works one more hour. When a certain number of hours has been reached, there is typically a change in the wage rate and, hence, in the slope of the budget constraint.
- Go over the substitution effects and the income effects carefully. Most of the time, leisure is a normal good, so the income effect is negative (higher wages mean higher income levels, which means more leisure, which means fewer hours of work). The substitution effect is always positive (higher wages mean more hours of work). Unless leisure is an inferior good, the two effects work in opposite directions. Along the backward-bending supply curve, the only question is which of

Labour Market Economics, Fifth Edition

the two effects dominates. The backward-bending part does not arise due to a change in the sign of the income effect; it arises due to an increase in the magnitude of the income effect.

Answers to Odd-Numbered End-of-Chapter Questions

1. If leisure were an inferior good, which is pretty inconceivable, then there would not be a backward-sloping portion to the labour supply curve, even for high wages. Note that according to this question, leisure is still a good; it is not a bad. Whether leisure is a normal or an inferior good is reflected in the form of the indifference map. As the wage rate is increased progressively, the budget line rotates clockwise. In this particular case, the points of tangency move successively to the left, approaching the vertical axis. Referring to Figure 2.10b, imagine the tangency with indifference curve U_3 lying to the left of the tangency with indifference curve U_2. The tangency with indifference curve U_4 is not shown, but it would lie to the left of the tangency with indifference curve U_3. This implies that the labour supply curve will always slope upwards, as higher wage levels always generate lower levels of leisure.

3a. The poor who are at minimum subsistence and who aspire to middle-class consumption patterns. This group values income highly, relative to leisure, so the indifference curve is relatively flat. As the wage increases, the income constraint line rotates clockwise, and we would expect a relatively large increase in hours worked. This response is dominated by a substitution effect, but there may be a small income effect working in the direction of increased leisure.

b. The wealthy who have acquired an abundance of material goods and who now aspire to be members of the idle rich. This group values leisure highly, relative to income earned from wages, so the indifference curve is relatively flat. They would presumably have high non-labour income, which would shift the income constraint line upward in parallel fashion from the bottom right-hand corner. As the wage increases, the income constraint line rotates clockwise, and we would expect a decrease in hours worked. In this income range — high up and to the left in the income-leisure diagram — very strong income effects work to outweigh the substitution effect. Recall that, for this model, the two effects always work in opposite directions. This group is on the backward-bending part of their labour supply curve.

c. Workers who have a strong attachment to the labour force and who are reluctant to change their hours of work. This situation can be depicted by the intersection between the upper left-hand corner of the income constraint and the highest indifference curve along the vertical axis (provided that the total time endowment available for working is feasible). The indifference curve is flatter than the income constraint line, so the marginal rate of substitution exceeds the wage. For a certain range, an increase in the wage will not cause a change in hours worked, and we could say that the wage elasticity of supply is perfectly inelastic.

d. Workers who have a weak attachment to the labour force and have viable alternatives to labour market work. This case is very similar to case b. If the wage falls, they may drop out of the labour force.

e. Workaholics are defined as those who have very strong preferences for labour market work. They have very flat indifference curves. One can expect a tangency near the vertical axis.

5. Any increase in non-labour income shifts the wage constraint line upward. The wage constraint line does not change its slope because there is no change in the wage. Instead, there is a vertical translation (shift) upward. The left-hand vertex intersects the vertical axis at a higher point, while the wage constraint line does not intersect the horizontal axis at all. Recall as well that the reservation wage is the slope of the indifference curve at the point of zero hours worked. Picture

a normal indifference map in which the indifference curves are (more or less) radial expansions of each other — sort of parallel. Now go over to the edge of the graph, where work is equal to zero and leisure is equal to the entire time endowment. As non-labour income increases, we move to higher and higher indifference curves, and the slope at the edge of these indifference curves increases. In other words, the marginal rate of substitution is increasing as we move up to higher indifference curves and higher income constraint lines. This can be seen because as we reach higher and higher curves along the same vertical line, we move closer to the middle portion of these curves, and as we move from right to left along indifference curves, they become steeper. This result makes intuitive sense. Remember that as we move up in the diagram, people get richer, so their reservation wage can be expected to increase.

7a. An offer to work as many hours as the worker would like at the going wage. She would move back to a tangency between the wage constraint and the highest possible indifference curve, like point D on indifference curve U_d.

  b. Payment of a moonlighting rate for hours of work beyond C. If the moonlighting wage rate is lower than the going wage, there is a kink in the wage constraint line at point C, and the portion to the left rotates downward. This should have no impact on the worker's choice, which would still be D with no constraints and C with the institutionalized workweek. The moonlighting opportunities do not allow her to reach higher indifference curves. Intuitively, at the going wage, he wanted to cut her hours. With a lower wage, she is not likely to want to work these hours.

Answers to Odd-Numbered End-of-Chapter Problems

1. This question pertains to the estimated linear equation of aggregate labour force participation for women. You are asked to interpret the coefficients. It is important to pay attention to the units that are given for each variable.

  a. *Ceteris paribus,* this effect is -7 percentage points. As the husband's expected earnings increase, there is a fairly strong negative effect on the wife's participation rate, which is called a cross-income effect.

  b. *Ceteris paribus,* this effect is +18 percentage points. As the wife's expected earnings increase, there is a very strong positive effect on the wife's participation rate. This is primarily attributable to a substitution effect.

  c. We can interpret the effect of the husband's income as a pure effect stemming from non-labour income. Assuming that this cross-income effect is the same as the wife's own income effect stemming from her own earnings, the substitution effect is +25 percentage points, which is partially offset by an income effect of -7 percentage points. This means that as the wife's earnings increase, the opportunity cost of her not working increases, which induces her to work longer. At the same time, she becomes richer and can maintain the living standard while purchasing more leisure. That effect pushes her to work less. The net effect of +18 induces her to work more.

  d. According to this equation, it would lead to a net increase of 25 percentage points. The pay cut for the husbands would increase the labour force participation of wives as they have to work more to maintain living percentage points.

  e. We are given no information on the hourly wage, so technically we cannot answer this question. The variables that appear in this equation for expected earnings include both wages and hours worked. For the less precisely defined quantities of uncompensated and the pure elasticities for expected income, the former is 18*(6/35) and the latter is 25*(6/35). We use only the coefficient pertaining to the wife for these "own" elasticities.

f. Yes, it does. The total effect of the expected earnings of women on their labour force participation far outweighs the negative effect of non-labour income earned by their husbands. As the returns from working for women increased a lot in recent decades, the labour force participation rate increased. The main reason is a substitution effect that dominated the income effects from both earners on women's labour force participation.

3. We are given the formula for the marginal rate of substitution of leisure for income (or consumption, since there is a one-for-one trade-off between the two of them). The MRS is the slope of the indifference curve. The formula that appears is actually the absolute value of the MRS, since that expression must be positive (A(x) must always be positive, and C and l must always be non-negative), and the indifference curves have a negative slope.

a. As we move from left to right, the amount of leisure increases, while A(x) remains constant, and the value of C falls. This implies that the value of the MRS decreases. The interpretation is that as the worker consumes more and more leisure, he/she values the marginal hour of leisure less and less and is willing to trade off less and less income. The variables (labelled X), which may affect the MRS, are the number of children that the woman has, as well as their ages, her level of education, and her marital status (tied with her husband's income).

b. Recall that the reservation wage is equal to the slope of the indifference curve at the lower right-hand corner solution, which corresponds to the situation in which no hours are worked. If h = 0 (the number of hours worked), then all of the time endowment (T) goes to leisure. We can thus write MRS = A(x) C / T = w*. In order for this woman to participate in the labour market, the market wage has to exceed the reservation wage, so we can write: w > A(x) C / T. Taking the natural logarithm of both sides of the equation yields ln w > ln (A(x)) + ln C - ln T. Since the logarithmic operation is the inverse of the exponential operation, and at the corner solution, C = non-labour income (Y_n), we obtain the desired result. The log of the time endowment (T) can probably be interpreted as a constant across almost all women, and so it can probably be ignored at this stage of the problem.

c. We treat Z as a random variable, which is distributed normally. That means that it has mean zero and a variance of unity. The graph has a bell shape on a diagram with the probability density of the vertical axis and the values of Z on the horizontal axis. Any factor that raises Z makes labour force participation more likely. The form of that distribution, however, is not really the focus of this question. An increase (decrease) in non-labour income ln y would shift the income constraint upward (downward), making participation less (more) likely. An increase (decrease) in ln w would rotate the income constraint upward (downward), making participation more (less) likely. The impact of the taste shifters depends on whether the sign of the beta coefficient is positive or negative. They have the effect of changing the slope of the indifference curve.

5a. For this case, we assume that the husband continues to work 40 hours per week, or 8 hours per day. This implies that his labour income falls from $160 to $120 per day. For the income-leisure choice diagram of the wife, refer to Figure 2.6b. The initial value of Y_n is $160, and the coordinates of point A are (T, $160). The budget line has a slope of -10. There is a solution at point E_0. Next, the budget shifts down in parallel fashion such that the coordinates of the right endpoint are (T, $120). There is a new equilibrium that lies to the southwest of the original one. It involves a lower amount of labour income and a higher number of hours worked for the wife.

b. In this case, we allow for the possibility that the husband may react to having his wages cut by altering the number of hours that he works. In his income-leisure choice diagram, the slope of the budget line changes from -20 to -15, which means that it becomes flatter. If the substitution effect dominates the income effect, he will work fewer hours, and he will earn much less income than before. If the income effect dominates the substitution effect, he will work longer hours, and he will be able to recoup some or all of his lost income. We are not given the information that is required the solve this problem. Until we know what his labour income is, we do not know what the wife's non-market income is, so we cannot say much about how she reacts to the wage cut that is imposed on her husband.

c. If the husband collects unemployment insurance (UI), he has to stop working on the labour market. The wife's non-labour income falls from $160 to $40 per day, and we repeat the analysis in Problem 5a with a major downward shift in the wife's budget line. She is likely to work many more hours. On the other hand, the husband does gain 8 hours of leisure per day by going on UI.

7a. For the income-leisure choice diagram, refer to Figure 2.6b in the textbook and the accompanying graph. The initial value of Y_n is $100, and the coordinates of point A are (T=60,$100). The budget line has a slope of - 5. There is a solution at point E_0, which in this case is the point (leisure=20,$300) Labour market income is 40*5 = $200.

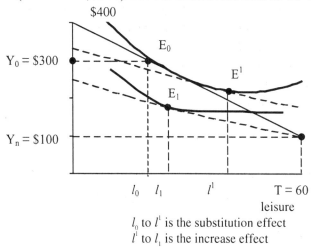

l_0 to l^1 is the substitution effect
l^1 to l_1 is the increase effect

b. For the income-leisure choice diagram, refer to Figure 2.6b in the textbook. As the effective wage is now cut in half, the budget line has a slope of -2.5, but it still has the right endpoint (T=60,$100). There will be a tangency at an indifference curve that is lower than the original indifference curve. Call this final point of tangency E_1. We do not know exactly what the resulting number of hours worked will be, but we do know that he will be worse off than before. Draw a hypothetical (dashed) budget line with slope -2.5, which is tangent to the higher, original indifference curve at point E^1. The horizontal distance between the two points of tangency on the higher indifference curve gives the substitution effect, and its direction is left to right. The horizontal difference between the final tangency E_1 and the hypothetical tangency E^1 is the income effect, and its direction is right to left. The horizontal distance between the original and the final tangency points is the total effect of the wage cut on his labour supply, or the difference between the two equilibria that we observe.

c. This event is not depicted on the graph because it becomes very crowded. George will pay only one of these taxes at a time, so the problem asks us to compare their effects on his labour supply using the same diagram. The poll tax has the effect of shifting the original budget line down in parallel fashion. It is the equivalent of cutting George's allowance. Taking the original budget line with a slope of -5, shift it down by the amount of taxes that George was paying in Problem 7b. This is given by the net income level that he was earning in Problem 7b. (Recall that he kept half of his earnings and forked over the other half to his caretaker.) The equilibrium should lie to the left of the equilibrium in Problem 7b, with more hours worked and less leisure taken. George will be worse off than he was in Problem 7a. The idea is that the poll tax gives George greater incentive to work. It produces only an income effect, which will actually raise work effort if leisure is a normal good. There is no substitution effect in this case.

Multiple Choice Questions

1. Consider the backward-bending portion of the labour supply curve. If there is a wage increase:
   a) The negative income effect dominates the positive substitution effect.
   b) The positive substitution effect dominates the negative income effect.
   c) The income effect and the substitution effect work in the same direction.
   d) There is only a positive substitution effect.
   e) There is only a negative income effect.

2. Consider the upward-sloping portion of the labour supply curve. If there is a wage increase:
   a) The negative income effect dominates the positive substitution effect.
   b) The positive substitution effect dominates the negative income effect.
   c) The income effect and the substitution effect work in the same direction.
   d) There is only a positive substitution effect.
   e) There is only a negative income effect.

3. Which of the following statements regarding labour supply is *false*?
   a) Leisure is a normal good.
   b) A wage increase brings about a positive substitution effect on hours supplied.
   c) An increase in non-market income will affect labour supply decisions.
   d) The wage is the opportunity cost of working.
   e) The wage is interpreted as the price of leisure.

4. Which of the following is *not* a factor in labour supply decisions?
   a) The technology of production
   b) The individual's time endowment
   c) The wage rate
   d) The individual's preferences for income versus leisure
   e) Alternative sources of income

5. Given that the worker chooses to work a positive number of hours, all of the following are equivalent *except* which statement?
   a) The marginal rate of substitution is equal to the wage rate.
   b) The slope of the budget line is equal to the slope of the indifference curve.
   c) The worker is maximizing her utility given her preferences and the wage rate and other sources of income.
   d) On the margin, the individual values another hour's worth of income and another hour of leisure equally.
   e) On the margin, the ratio of the individual's valuation of another hour of leisure to another hour's worth of income is equal to the wage rate.

6. The reason why indifference curves between leisure and income slope downward is because:
   a) Of the law of diminishing marginal utility of income and leisure.
   b) Preferences for income and leisure must be transitive.
   c) Steep indifference curves indicate that the worker is lazy, whereas fairly flat indifference curves indicate that she is very motivated.
   d) Both income and leisure are valued by the worker.
   e) None of the above.

7. In the context of the labour supply model, if the worker receives a demogrant:
   a) There is only an income effect, as there is no substitution effect.
   b) There is an income effect and a substitution effect.
   c) It will not affect the worker's choice of hours.
   d) There is only a substitution effect, as there is no income effect.
   e) It may lead to a decrease in the worker's utility level.

8. The wage elasticity of supply is defined as which of the following:
   a) The marginal rate of substitution divided by the wage rate
   b) The percentage change in the quantity of labour supplied divided by the percentage change in the wage rate
   c) The change in the quantity of labour supplied divided by the change in the wage rate
   d) The income effect divided by the substitution effect
   e) The substitution effect divided by the income effect

9. For a worker who is deciding how many hours of labour to supply, all of the following are true *except* which statement?
   a) Leisure is a normal good.
   b) A demogrant will have the same effect on hours as a wage increase.
   c) In equilibrium, the worker cannot increase total utility by working more or fewer hours.
   d) In equilibrium, the rate at which she is willing to trade leisure for income equals the rate at which the market allows that exchange.
   e) In equilibrium, there is normally a tangency between the budget line and the indifference curve.

10. If a worker is currently in the position where his/her indifference curve and budget constraint intersect, and the marginal rate of substitution exceeds the wage, then:
    a) The worker is maximizing his/her utility.
    b) The worker could increase his/her utility by working more hours.
    c) The worker could increase his/her utility by working fewer hours.
    d) The slope of the budget constraint equals the slope of the indifference curve.
    e) None of the above.

11. Suppose that leisure is an inferior good (a good whose consumption goes down as income goes up). As the wage rate goes up:
    a) The hours of labour supplied should increase.
    b) The hours of labour supplied should decrease.
    c) The hours of labour supplied should increase, provided that the substitution effect dominates the income effect.
    d) The hours of labour supplied should increase, provided that the substitution effect dominates the income effect.
    e) The effect is indeterminate.

12. The labour force participation rate is defined as which of the following:
    a) The employed plus the unemployed over the working-age population
    b) The unemployed over the sum of the employed plus the unemployed
    c) The employed over the sum of the employed plus the unemployed
    d) The employed divided by the labour force
    e) None of the above

13. All of the following groups of individuals are considered to be out of the labour force *except* which group?
    a) Discouraged workers
    b) Retired persons
    c) Unemployed workers
    d) Students
    e) Household workers

14. Consider Figure 2.8 in the textbook. The distance OY_N represents:
    a) The level of non-market income.
    b) The level of market income.
    c) The wage rate.
    d) The marginal rate of substitution between income and leisure.
    e) The number of hours worked.

15. Consider Figure 2.8 in the textbook. Given a wage increase from W_0 to W_1, the distance between I' and I_0 represents:
    a) The substitution effect.
    b) The income effect.
    c) The net effect of both the substitution effect and the income effect.
    d) The equilibrium choice for hours worked.
    e) The equilibrium choice for leisure.

Answers to Multiple Choice Questions

1. A Response B applies to the upward-sloping portion of the labour supply curve. For responses C and E, only if leisure is an inferior good can the income effect be negative. For response D, there must be an income effect in this case.
2. B See the explanation for question #1.
3. D The wage is the opportunity cost of leisure. All of the other points are raised in the section entitled "Basic Income-Leisure Model."
4. A The technology of production affects labour demand. All of the other responses refer to elements of the basic income-leisure model.
5. D If the marginal utilities are equal, then the MRS = -1. That is a very particular case that does not generally apply.
6. D Responses A and C refer to the curvature of the indifference curve. Response B implies that indifference curves cannot cross.
7. A For responses B and D, in order for there to be a substitution effect, a change in the wage is required. Response E is absurd, as the worker has received an increase in income. Response C is wrong if leisure is a normal good.
8. B Straightforward definition.

9. B   The fact that a demogrant has a very different effect than a wage change is a crucial lesson from this chapter. All of the other points are true and are raised in the section entitled "Basic Income-Leisure Model."

10. C.   Ruling out the case of non-participation, the worker could reach a higher I curve by working fewer hours. Response A violates the equilibrium condition. Response D contradicts the premise of the question.

11. A   If leisure is an inferior good, the income effect of a wage increase on hours worked becomes positive rather than negative. Combined with a substitution effect that is always positive, we obtain a positively sloped labour supply curve. In this case, the two effects work in the same direction, so one cannot talk about them dominating each other.

12. A   Straightforward definition.

13. C   This is stated explicitly in the textbook in the section entitled "Hidden Unemployment."

14. A   This is stated explicitly in the textbook in the basic development of the income-leisure model.

15. A   This is indicated at the bottom of the graph, but the identifying information would not appear on an examination.

CHAPTER 3

Chapter Highlights

The central issue for this chapter is social insurance for low-income status, most of which can be called income maintenance programs. At the broadest level, there are two types of programs: universal programs and targeted programs. The former type awards benefits to virtually anyone, regardless of individual need. Most income maintenance programs are of the latter type and direct benefits to those who have suffered an income loss for a particular reason. They typically involve disincentive effects. The type of income maintenance program should depend on whether the deficiency in income is temporary or permanent. For persistent low-income status, it is useful to differentiate between the case of low hourly wages and a low number of hours. The income-leisure choice framework can be utilized to analyse the workings of many of these programs.

1.   Static Partial Equilibrium Effects in Theory

Eight different applications are illustrated in the textbook. The key point in analysing them is to determine the form and position of the budget constraint. The indifference curves always have a negative slope reflecting the disutility of work and the utility of income. Under these circumstances, there is always the potential for disincentive effects to emerge from any program that grants money to recipients. If a program has a disincentive effect, it causes an individual to work fewer hours on the labour market than he/she would in the absence of the benefit.

The simplest case involves demogrants, which consist of lump-sum grants that are awarded with no strings attached. The budget constraint shifts upward in parallel fashion, causing a negative income effect if leisure is a normal good. Since the wage does not change, there is no substitution effect.

If an individual is able to work, social assistance programs have strong disincentive effects for low-wage workers. If a recipient takes a job, social assistance benefits (which are in the form of a demogrant) are reduced one dollar for every dollar of labour market earnings, which constitutes a 100% implicit tax rate on labour market earnings. Most recipients would choose not to work at all given these stakes.

The negative income tax (NIT) program has been implemented only in a few jurisdictions. It is a form of social assistance program that is designed to address the work disincentives that spring from the 100% implicit tax rate that is applied to the labour market earnings by the conventional social assistance program. The recipient can earn income on the labour market without losing all of his/her benefits. The NIT benefit consists in part of a demogrant and in part of a positive implicit tax rate that is much less than 100%, thus making it worthwhile to work.

A wage subsidy involves a positive benefit for each hour that the recipient works. It is designed to assist low-wage workers, with no demogrant involved. As the worker receives a higher wage, the budget line rotates clockwise. There is a positive substitution effect but a negative income effect.

Unemployment insurance (UI) is a very important policy measure in Canada, and it is multi-faceted. This program can actually increase the incentive for non-participants to enter the labour market, because they sometimes can qualify for benefits after working a short-term job. The disincentive effect stems from the case in which, in the absence of the UI program, some workers would work longer hours than what is required for entitlement to benefits. The disincentive effects can be quite strong for workers with regular seasonal jobs.

Workers' compensation, or disability insurance, benefits are disincentive effects only if disability is partial and returning to work in some way or form is feasible. It is necessary to determine the shape of the budget constraint as it relates to labour market earnings, which depends on the nature and extent of the disability. The next step is to determine the impact of the compensation on the shape of the budget constraint. Typically, there is a substitution effect and an income effect, both of which push the worker to work fewer hours.

A child-care subsidy is a current and controversial policy issue, and it can have an effect on the labour supply choices of women. It tends to have a positive effect on the labour force participation of women, but there is the potential for reducing the number of hours supplied given that the person is already participating in the labour force.

2.   Illustrative Evidence of Incentive Effects

All of the predictions mentioned above are theoretical. This section deals with the empirical evidence regarding social assistance programs, which seems to indicate that both labour market opportunities that the recipients face and the program parameters (that is, how generous the benefits are and how easily one can qualify for them) play a role in explaining the incidence of social assistance benefits.

Non-experimental evidence is produced from data on observed participation in social assistance programs. These empirical studies involve only low-income workers. They try to explain program participation status as a function of labour market opportunities and program eligibility/generosity. The findings indicate that workers with low predicted earnings and unfavourable job market opportunities are more likely to use welfare, *ceteris paribus,* and that program generosity has the expected effect on participation.

In order to generate experimental evidence, program participants are actually selected for an experimental treatment. In some cases, this treatment is similar to an NIT arrangement. Their labour market activity is followed over time and compared to otherwise similar individuals who do not participate in the experiment (that is, a control group). These studies have indicated the presence of strong disincentive effects compared to the situation of no social assistance benefits at all.

The self-sufficiency program (SSF) was a Canadian social experiment. This pilot project was directed at selected social assistance recipients, who were offered wage benefits if they left social assistance within a year in order to take a job on the labour market. The program was evaluated and judged to be a success.

Helpful Hints

These points are in no particular order:

*   Recall that in any application of the income-leisure choice model, the slope of the budget constraint gives the economic returns to working, while the intercept on the right edge (the point

of zero hours worked) gives the level of non-market income.

- Recall the interpretation of the budget constraint; it gives the maximum potential income that can be obtained by working that number of hours.
- Recall that as we go from right to left along the horizontal axis, hours of work increase and hours of leisure decrease.
- In order to analyse a disincentive effect, first consider the choice of the worker in the absence of any income maintenance program. Next, examine the income-leisure choice after the benefits have been awarded. If the new equilibrium is on a higher I curve, and there are no more hours of work than before, there is a disincentive effect.
- When we say that the NIT program has disincentive effects, we are comparing it to the situation of the absence of social assistance benefits. The work incentives associated with the NIT arrangement are stronger than they are for conventional social assistance programs.
- The UI application is the most difficult one. Whereas the time horizon for many applications is one day or one week, it is one year for this application. Whereas the units for many applications are hours per day or days per week, they are weeks per year for the UI application. The goal is to predict how many weeks will be worked in a year with and without the UI program. As you move from right to left by weekly increments, think of how many weeks of potential UI benefits are passed over by working during that particular week. In other words, think of how each week worked affects the entitlement to benefits. There are essentially two kinks. At the first kink, after 14 weeks of pure work, the worker becomes eligible for 20 weeks of UI benefits, which greatly increases total income at that range. At the second kink, after 32 weeks of pure work, the worker would be eligible for 20 weeks of UI benefits, but with only 52 weeks in a calendar year, entitlement diminishes after that point. For instance, 33 weeks of work opens up entitlement for only 19 weeks of benefits, 34 weeks of work opens up entitlement for only 18 weeks of benefits, and so on. The loss of benefit entitlement lowers income possibilities, which gives a slope for that final segment that is less than the market wage (in absolute value terms) as potential UI benefits have not been claimed.
- For the case of social assistance benefits, the key diagram is Figure 3.2. The budget line has a kink at the point where labour market earnings, given by w*h, are equal to the demogrant. The lower right-hand corner of the budget constraint takes the form of a right triangle whose hypotenuse is the former budget line.
- Any time that the income maintenance program involves a demogrant, the right-side endpoint of the budget constraint $(T,0)$ becomes the point (T,Y_n), as some non-labour income is received even when no hours are worked.

Answers to Odd-Numbered End-of-Chapter Questions

1. This can be seen by examining Figure 3.1. The income level at the post-demogrant equilibrium E_d is higher than that associated with E_o. The reason underlying this result is the income effect. As income rises, she purchases more leisure, which is a normal good. She will thus work fewer hours, and income earned from working will fall. Total income, including both the demogrant and the earned income, will rise.

3a. Unwilling to go on welfare because the welfare payment is too low: The wage constraint line is tangent to an indifference curve that is higher than the indifference curve that touches the corner of the wage constraint line at the right corner of the diagram. In other words, there is an interior solution giving a positive amount of work, and that indifference curve is higher than the one that intersects the demogrant segment — the vertical segment rising from the horizontal axis at T hours of leisure. Recall that, at these corner solutions, the slope of the indifference curve does not equal the slope of the budget line.

b. Indifferent between welfare and work: The wage constraint line is tangent to the same indifference curve that touches the corner of the wage constraint line at the right corner of the diagram. In other words, there is an interior solution giving a positive amount of work, and that indifference curve intersects the demogrant segment — the vertical segment rising from the horizontal axis at T hours of leisure.

c. Induced to move off of welfare because of an increase in his wage (see Figure 3.3, panel b): The welfare equilibrium is E_w, while the working equilibrium is E_1.

d. Induced to move off of welfare because of a change in preferences (see Figure 3.3, panel d): Imagine the slope of the indifference curves becoming flatter. That corresponds to the individual valuing income relative to leisure more than she did in the past. The equilibrium would jump from the right-hand corner (welfare) to a smooth interior solution (working).

e. Induced to move off of welfare by a reduction of the 100% implicit tax on earnings (see Figure 3.3, panel c): When welfare benefits are withheld dollar for dollar against earnings, the wage constraint line is flat at the level of the demogrant. If this confiscatory tax is lowered, the budget line has a negative slope, but it will not be as steep as the remainder of the wage constraint line unless the implicit tax rate is 0. The equilibrium E_w', which involves working, dominates E_w, which does not involve working.

5. This is depicted in Figure 3.9a. We are assuming that the disability is partial, so the worker can work a little. The segment E_oY would be almost flat. Without a compensation program, the worker would forfeit the wage for each hour not worked. Now she forfeits only 10% of the wage that would be paid. There is an incentive to work, albeit a slight one. There is a minor substitution effect. For each hour worked (a movement from right to left), the worker gains 10% of her wage.

Answers to Odd-Numbered End-of-Chapter Problems

1. The simple response is that compared to the design of present social assistance programs, the work disincentives of the negative income tax program are a major improvement. However, compared to an economy with no social assistance whatever, it is true that the work disincentives of the negative income tax program are notable. In addition, there is widespread agreement among most observers that it is crucial for social assistance recipients to have some work experience, even if it is initially low paid. Even in the face of some work disincentives caused by a negative income tax program, the hours that they are working may well lead to more favourable labour market outcomes in the future. Further discussion appears in the text.

3. This is a difficult question. Compare Figure 3.4 (the case of the negative income tax) to Figure 3.5 (the case of a wage subsidy). It is probably easier to think of holding the post-subsidy income constant. For the latter, it is the ordinate of E_s. For the former, it is the ordinate of E_n. If we were to superimpose them on a diagram with U_o and the no-subsidy equilibrium of E_o, the work level would be higher for the wage subsidy. This is because the wage subsidy has no demogrant portion, and a demogrant reduces work incentives. The wage subsidy increases the opportunity cost of not working, which has a positive substitution effect of inducing more work. On the other hand, the negative income tax program has a positive substitution effect too, but since the wage received is lower under this plan, the magnitude of the substitution effect is not as strong.

5a. On the graph, note that the units are hours worked per year on the horizontal axis and earnings per year on the vertical axis. This program functions as a wage subsidy, but because no one can collect a total benefit that exceeds $2,400 per year, we say that the program has a ceiling. The budget line has kinks. Since there is no demogrant, the vertex on the right side is the point (T,0), meaning that if zero hours per year are worked, the worker earns nothing from the employer and collects no EITC benefit. The wage for the first hour worked is W + 0.34*W = 1.34*W. In fact, until the total amount of the EITC reaches $2,400, the return to working is 1.34*W, which is therefore the absolute value of the slope of the first segment. When W* hours = $7,000, the total EITC = W* hours * 0.34 = $2,400 (approximately), and the worker earns only W for each hour worked beyond that point. The absolute value of the slope of the next segment is W. This kink occurs at T - 7,000 / W hours of work. When the worker earns more than $12,000, the EITC benefit that he/she has collected is subject to clawback, which means that he/she has to start giving it back if he/she earns more money on the job market. We are told that the clawback rate is $0.16 per dollar earned, so the wage for the next hour worked is W - 0.16*W = 0.84*W, which is therefore the absolute value of the slope of the third segment. The second kink occurs at T - 12,000 / W hours of work. When the worker reaches the earnings level of $27,000, he/she has paid back the total EITC benefit of $2,400 ($27,000 - $12,000 = $15,000 of earnings subject to clawback, and $15,000*0.16 = $2,400). After that point, the absolute value of the slope of the budget line reverts to W. The position of the final kink is T - 27,000 / W hours of work.

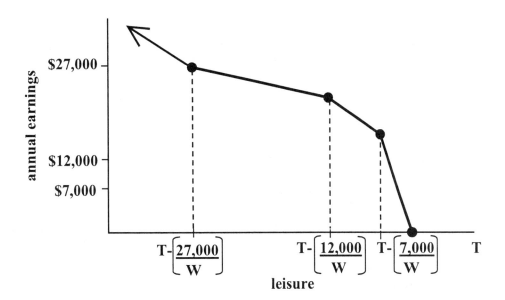

b. It is designed very much to affect the worker's behaviour through a positive substitution effect. As the wage level increases, the substitution effect implies that the number of hours worked increases, and the income effect works toward fewer hours of work. For low-wage workers, assuming that their level on non-labour market income is low, it should increase the number of hours that they work. If the level of non-labour market income is fairly high, however, it may not have this effect.

Multiple Choice Questions

1. Consider Figure 3.1 in the textbook. The original equilibrium is E_0, while the new equilibrium is E_d. This change could be brought about by which of the following policies?
   a) The negative income tax plan
   b) Unemployment-insurance-assisted work sharing
   c) Unemployment insurance
   d) A demogrant payment
   e) A conventional social assistance program

2. Consider the case of a social assistance program in the framework of the income-leisure model. When the benefits become available, what changes occur to the diagram?
   a) There is a kink in the budget line.
   b) The budget line becomes steeper.
   c) The budget line becomes flatter.
   d) The budget line shifts outward in parallel fashion.
   e) The shape and slope of the indifference curve changes.

3. Consider the framework of the income-leisure model and the context of a social assistance program. If the budget line is flat over any range of working hours, the interpretation is which of the following?
   a) The level of non-market income is high.
   b) The rate of remuneration for those hours is zero.
   c) The individual does not value income very highly relative to leisure.
   d) The marginal rate of substitution is zero.
   e) Such a case is not possible.

4. Welfare reform tends to be oriented around which of the following strategies?
   a) Lowering demogrant benefits
   b) Reducing fraud and abuse of benefits
   c) Altering the incentive structure of benefits so that the returns to working are greater
   d) Altering the income-leisure preferences of recipients
   e) All of the above

5. Which of the following statements concerning social assistance programs is *false*?
   a) The high implicit tax rate on welfare benefits is an important work disincentive.
   b) Lowering benefits can cause undue hardship on certain recipients, even if it increases incentives to work.
   c) The negative income tax program gives more incentives to work than a situation of a labour market with no welfare program at all.
   d) Under a negative income tax program, workers do face a clawback in labour market earnings.
   e) There is a fundamental trade-off between creating incentives for working and providing a social safety net for disadvantaged individuals.

6. Consider Figure 3.5 in the textbook. The original equilibrium is E_0, while the new equilibrium is E_s. This change could be brought about by which of the following policies?
   a) The negative income tax plan
   b) Unemployment-insurance-assisted work sharing
   c) Unemployment insurance
   d) A wage subsidy program
   e) A conventional social assistance program

7. All of the following are characteristics of a wage-subsidy program except:
   a) It can be fiscally costly.
   b) It has an ambiguous effect on work incentives.
   c) It involves a substitution effect and an income effect.
   d) It is an effective tool for providing assistance to disadvantaged families.
   e) It should provide greater incentives for working than the negative income tax program.

8. The basic idea that underlies the design of a negative income tax program is that:
   a) Welfare payments should be designed solely to provide an adequate income floor to recipients.
   b) Welfare programs should be designed solely to give recipients incentives to work.
   c) Negative taxes are not as painful as positive taxes.
   d) Compared to a situation in which no assistance whatsoever is given to the poor, this program gives more incentives to work.
   e) Compared to the situation of conventional social assistance, this program gives recipients more incentives to work.

9. In order for a welfare recipient to prefer being on the dole to getting a job, which of the following conditions must hold?
   a) The equilibrium with social assistance must leave the worker on a higher indifference curve than does the equilibrium without it.
   b) The equilibrium with social assistance must leave the worker with more income than does the equilibrium without it.
   c) The equilibrium with social assistance must leave the worker with more leisure than does the equilibrium without it.
   d) The substitution effect of the benefits must dominate the income effect.
   e) The worker must receive a demogrant as well as variable compensation.

10. Consider the effect of workers' compensation within the income-leisure framework. Assume that the compensation level is approximately $2/3$ of the level of original earnings before the injury. In Figure 3.10b, what is the significance of the points E_0, E_C, and H_f, respectively?
   a) The point corresponding to the original equilibrium, the equilibrium with compensation, and the post-injury equilibrium without any compensation
   b) The point corresponding to the equilibrium with compensation, the original equilibrium, and the post-injury equilibrium without any compensation
   c) The point corresponding to the post-injury equilibrium without any compensation, the original equilibrium, and the equilibrium with compensation
   d) The point corresponding to the equilibrium with compensation, the equilibrium without any compensation, and the original equilibrium
   e) None of the above

11. Which of the following statements does not apply to Figure 3.10c? Assume that the compensation level is Y_0.
    a) The worker is better off post-injury with the compensation than she was while working.
    b) The worker was better off while working than she would be if there were no compensation available after the injury.
    c) In order to make the worker as well off as she was before the injury, the compensation level must be equal to the distance H_fC.
    d) The earnings levels are the same before and after the injury, given compensation.
    e) The worker's utility level would be negative without the compensation, as she would be on indifference curve U_d.

12. Assuming that an individual is capable of performing some work, what is the nature of work disincentive effects associated with workers' compensation?
    a) The income effect of the benefit tends to increase hours worked, but the substitution effect of the benefit tends to increase hours worked.
    b) The income effect of the benefit tends to reduce hours worked, but the substitution effect of the benefit tends to increase hours worked.
    c) Both the income effect and the substitution effect of the benefit tend to decrease hours worked.
    d) Only the income effect of the benefit tends to reduce hours worked, while the substitution effect does not apply in this case.
    e) None of the above.

13. A common theme of the various commissions' reports on social policy that were released in the 1980s (the Forget Commission, the MacDonald Commission) was that:
    a) Canada's social insurance programs are too costly for taxpayers.
    b) Canada's social insurance programs provide adequately for the needs of the working poor.
    c) Canada's social insurance programs contain design flaws, which often discourage recipients from finding gainful employment.
    d) Canada's social insurance programs could be improved, but major reforms are not desirable.
    e) Benefits should be determined on the basis of need, regardless of how employable a recipient is.

14. Canada's unemployment insurance program has received much criticism from most policy analysts. Their greatest concern is that:
    a) Unemployment insurance (UI) has evolved in many circumstances into a long-term income maintenance program.
    b) Benefits are paid for too long a period, causing individuals to delay their job search.
    c) It serves to insure workers from income loss associated with the risk of unpredictable unemployment.
    d) It has an unfunded liability.
    e) The premiums are judged to be too high.

Labour Market Economics, Fifth Edition

15. A negative income tax policy program is supposed to combat poverty by:
    a) Granting a demogrant to poor individuals.
    b) Granting a wage subsidy to low-wage workers, which is reduced progressively as earnings increase.
    c) Granting a subsidy to employers to induce them to hire more disadvantaged workers.
    d) Taxing well-paid workers with a negative tax, and taxing low-wage workers with a positive tax.
    e) Granting job-training subsidies to the disadvantaged.

Answers to Multiple Choice Questions

1. D See the caption for Figure 3.1. Response C precludes any work being performed, so there is no budget line. Responses A, B, and E involve kinks in the budget line, as not all hours worked are remunerated at the same rate.
2. A See Figure 3.2. Social assistance, or welfare, involves a 100% clawback.
3. B For response A, the level of non-market income is given by the intercept on the right edge of the diagram. Responses C and D deal with the indifference curve. Response E is totally wrong.
4. C Although response B makes sense, that is not the highest priority. Response A implies a cutback of benefits rather than a reform. Response D is hard for the government to bring about.
5. C The incentives of the negative income tax program are superior to those of the conventional welfare program with its 100% clawback rule. See pages 82–86.
6. D A wage-subsidy scheme is one of the easier programs to model within this framework. Most of the other programs involve kinks in the budget line.
7. D The program is not necessarily well targeted, as workers belonging to middle- and upper-class families can be eligible. See pages 86–88.
8. E Response A refers to the conventional social assistance program. There would be no need for a welfare program at all given response B. Response C is true, but that doesn't answer the question. Response D is false.
9. A The level of welfare can only be ascertained by the indifference curve, which considers both the level of income and the level of leisure. For response D, there is no substitution effect for conventional welfare programs, as the payments are in the form of a demogrant. Response E will not necessarily make the worker better off.
10. A See the caption for Figure 3.10.
11. E Response A is true because he/she is on a higher indifference curve. Response B is true because the original indifference curve U_0 is above any indifference curve passing through H_f. Response C is true because that would put the worker back on indifference curve U_0. Response D is true, as that level of income is Y_0.
12. D Response A is false, as the income effect reduces hours worked. For responses B and C, a positive substitution effect applies only if the worker receives a wage supplement for hours worked. If so, it would not be a disincentive.
13. C
14. A See page 90.
15. B Response A refers to the conventional social assistance program. Response C refers to the wage-subsidy program. Response D makes no sense, as it is a Robin Hood scheme in reverse.

CHAPTER 4

Chapter Highlights

Introduction and Motivation

An essential difference between this chapter and the preceding two chapters is the time frame, which now spans all of an individual's potential working life. The focus of this chapter is on variations in labour supply, or patterns in labour supply, in the time that an individual is between the ages of 20 and 65 years (roughly). This type of framework is sometimes called the life cycle. Choices of whether or not to participate in the labour market, or how many hours to supply, depend in part on the career stage and the family status of a worker.

1. Dynamic Life-Cycle Models

Unlike the static labour supply models presented in Chapters 2 and 3, dynamic life-cycle models involve a multi-period analysis. The question is how much labour the individual plans to supply (and hence how much labour income he/she expects to earn) at each stage of the life cycle or the entire career. In this model, the worker chooses consumption levels and leisure for each period of his/her life cycle, based on his/her preferences given a lifetime income constraint. How does a change in a variable such as the wage or the non-labour income at one stage of the life cycle affect the choice of hours to supply at another stage? For example, if a pay raise is anticipated in the future, what effect will it have on labour supply in the current period? The simplest case is the 2-period model, which essentially divides the 45-year career into an earlier part and a later part. Borrowing money in the earlier period to be repaid from higher earnings in the later period is feasible. The quantity of labour supplied in each of the two periods is a function of wages and preferences in all periods and the discounted present value of lifetime earnings.

The two graphs in Figure 4.2 are called age-earnings profiles, and they illustrate three different types of wage changes. The difference between the two curves is called a profile shift, as the permanent earnings of a worker increase. An evolutionary wage change for an individual is represented by a movement along the curve, which corresponds to normal career advancement. A transitory wage change is represented by a temporary blip from a given wage profile. Each of these three types of wage changes will have a different effect on the labour supply choices over the life cycle, with different income effects and substitution effects applying in each of the three cases.

2. Fertility and Child-Bearing

The dynamic life-cycle earnings framework can be applied to a number of specific choices tied to labour supply behaviour, including the interface between fertility and labour market activity. For women, the fertility patterns are closely related to labour supply patterns. The choices have an intertemporal dimension, which means that the decision to bear children in one time period (and raise them in the next time period) has repercussions for earnings much later in the life cycle. The essential variables are family income, the price or cost of a child, wages, tastes and preferences (career aspirations, desire to have children), and the foregone earnings of the parent charged with raising the children. These earnings have income effects and substitution effects on labour supply patterns.

The challenge for empirical work is to isolate the impact of one variable, such as baby bonuses or women's wages, on fertility patterns. The existing evidence indicates the presence of a strong substitution effect among working-age women. As the economic returns to work increase, the opportunity cost of parenthood increases. Female workers supply more labour, which implies higher labour force participation rates, longer working hours, and lower fertility rates. There tends to be a negative relationship between the number of children and the cost of having and raising children, particularly as measured by the foregone labour market earnings. There tends to be a negative relationship between income and family size across countries; in less developed countries, children can be put to work at fairly young ages and contribute to family income. In this respect, having children can be viewed as an inferior good.

3. Retirement Decisions/Pensions

The decision to retire is a decision to no longer participate in the labour force. As this choice is affected by labour supply (and savings) decisions made throughout the worker's career, it is an ideal application for the dynamic labour supply model. Like the case of fertility behaviour, retirement is rife with issues concerning government policy, particularly pensions and the size of the labour force. The government is very active in the policy domain of retirement from the labour force.

The theoretical determinants of retirement include regulations such as mandatory retirement. This practice is common in unionized settings or among employers with pension programs and formal wage policies. Other variables that can influence retirement behaviour are wealth and earnings of the individual, his/her health, the nature of work and family responsibilities, and spousal income. As wealth increases, there is a pure income effect working towards earlier retirement, as one can afford to retire earlier. As the worker's wage increases, there is a substitution effect discouraging retirement (higher foregone labour market earnings), and an income effect working in the opposite direction (he/she could afford to retire earlier).

There are three major types of pensions in Canada. The two government-sponsored pension plans are the universal Old Age Security (OAS) plan and the social insurance pensions of QPP in Quebec and CPP in the rest of Canada. There are also employer-sponsored pension plans. Their primary function is to provide income during old age when labour market opportunities are low. In addition, all of these sources of pension income have potentially different influences on labour market choices and retirement behaviour — that is, at what stage of the life cycle retirement will occur. Their provisions are summarized in Exhibit 4.8. The OAS program takes the form of a demogrant; it thus entails only an income effect. The social insurance pensions can involve (although this does not apply to Canada) very significant implicit taxes on the labour market earnings of those who continue to work while collecting benefits, which lowers the returns to working after retirement. In the extreme case, pension benefits are clawed back one dollar for every dollar that is earned on the labour market. This entails a negative substitution effect on working and tends to encourage retirement.

The private pension plans are typically categorized as defined contribution plans and defined benefit plans. These plans are an integral part of the overall compensation packages benefiting workers. Various institutional features of these plans, such as early retirement and postponed retirement provisions, have important incentive effects for the retirement decisions of older workers (whether to take early retirement, postponed retirement, or normal retirement) and the turnover decisions of younger workers (whether to stay with the employer or quit). For instance, if a pension scheme is back-loaded, the worker's accrued benefits upon retirement grow rapidly during the later years of his/her career. This discourages workers from quitting a firm too early. A key concept is that almost all pension schemes — public or private — serve an important role beyond merely providing income support to retired workers.

The empirical evidence indicates that the characteristics of public and private pension plans affect the retirement decision in ways in which the theory predicts, but the estimated responses in terms of retirement behaviour to changes in these economic variables have been minor. A good portion of the major trends in retirement behaviour over the past three decades remain unexplained by economic variables that we can observe.

Helpful Hints

- You should review the basic elements of present value discounting, which appears in any textbook of introductory econometrics. It is a procedure for calculating the value today of the right to receive a stream of payments in the future. In essence, it is a way of comparing money received in the future (or the past) with money received in the present.
- The primary graph for this chapter is not the income-leisure choice model, but rather the age-earnings profile in Figure 4.2. Although the graph does not appear complicated, it reflects more economic substance than what first meets the eye. Each profile gives the locus of earnings levels that a worker can be expect to earn as he/she progresses through his/her career. A shift from A to B could emerge from obtaining a particular degree or qualification and working in that occupation for many years. A movement from B to C is associated with normal career advancement as the worker ages. A blip from C to D reflects an unanticipated temporary wage gain.
- Always keep in mind the distinction between a substitution effect and an income effect. In this life-cycle context, it matters whether it is permanent or temporary, anticipated or unanticipated. A strong substitution effect is most likely when a wage change is temporary. For instance, if a firm is scheduling a lot of overtime for an upcoming period of six months, many workers will increase their work hours in order to benefit "while the going is good." For temporary wage changes, income effects should be minor. Substitution effects are also likely to enter when the worker expects to receive seniority raises on a regular basis (that is, anticipated wage increases). He/she has an incentive to work longer hours when wages are high (mid-career) and shorter hours when wages are lower (at the earlier stages of a career). If all of these wage changes are unanticipated over the course of the career, income effects should not be important.
- For the fertility section of this chapter you should be aware of the major developments over the past 50 years, as well as the differences between developed and less developed countries. There is no graph to learn, but you should be able to think of economic explanations for some of the observed patterns.
- For the retirement section of this chapter, the income-leisure choice diagram can be applied to the case of an older worker. Focus on the impact of the retirement plan on the budget line. The primary parameters are the implicit tax rate for those workers who receive the pension but continue to work, the wage rate paid for labour market income, and the pension benefit. This is essentially the same theme that was present with social assistance programs: The rate at which benefits are clawed back as the level of earnings rises (the implicit tax rate) creates extremely strong disincentive effects.

Answers to Odd-Numbered End-of-Chapter Questions

1. Exhibit 4.3 and the corresponding passage in the textbook provides a partial response to this question. There has doubtless been a change in social mores that could reduce fertility, as well as new medical developments in family planning. The most important single economic reason is that higher salaries and real wages have caused a positive substitution effect on labour supply of women, which diminishes fertility.

3. If the mandatory retirement age is an exogenous determinant of the retirement decision, the former causes the latter. If it is an endogenous result of the retirement decision, the latter causes the former. For the first case, certain workers have strong preferences for income and work relative to leisure, such as the workaholic type. Such an institutional arrangement may force them to withdraw from the labour force sooner than they would prefer. On the other hand, the age for mandatory retirement is sometimes predicated on the parameters for the salary scale and the pension scheme. In order for the employer to finance her payroll, with its hierarchy of salaries and career paths (for example, raises according to number of years of service), it may be necessary to oblige long-serving workers to retire. A similar story could apply to the employers' labour force requirements. In many cases, the recruitment of younger workers with more up-to-date skills is facilitated by mandatory retirement. This concern falls under the rubric of personnel policy. More discussion of mandatory retirement appears in Chapter 13.

5. This indifference curve would be tangent to the wage constraint line Y_mB at an interior solution and would intersect it again at point B at a corner solution. At point B, the indifference curve would be steeper than the budget line, which is flat. At the interior solution, she is still working and is earning a higher income than she would earn if she were retired. She also incurs a disutility from work, however. If she were to retire, she would not work at all, but the income level would be only Y_b, and she would have a higher utility from leisure. She trades off two goods — income and leisure — along an indifference curve such that all combinations are equally valued. In order to discourage retirement, one could lower the pension amount Y_b, which would lower the horizontal part of the wage constraint line near point B. One could also cut taxes on earnings, which would rotate the other segment of the income constraint line clockwise. As the opportunity cost of leisure increases, the returns to working (as opposed to retiring) increase.

7. This question deals with material that has been mentioned in the previous questions. As far as deliberate government policy is concerned (factors over which the government has some influence), the relevant measures include provision of child care, educational services, tax exemptions, and child benefits and allowances. In Canada, the Quebec government has been quite active in attempting to raise fertility rates.

Answers to Odd-Numbered End-of-Chapter Problems

1. First, it is necessary to understand what we mean by these terms. The static model refers to a relatively short time frame in which all variables except wages, non-labour income, and factors such as social programs remain fixed. The idea is to explain choices of hours over the course of a workday, workweek, or perhaps work year. With the dynamic model, or the life-cycle model, we are looking at how time spent working is allocated over a 40-year period. The basic idea is that as people become older, their preferences for income versus leisure evolve, their earnings change,

and the constraints that they face change. Probably the two most important factors to consider are child-bearing/raising activities and retirement decisions. In addition, within a dynamic framework, it is possible to save income earned from one period in order to consume more than what one earns in another period.

As far as tax cuts are concerned, in the static setting, the time frame is too short to distinguish between a permanent versus a transitory tax cut. We would examine an income effect and a substitution effect. As taxes are reduced, take-home pay increases, and the substitution effect tells the worker to work longer hours. As total take-home pay increases, however, it is possible to maintain living standards by working fewer hours. This negative income effect pushes the workers to work fewer hours.

For the static setting, if a tax cut is temporary, we would not expect for it to have much of an impact on labour supply patterns. For the dynamic setting, a temporary tax cut is depicted as the move from C to D in Figure 4.2. As explained in the text that corresponds to that graph, there is probably a positive substitution effect inducing longer hours during the time that the tax cut is in effect. There is not much of an income effect working in the opposite direction. A permanent tax cut means higher wages now and into the future. This corresponds to the movement from A to B in Figure 4.2, except that we are talking about two different tax levels for the same person rather than two different individuals with higher and lower wages. As explained in the text that corresponds to that graph, we would expect a positive substitution effect pushing toward more hours worked, but an income effect working in the other direction.

3a. Women's wages: As they increase, the substitution effect induces them to work longer hours, which should reduce fertility.

   b. Family allowances: This is an increase in non-labour income. There is only a pure income effect causing them to purchase more leisure and work fewer hours. The allowance allows them to maintain living standards while working fewer hours. This should increase fertility.

   c. The basic income tax exemption for each dependent: First, one should note that in Canada, this does not exist. Instead, there is a child tax benefit for lower- and middle-class families that works like Problem 3b. This policy should generate an income effect inducing the worker to work fewer hours, as again a certain living standard can be had by working less and taking more leisure. There is not much of a substitution effect working in the other direction because this tax exemption does not affect earnings at the margin. In other words, when faced with the decision of whether or not to work overtime, the worker does not care about these tax exemptions, because they apply only to her basic salary. This tax policy can be expected to increase fertility.

   d. For reasons explained in the text, as the education level of women continues to rise, we can expect even further decreases in fertility. Some of this is due to a substitution effect stemming from higher earnings, while some of it is attributable to a change in tastes and custom regarding child-bearing.

5a. See Figure 4.3c in the textbook. The units on the horizontal axis are weeks, and they range from 0 to 52. At the right-most point on the graph, where there is no work, all 52 weeks of the year are allocated to leisure. The non-labour income is B = $6,000, so the endpoint is (52,$6,000). Moving from right to left, W = $600 for each week of work. Over the first 15 weeks of work, labour market earnings rise from $0 to $9,000, there is no penalty, and total income rises to $15,000. The slope of the budget line is -600. Over the next range of 20 weeks of work, gross earnings rise from $9,000 to $21,000. The $12,000 that he/she earns on the labour market is

Labour Market Economics, Fifth Edition

subjected to a 50% clawback, so the benefits of $6,000 are paid back, and net earnings are $300 per week. The point of the first kink is (37,$15,000), the point of the second kink is (17,$21,000), and the slope of the segment between them is -300. For the remaining 17 weeks of the year, the wage = 600, so the slope is -600.

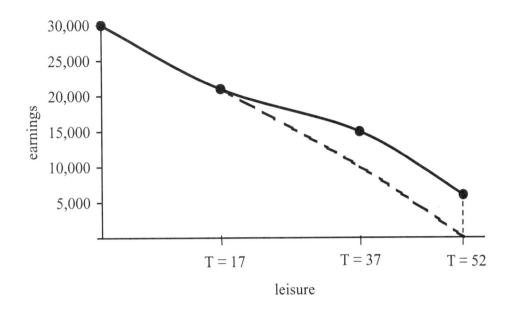

b. There should be a tangency on the segment between the points (37,$15,000) and (17,$21,000).
c. If the retirement test is eliminated, the slope of the budget constraint becomes -600 everywhere. The right endpoint is still (52,$6,000), but the kinks are removed. There is a positive substitution effect and a negative income effect as work pays more than before. The current indifference curve intersects the new, higher budget line, and the worker can reach a higher indifference curve, so he/she is better off. The statement is therefore true if leisure is a normal good. In the event that leisure is not a normal good, it is possible, however, to draw a tangency to the right as well as to the left of the tangency in Problem 5b, in which case the number of hours worked could decrease.

7a. The best way to think of the break-even level of earnings is that for which the pension is taxed away in its entirety, so $B = E_b{}^* t$ at the break-even level. Another approach, suggested by the hint, is to substitute information into the budget line to obtain $E_b = B + (1 - t)^* E_b$, which one can solve algebraically to obtain $E_b = B / t$.
b. Using the same method as above, set $E_b = B + Y_t + (1 - t) E_b$, which implies that $E_b = 1/ t (B + Y_t)$.
c. For case a, $B / t = \$12,000$. For case b, the result is $32,000.

Multiple Choice Questions

1. All of the following economic decisions can be modelled within the life-cycle approach to labour supply *except* which decision?
    a) The school/work decision
    b) The decision of whether and when to have children
    c) The decision to work overtime
    d) The decision to retire from the labour force
    e) All of the above

2. What type of wage increase will cause the greatest labour supply response in a dynamic life-cycle context?
   a) A permanent, unanticipated wage increase (due perhaps to gaining a union job).
   b) An evolutionary, anticipated wage increase (due to standard career progression).
   c) A transitory, unanticipated, one-time-only wage increase (due perhaps to earning a lot of overtime hours during a certain year).
   d) All of these changes will have an equal impact on labour supply.
   e) One needs more information in order to determine.

3. What is the primary difference between labour supply decisions in the life-cycle context and labour supply decisions in the shorter time frame?
   a) The substitution effect does not apply in the life-cycle model.
   b) The income effect does not apply in the life-cycle model.
   c) Intertemporal substitution effects, whereby a wage increase in one period only has an effect in another time period, occur in the life-cycle model.
   d) The budget constraint in the life-cycle model never has a kink.
   e) None of the above.

4. Consider the economic model of the decision to bear children. Which of the following variables is the least directly correlated with fertility rates?
   a) The potential income of wives
   b) The price of (or cost of having) children
   c) Technological developments
   d) The prices of related goods and services
   e) Tastes or preferences

5. All of the following are government programs related to old-age pensions *except* which program?
   a) The Canada/Quebec Pension Plan
   b) The Old Age Security program
   c) The Social Security program
   d) The Guaranteed Income Supplement program
   e) All of the above programs are related to pensions

6. Retirement decisions have important implications for public policy in all of the following issues *except* which issue?
   a) Fiscal constraints for old-age security programs
   b) Saving behaviour and capital formation for the economy
   c) The financial well being of elderly people
   d) Unemployment and the size of the labour force
   e) Health care

7. All of the following variables are expected to affect the retirement decision *except* which variable?
   a) Wealth and earnings levels
   b) Unemployment
   c) Health and the nature of work and family
   d) The demand for leisure
   e) The design features of pension plans, such as accruals

8. What is the primary difference between a universal Old Age Security pension and a social insurance pension?
   a) The former is funded from tax revenues, while the latter is not.
   b) The former is typically in the form of a demogrant, while the latter pays benefits according to prior contributions.
   c) For the Canada Pension Plan, a worker's contributions are held in escrow by the government and returned to the worker upon retirement.
   d) For the Canada Pension Plan, one cannot receive the benefits and continue to work (called a retirement test), while one can for the universal Old Age Security pension.
   e) All of the statements above are false.

9. Consider a government pension program that claws back some benefits as the recipient earns wages in the labour market. What are the effects on work incentives for an able-bodied individual?
   a) An income effect inducing more work and a substitution effect inducing less work
   b) An income effect inducing less work and a substitution effect inducing less work
   c) An income effect inducing less work and a substitution effect inducing more work.
   d) An income effect inducing more work and a substitution effect inducing more work
   e) Only an income effect inducing less work

10. What happens to a budget constraint when a retirement test is applied and any earnings from the labour market are deducted dollar for dollar from benefits?
    a) The budget line is flat.
    b) The budget line becomes steeper.
    c) The budget line becomes flatter.
    d) The budget line collapses to a single point.
    e) The budget lines shifts outward.

11. All of the following are aspects of public pension programs that are subject to government regulation *except* which?
    a) The retirement test
    b) The rate for contributions
    c) The replacement ratio for benefits
    d) The coverage and eligibility provisions
    e) The labour market opportunities of older workers

12. It may be in the interest of an employer to contribute to an early retirement program for his/her workers because of all of the following reasons *except* which reason?
    a) It will reduce the labour costs associated with pensions.
    b) It may open up new promotion opportunities for the existing labour force.
    c) It will contribute to downsizing the labour force, provided that the employer wants to reduce it.
    d) It may reduce the turnover of the existing labour force.
    e) It may maintain his/her reputation as a good employer by downsizing through less painful methods.

Answers to Multiple Choice Questions

1.   C   This decision is made within the framework of the static model, and the planning horizon is typically a week or a day. All of the other decisions are made over a long time frame within the dynamic life-cycle model.

2.   B   This is explained explicitly in the textbook in reference to Figure 4.2.

3.   C   Responses A, B, and D are totally false statements. See the section in the text entitled "Dynamic Life-Cycle Models."

4.   C   This is explained explicitly in the textbook in the section entitled "Fertility and Child-Bearing."

5.   C   All of the public pension programs are described on pages 128–129 in the textbook.

6.   D   These factors are mentioned in the section of the textbook entitled "Retirement Decisions and Pensions," although response D does play a role in some countries in Western Europe.

7.   B   These factors are mentioned in the section of the textbook entitled "Retirement Decisions and Pensions," although response B does play a role in some countries in Western Europe.

8.   B   This is explained explicitly in the textbook on pages 128–129.

9.   A   Benefit clawbacks can be interpreted as wage cuts, or a decline in the returns to working. If leisure is a normal good, wage changes always have positive substitution effects (meaning less work in this case) and negative income effects (meaning more work, in this case).

10.   A   This is explained explicitly in the textbook in reference to Figure 4.3b. The returns to working are zero.

11.   E   The first four responses are mentioned in the descriptions of public pension plans provided in the textbook on pages 128–129. Public pension policy does not directly affect the labour market opportunities of older workers; it changes the returns to those work activities.

12.   A   In order to induce a worker to take the early retirement option, it is usually necessary to make the benefit package more attractive than the standard benefits awarded upon a normal retirement.

CHAPTER 5

Chapter Highlights

1. Categorizing the Structure of Product and Labour Markets

In order to determine the equilibrium wage and employment levels in the labour market, one needs to assess the structure of the labour market as well as the structure of the product market. One has to consider the degree of competition that prevails in both of these markets. For our purposes, the four major cases are i) perfect competition in the labour market and perfect competition in the product market, ii) perfect competition in the labour market and monopoly in the product market, iii) monopsony in the labour market and perfect competition in the product market, and iv) monopsony in the labour market and monopoly in the product market.

2. Demand for Labour in the Short Run

The starting point for deriving the demand for labour is the firm's technology of production, which is contained in the production function (Equation 5.1). The stock of capital is fixed, so the only variable factor of production is labour. It is assumed that the firm is motivated by profit maximization. The firm will always select the level of labour input such that marginal revenue product (MRP), which is the increment to total revenue obtained by hiring one more unit of labour, is equal to the marginal cost of obtaining that unit of labour on the labour market. The firm's demand curve for labour is the portion of the MRP curve that lies below the average revenue product curve. The firm's demand curve for labour slopes downward due to the law of diminishing marginal returns.

3. Wages, the Marginal Productivity of Labour, and Competition in the Product Market

In the special case where the product market is perfectly competitive, the marginal revenue product (MRP) is called the value of the marginal product (VMP). The relationship between them is demonstrated in Equation 5.2. The equilibrium level of labour hired in the special case of perfect competition in both the labour market and the product market occurs when the VMP is equal to the wage paid to labour (Equation 5.3). The equilibrium level of labour hired in the special case of perfect competition in the labour market and monopoly in the product market occurs when the MRP is equal to the wage paid to labour (Equation 5.4).

4. Demand for Labour in the Long Run

In the long run, the capital stock is variable, and the firm selects both the equilibrium level of capital and the equilibrium level of labour hired. For the first case, one assumes that the level of output has been determined, and that the firm seeks to minimize the costs of production. Given the wage level (w) and the rate of return on capital (r), the firm selects the level of labour and the level of capital such that the marginal rate of technical substitution between those two factors is equal to the wage divided by the rate of return on capital (Equation 5.4). In the second and more complicated case, the firm selects the profit-maximizing level of output, and subsequently the equilibrium levels of labour and capital.

5. Demand for Labour in the Short Run

A change in the wage brings about a change in the quantity demanded of labour, and this change can be decomposed into a scale effect and a substitution effect. The former refers to the component that is attributable to the change in the level of output, holding relative factor prices (the wage and the rate of return on capital) constant. The latter refers to the component that is attributable to the change in the relative factor prices, holding the level of output fixed. Both the scale effect and the substitution effect work in the same direction to yield an unambiguous downward-sloping demand for labour.

6. The Relationship between the Short- and Long-Run Labour Demand

In the short run, the capital stock is fixed, so there is no substitution effect; there is only a scale effect. The downward slope of the short-run labour demand curve is a consequence of the scale effect and the law of diminishing marginal returns to labour. The long-run labour demand curve has a steeper slope because both the scale effect and the substitution effect apply.

7. Labour Demand under Cost Minimization

This is a particular case mentioned above in which the capital stock can vary, but the level of output is given. This implies that there is no scale effect.

8. Elasticity of Labour Demand

Hicks' four laws deal with the relationship between four economic variables and the wage elasticity of demand for labour. The basic determinants are the availability of substitute factors of production (the greater the availability, the higher the elasticity), the elasticity of supply of these substitute inputs (not usually an important point), the price elasticity of demand for output (the higher this elasticity in the output market, the higher the elasticity of labour demand), and the ratio of labour cost to total cost (the higher this proportion, the higher the elasticity). The empirical evidence suggests that the wage elasticity of demand is fairly low, with -0.30 being a ballpark estimate.

The wage elasticity of demand is related to globalization and international trade. Changes in international trade and investment patterns have an impact on product market conditions, which in turn have an impact on the demand for labour. When the demand for labour shifts, the resulting change in equilibrium employment and wage levels is affected by the wage elasticity of demand for labour.

The remainder of this chapter deals with the impact of international trade on a single labour market. In order to determine whether foreign trade hurts employment in Canada, one has to consider the relative marginal products of labour in the two trading partners, as well as the relative wages that are paid. Both of these ratios are equally important (in fact, they are equalized) in the profit maximization condition that governs the allocation of labour across the two countries. Jobs will remain in Canada to the extent that unit labour costs are competitive with those of our trading partners. Almost all economists agree with the principle that lower trade barriers generate higher levels of productivity and hence higher incomes. The gains from trade stem from specialization of production patterns, but the transition to freer trade entails substantial adjustment costs. The empirical evidence seems to indicate that the FTA and NAFTA are quite beneficial to the Canadian economy.

Labour Market Economics, Fifth Edition

Helpful Hints

- The primary and unifying theme of this chapter is that the demand for labour is derived from the demand for the product or service that the workers produce.
- Beyond that theme, however, various cases of labour demand vary according to two dimensions: the time frame and the structure of the labour and product markets.
- As far as the time frame is concerned, there are three cases, and they each have somewhat different graphs. First, there is the short run, in which the capital stock is fixed. The isoquant-isocost diagram does not apply here. In the long run, there are two cases: fixed output and variable output. For the former, there is only the isoquant-isocost diagram, and the firm minimizes costs along a given isoquant. The latter case is complicated, as it involves the firm's cost curves, as well as the isoquant-isocost diagram. First, it determines the profit-maximizing level of output given a set of factor prices, and then it minimizes costs along a given isoquant.
- As far as the structure of product and labour markets is concerned, there are four primary cases, which are listed in the chapter highlights above. The structure of the output market is relevant for the MRP curve. The labour demand curve (also the MRP curve) is always downward sloping, but it is steeper in the case where the product market is a monopoly. The structure of the labour market is relevant for the labour supply curve. If it is perfectly competitive, the firm faces an infinitely elastic labour supply curve. If it is monopsonistic, the firm faces an upward-sloping supply curve; this topic is discussed further in Chapter 7.
- If you are a bit uncomfortable with the isoquant-isocost analysis, which is not easy to master, you can find a review in most introductory textbooks, which typically contain an appendix that explains this model.
- It is easy to confuse the two expressions for the marginal rate of technical substitution (MRTS) in Equations 5.5 and 5.6. The first equation relates the marginal product of labour to the marginal product of capital, while the second one relates the marginal product of labour in Canada to the marginal product of labour in foreign countries.
- Provided that labour is a normal (as opposed to an inferior) factor of production, the scale and substitution effects of a wage change always work in the same (negative) direction.
- As indicated in the chapter highlights, only three of Hicks' laws are important. As they are quite intuitive, they need not be memorized.
- The final part of the chapter deals with the link between international trade and labour demand. One of the key points is the importance of relative unit-labour costs across trading partners. Low unit-labour costs are associated with comparative advantage and are conducive to employment growth.
- For further exposition of the model of international trade section involving the production possibilities frontier, see the international trade chapter of many basic principles textbooks.

Answers to Odd-Numbered End-of-Chapter Questions

1. This is an interior solution where the isoquant is tangent to the isocost line. The marginal rate of technical substitution between labour and capital is equal to the ratio of their prices. Any other point in the diagram is either unattainable for the firm, or is suboptimal, meaning that the firm can make higher profits by a substitution of one input for another. The firm's expansion path is the locus of points (capital/labour combinations) that the firm chooses as it expands production. Do not confuse it with the labour demand curve, which is in employment-wage space. The expansion path is always in labour-capital space, just like the isocost and the isoquant curves.

Normally, we would expect the expansion path to be positively sloped — as output expands, the firm hires more labour. It need not be a straight line, however, and in general, it is not.

3. This statement is false. See the end of the section entitled "Demand for Labour in the Short Run." The theory of labour demand assumes that labour is homogenous in quality. The negative relationship is due to a negative scale effect and a negative substitution of a wage change on the quantity demanded of labour.

5. Unit labour costs are obtained by dividing labour cost by the output level. In the context of international competitiveness, the three components to unit labour costs are indicated by the solid line in Figure 5.8. First is the exchange rate. A strong Canadian dollar in the early 1990s raised the unit labour costs relative to those of some of its trading partners, and a depreciating dollar thereafter had the opposite effect. The next factor is the labour costs per hour expressed in Canadian dollars, which are indicated by the dashed line in Figure 5.8. In the late 1990s, these costs fell relative to those of our trading partners. The figures of Table 5.1, which show the levels of compensation costs relative to Canadian levels, indicate that Canada is reasonably competitive in terms of compensation costs relative to other industrialized countries. In addition, the growth in hourly compensation (after converting into U.S. dollars) between 1979 and 1999 was in line with most of Canada's trading partners (see Table 5.2). The third factor is physical productivity, or output per hour, which is indicated by the dotted line in Figure 5.8. The first column of Table 5.2 shows that Canada fared badly compared to most of its trading partners in this dimension, as productivity grew slowly between 1979 and 1999. Combining these three factors, Canada's unit labour costs grew in the middle range of these countries over this period. Canada did not lose much competitiveness in relation to its largest trading partner, the United States.

7. This statement might have been true in the late 1980s and early 1990s (see pages 162–163), but due in part to a weak Canadian dollar, Canadian goods and services were quite competitive with American products in the late 1990s and early in the following decade. That competitiveness was manifested in a series of very strong trade surpluses. One cannot sustain, however, a gain in competitiveness based on a continual depreciation of the currency, as that can serve to divert attention away from the continual challenge of increasing productivity — modernizing production facilities, restructuring, and so on. The last section of the chapter talks about the constant presence of all demand-side factors, and not just international trade, in necessitating cost efficiency in production — a flexible, highly trained, and adaptable labour force, flexible, modular factories, just-in-time inventory and delivery system, and so on.

Answers to Odd-Numbered End-of-Chapter Problems

1a. Given that the production function is $Q = 2L^{1/2}$, we can derive the function for the marginal product of labour, which is the derivative of that function with respect to labour input: $1 / L^{1/2}$. The next step is to derive the function for the marginal revenue product of labour. Assuming that the product market is perfectly competitive, the MRP = VMP = Price * marginal product of labour, which works out to $10 / L^{1/2}$. Since the firm's demand curve for labour is the same as its MRP curve (provided that we are below the firm's average revenue product curve), it follows that the expression for the demand curve is $W = 10 / L^{1/2}$. Solving for L, we have $L = 100 / W^2$. Note that there is a negative relationship between L and W, as there should be.

b. The values for the second column can be obtained by simply inputting the suggested value for the wage that appears in the first column. Once one has obtained these values for labour input, they

Labour Market Economics, Fifth Edition

can be inputted into the production function $Q = 2L^{1/2}$ to obtain the values for the third column. In order to obtain the values for profit, it is necessary to ignore the costs incurred by the other factors of production. These figures are thus interpreted as the profits net of labour costs. The expression is total revenue - total labour costs = Price*output - wage*labour input = 10*output (from column 3) - wage (from column 1)*labour input (from column 2). The figures appear in the table below.

Wage	Labour Demand	Output	Profit
$1.00	100	20	$100
$2.00	25	10	$50
$5.00	4	4	$20
$10.00	1	2	$10

The profit level falls as the wage level increases.

3. The answer to this question depends on whether the output level is fixed. If the case mentioned in the textbook under the heading "Labour Demand under Cost Minimization" applies, the level of output is not generated by profit-maximizing behaviour. The employer is likely to minimize costs subject to a certain level of service being provided. Unless the services of doctors and the services of nurses are perfect complements, which means that they are not substitutable at all, the statement is true. Place the level of nursing services on one axis of the isoquant-isocost diagram and the level of doctor services on the other axis. As the wage paid to nurses increases, the relative wage paid to doctors decreases, and the isocost line rotates along a given isoquant. The health care organization will reallocate its labour input toward doctors and away from nurses. This is due to a pure substitution effect.

In the case in which the level of output is variable, and the health care provider sets this level by maximizing profits, an increase in the wage paid to nurses will shift the marginal cost curve upward. This will normally result in a lower level of output. Due to the scale effect, the quantity demanded for doctors will fall. On the other hand, the relative wage of doctors has fallen, so due to the substitution effect, the quantity demanded for doctors will increase. The net effect of this wage change on the quantity demanded for doctors depends on the magnitudes of the scale effect and the substitution effect, which work in opposite directions. If the scale effect dominates, the statement is false; if the substitution effect dominates, the statement is true.

5. The information that is provided regarding a wage of $15.00 per hour is irrelevant to this question. To respond to any of these questions, think of Hicks' laws. Note that, in some instances, more than one of these laws can apply. The responses below consider the influence of one variable at a time, holding all other factors fixed (including any other of Hicks' laws).

5a. Chemical herbicides can be thought of as a substitute factor for the manual labour of weeding. If they are banned from a jurisdiction, the firm does not have a viable substitute for the factor of manual labour, which works to reduce the wage elasticity of demand.

b. If the product market in which the coal is sold is characterized by a monopoly, the wage elasticity of demand is likely to be inelastic, *ceteris paribus.*

c. This case is similar to the previous question. The price elasticity of demand in the output market for cigarettes is lower than it is in the output market for fast food, so *ceteris paribus,* we would expect for the wage elasticity of demand to be higher (more elastic) in the latter.

d. Given the technology of production for firms in Silicon Valley, they are likely to employ many more computer programmers than secretaries. This implies that the payroll for the former comprises a much higher share of total production costs than does the payroll for the latter. *Ceteris paribus,* this implies that the wage elasticity of demand for programmers is likely to be more elastic than it is for secretaries.

e. It is probably harder to replace quality control engineers, either with machinery or with other workers, than it is to replace beer-production-line workers. *Ceteris paribus,* this implies that the wage elasticity of demand for the tasters is likely to be more elastic than it is for the beer-production-line workers.

Multiple Choice Questions

1. If the firm is a perfect competitor in the input market, then:
   a) It is a monopsonist.
   b) It must have market power in the product market.
   c) It can hire all of the labour it wants at the going market wage.
   d) The market labour supply curve is horizontal.
   e) The individual's labour supply curve is backward bending.

2. All of the following statements are equivalent *except* which statement?
   a) The supply of labour to a firm is perfectly elastic.
   b) The firm can hire all of the labour it wants at the going market wage.
   c) The labour supply curve facing the firm is horizontal.
   d) The firm possesses a degree of market power in the input market.
   e) The firm is unable to affect the going market wage.

3. Assuming that the output market is perfectly competitive, what occurs to the demand for labour as the physical productivity of workers increases?
   a) It shifts to the right as the workers are now producing more output.
   b) It shifts to the left as the employer now needs fewer workers to produce its usual output levels.
   c) Nothing, as one moves up the labour demand curve.
   d) Nothing, as one moves down the labour demand curve.
   e) Nothing, as the productivity of labour is not an element in labour demand.

4. Which of the following statements concerning the marginal revenue product of labour is *false*?
   a) It equals the change in total revenue obtained by hiring one more unit of labour.
   b) It equals the change in total revenue obtained by producing one more unit of output.
   c) It equals the marginal physical product of labour multiplied by the marginal revenue of production.
   d) Its downward-sloping part is equal to the demand curve for labour.
   e) It intersects the average revenue product curve at its highest point.

5. If the marginal revenue product exceeds the wage paid, then:
   a) The firm should increase its use of labour input.
   b) The firm should decrease its use of labour input.
   c) The firm is making a loss.
   d) The firm is making a profit.
   e) The law of diminishing marginal returns does not apply.

6. All of the following are ingredients in the derivation of the demand for labour *except* which?
   a) The technology of production
   b) The market structure of the output market
   c) The demand for the output that the workers produce
   d) Profit-maximizing behaviour on the part of firms
   e) Utility-maximizing behaviour on the part of workers

7. In the short run, the marginal revenue product of labour curve slopes downward because:
   a) Of the backward-bending supply curve of labour.
   b) Of the law of diminishing marginal returns.
   c) Of the substitution effect of wage changes.
   d) The stock of capital is fixed.
   e) Of Hicks' laws regarding the wage elasticity of labour demand.

8. In the long run, the labour demand curve slopes downward because:
   a) The substitution effect of a wage increase or decrease dominates the scale effect.
   b) The substitution effect of a wage decrease or increase and the income effect both work in the same direction.
   c) Solely the scale effect of a wage change matters.
   d) The scale effect of a wage increase or decrease dominates the substitution effect.
   e) Solely the substitution effect of a wage change matters.

9. Consider Figure 5.5 in the textbook. The original equilibrium is E_0, and the final equilibrium is E_1. Which distance gives the substitution effect of the wage change?
   a) N_1N_s
   b) N_sN_0
   c) N_1N_0
   d) K_1K_0
   e) None of the above

10. Consider Figure 5.5 in the textbook. The original equilibrium is E_0, and the final equilibrium is E_1. Which distance gives the scale effect of the wage change?
    a) N_1N_s
    b) N_sN_0
    c) N_1N_0
    d) K_1K_0
    e)   None of the above

11. Consider the long-run equilibrium for the firm's choice of labour and capital input. Which of the following statements is *false*?
    a)   The marginal area of technical substitution is equal to the ratio of the wage to the rate of return on capital.
    b)   The firm seeks to minimize the costs of producing a given level of output.
    c)   The ratio of capital input to labour input is equal to the ratio of the wage to the rate of return on capital.
    d)   The slope of the isoquant is equal to the slope of the budget line.
    e)   The rate at which the employer wants to substitute between capital and labour input is equal to the rate at which the market allows her to exchange them.

12. Which of the following statements is *false*?
    a)   The long-run labour demand curve is less elastic than the short-run labour demand curve.
    b)   The capital stock is fixed for the short-run labour demand curve.
    c)   There is no substitution effect in the case of the short-run labour demand curve.
    d)   An increase in the capital stock will normally cause an increase in the short-run demand for labour.
    e)   The firm seeks to maximize profits regardless of the time frame.

13. Which of the following is associated with a high elasticity of demand for labour (elastic case)?
    a)   Labour costs are low in relation to total production costs.
    b)   A low price elasticity of demand for the product.
    c)   A low degree of substitutability of labour with other factors.
    d)   Labour costs are high in relation to total production costs.
    e)   None of the above.

14. Which of the following is associated with a low elasticity of demand for labour (inelastic case)?
    a)   Labour costs are high in relation to total production costs.
    b)   A high price elasticity of demand for the product.
    c)   A high degree of substitutability of labour with other factors.
    d)   A high wage elasticity of supply.
    e)   A low price elasticity of demand for the product.

Labour Market Economics, Fifth Edition

15. The figures below give the production schedule and the product demand schedule for the firm, which has to decide how many workers to hire.

Workers Hired	*Average* Physical Product	Price of Output
0		$10
1	10	$10
2	9	$10
3	8	$10
4	7.5	$10
5	7	$10
6	6	$10

What would the wage have to be in order for the profit-maximizing firm to hire three workers?
a) $30
b) $40
c) $50
d) $60
e) Indeterminate

Answers to Multiple Choice Questions

1. C Alternatively, the labour supply curve facing the firm is infinitely elastic at the going market wage. Response A is the exact opposite, while responses D and E are irrelevant. Response B is wrong because a firm can be a perfect competitor in the input market without being a perfect competitor in the output market, and vice versa.

2. D This statement has the opposite meaning of the other four statements. In that case, the supply curve of labour for the firm slopes upward.

3. A Response B is a common misperception. Responses C and D refer to changes in the wage rate, while response E is totally wrong.

4. B Response B refers to the marginal revenue (not marginal revenue product) obtained by producing one more unit of output. All of the other statements are true.

5. A One can say nothing about the level of profit that is being earned, so responses C and D are wrong. Response E is irrelevant.

6. E Responses A, B, C, and D are made explicit in the section of the textbook entitled "Demand for Labour in the Short Run," and response E is totally irrelevant as it is related to labour supply.

7. B Responses D and C are tied to the negative slope of the demand curve for labour, but they are not the best, most direct answer. Response A is totally irrelevant. Response E pertains to the magnitude of the elasticity and not to the slope of the MRP curve.

8. B As mentioned in the chapter highlights, in the long run, there is both a scale effect and a substitution effect, and they both work in the same direction.

9. B This is demonstrated in the textbook. See the caption for that figure.

10. A This is demonstrated in the textbook. See the caption for that figure.

11. C This is false because the marginal rate of technical substitution is equal to the ratio of the marginal products of the factors and not to the ratio of the employment levels of the factors. See the section in the textbook entitled "Demand for Labour in the Long Run."

12. A   The opposite of this statement is true. Statement D is true because the employment of more capital will often raise the marginal product of labour.

13. D   This is one of Hicks' laws. Look for the case in which labour demand becomes more elastic. Refer to those laws to evaluate the validity of any of the responses.

14. E   This is another one of Hicks' laws. Look for the case in which labour demand becomes less elastic. Refer to those laws to evaluate the validity of any of the responses.

15. D   One has to calculate the total product of labour and then the marginal product of labour. The marginal product of the third worker is 6, so his/her MRP is $60.

CHAPTER 6

This chapter is an extension of the labour demand material that was covered in Chapter 5. In the previous chapter, labour is a totally variable and divisible factor. This means that the firm can adjust its quantity demanded of labour without limitation, hiring one hour more or less, or one worker more or less. It also means that the quantity of labour varies directly with the production level of the firm – as the level of output increases (decreases), the quantity demanded of labour increases (decreases). Finally, it implies that all labour costs are strictly variable costs. In this chapter, the topic of labour as a quasi-fixed factor of production is covered. With certain qualifications, this means that as the level of output increases (decreases), the quantity demanded of labour remains constant. This in turn has important consequences for the structure of labour costs, which now have a fixed component and a variable component.

1. Non-Wage Benefits and Total Compensation

In Chapter 5, the only remuneration that the worker receives for his/her services is the hourly wage, and this is the only cost that the employer incurs in hiring labour on the labour market. In practice, however, a good part of the remuneration is in the form of non-wage benefits, often called social benefits or transfers-in-kind. Additionally, the worker sometimes receives wages for time not spent at work. In recent decades, the absolute and relative importance of non-wage compensation has grown in the Canadian labour market. A number of reasons why both employers and employees may prefer to have a greater share of the total compensation take this form than was previously the case are listed. Government policy has certainly not discouraged this trend.

2. Quasi-Fixed Labour Costs

This is the key concept of this chapter. The basic idea is that the firm can alter its labour input in two ways: either change the number of workers or change the number of hours per worker, or both. The composition of labour input between employment and hours per employee is a very important choice for the firm, and it is affected by the structure of the labour costs between the quasi-fixed component and the strictly variable component. Quasi-fixed labour costs vary only with the number of employees. They are fixed with respect to that particular worker. The variable labour costs vary directly with the number of workers hired as well as the number of hours worked per worker. Once the worker has been hired, the quasi-fixed labour costs remain constant no matter how many hours he/she works. In other words, the marginal quasi-fixed labour cost is zero until another worker is hired. Once the employer has incurred the quasi-fixed labour costs, the employer has an incentive to work that employee as many hours as possible in order to amortize these quasi-fixed labour costs (such as training costs and hiring costs). The employer also has a disincentive to hiring more workers, as that would incur additional quasi-fixed labour costs. An implication is that it is generally much more costly to adjust the employment level than it is to adjust the number of hours worked. The textbook explains some of the phenomena that we observe in real-work labour markets, such as labour hoarding during economic downturns, in terms of the structure of labour costs between the quasi-fixed component and the strictly variable component.

The rule for the optimal choice of the number of workers to hire in the face of hiring and training costs is expressed in Equation 6.1. It is a derivative of the wage = marginal revenue product condition that was presented in Chapter 5.

3. Work Sharing and Job Creation

This section deals with a number of government policy measures that have been either introduced or suggested. The underlying idea is to "spread the work around more evenly," which means to induce firms and their workers to alter the composition of labour input such that there are fewer hours per worker and higher employment levels than would otherwise be the case. Measures of this type have been widely implemented in continental Europe and take the form of regulatory restrictions on overtime use (which includes reductions to the length of the standard workweek and subsidies to work-sharing schemes). Most economists are very sceptical of the long-run efficacy of these measures in creating jobs.

Helpful Hints

- The major concepts for this short chapter are listed in the chapter outline, and they are twofold. First, there are essentially two types of labour input: labour as a strictly variable factor and labour as a quasi-fixed factor. Second, always evaluate the cost of more or fewer employees relative to the cost of a shorter or a longer workweek.
- If the firm has to cut production and labour input, the relevant decision is whether it should carry out layoffs or reduce the working time of its existing labour force.
- If the firm is going to increase production and labour input, the relevant decision is whether it should hire new workers or increase the working time of its existing labour force.
- For Equation 6.1, you should be able to determine what would happen to the number of workers hired if there were a change in any of the variables listed below the equation. Always keep in mind the central microeconomic concept that the firm's choice depends on the *structure* of the costs — that is, a change in the variable costs has a different effect than a change in the fixed costs.

Answers to Odd-Numbered End-of-Chapter Questions

1. There are a number of such factors. Conceptually, think of the cost of each, relative to the other. One would expect the employer to choose the cheapest one. The factor that is emphasized the most in the text is quasi-fixed labour costs, which are defined on page 178. Examples of quasi-fixed labour costs include recruitment and training costs, payroll taxes, and many elements of non-wage compensation. As explained on pages 178–179, one general effect of quasi-fixed labour costs is to increase the marginal cost of hiring an additional worker, relative to the marginal cost of working an existing worker longer hours. The higher the level (or proportion) of quasi-fixed labour costs, the more one would expect employers to resort to overtime rather than hire new workers. Another factor is the technology of production. Certain industries and occupations lend themselves well to a division of labour input into many part-time jobs (hours per employee and the number of workers are interchangeable for the employer), while others seem to require full-time workers working long hours. An example of the former appears to be nursing, whereas many supervisory jobs seem to be characterized by the latter.

3. The answer is an emphatic yes. This phenomenon, called labour hoarding, is explained on pages 180–181. The essence of the model is covered on pages 178–179. For many workers, the hiring

and training costs are non-trivial. Most workers do not pay their own way at the firm when they are first hired. To the extent that these fixed and sunk costs (sometimes called non-recurrent costs) are paid by the employer, the returns from employing the person have to be amortized (recuperated through a VMP, which exceeds the wage paid) very gradually over a longer time horizon. During certain time periods — either the beginning of the worker's tenure or times of slack output demand — the wage exceeds the marginal revenue product (or the value of the marginal product), but in most other periods — after training has occurred or when demand is strong — the opposite should apply. What the equation does suggest is that over the expected tenure of the worker at the firm, the discounted present value of all of the employment-related expenses — including the flow of wages in the future — is at least as great as the discounted present value of the flow of revenues that the worker generates for the employer.

5. The basic idea is to compare the marginal cost of working a group of the employees of the existing labour force one more hour versus the marginal cost of hiring one more worker. Compare the expense of these two options on the margin. Suppose that eight workers, each working one hour of overtime per day, produce the equivalent output of one more worker added to the labour force per day. In other words, the marginal product is equal in each case. If the overtime premium is raised from 1.5 times to 2 times the base pay rate, each hour of overtime becomes more expensive relative to the choice of hiring another worker. One would expect the overtime option should be adopted less frequently. A subsidy for work sharing would have a similar effect. If the firm is expanding and thus hiring more labour input, it would render the option of hiring more workers cheaper, relative to the option of lengthening the standard length of working time. If the firm is cutting back and thus shedding labour input, a subsidy for work sharing would render the option of laying off workers more expensive than the option of shortening the standard length of working time.

    If the overtime premium were increased, workers who were hired for overtime hours would tend to lose some of these hours and, hence, lose some income. On the other hand, a few marginal workers who would otherwise be on layoff or waiting in the queue to be hired would gain employment and, hence, would be better off. Generally, work-sharing schemes favour the interests of marginal workers who would otherwise be on layoff or waiting in the queue to be hired. They do not favour the interests of workers who enjoy a high degree of job protection, as they are unlikely to be laid off in the event of a downturn. They work fewer hours under the work-sharing scheme. Even when they receive subsidies, they still tend to lose some income.

Answers to Odd-Numbered End-of-Chapter Problems

1. This problem illustrates the frequent compensation practice of social benefits that are paid explicitly by the employer. In this problem, the employer is paying the premiums on Jane's behalf. She does not have to pay an explicit premium, but she also cannot convert them into cash or some other benefit. Income received from working and insurance benefits are assumed to be goods that yield positive marginal utility to Jane. The key to this question is distinguishing between employer-provided insurance (which is the good on the horizontal axis) and insurance that she can buy on her own on the open market.

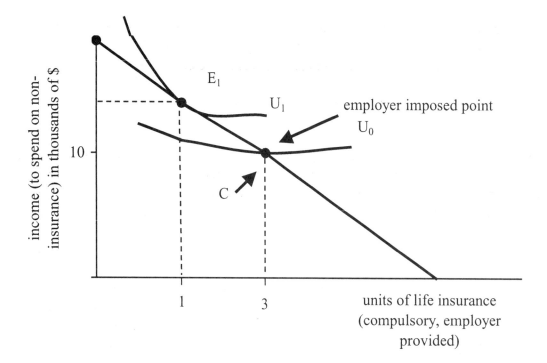

1a. The employer is offering her one bundle consisting of $10,000 in remuneration and $30,000 of insurance benefits. She has no other options, so her budget constraint consists of that one point. Do not draw a line.

b. If she were to receive only one unit of life insurance, she would have to receive a salary that is greater than $10,000 in order to be equally well off, because she has sacrificed two units of insurance that are worth something to her. We do not know how much additional income she would require in order for her to be equally well off with only one unit of insurance. If the salary were substantially higher than $10,000, she would likely prefer to receive that pay level and spend $2,000 on that unit of insurance (or $4,000 for two units of insurance). If the salary were only slightly higher than $10,000, she would likely prefer the firm's offer. E_1 refers to the former case. She is better off when she receives only one unit of employer-paid benefits. She will presumably spend a portion of the higher salary that she received (called "pay in lieu of benefits" in practice) on obtaining extra coverage on her own on the private insurance market. Even after this purchase, she will presumably have a higher income level than she would have if she were to receive three units of employer-paid insurance.

c. If the explicit cost to the firm is under $2,000 per unit of insurance, then the wage that the firm pays is not likely to be $2,000 lower than what would be the case if the firm did not provide benefits. In other words, the firm has to pay the cost in explicit terms, and it will pass along some of the cost to Jane in the form of lower wages. But this wage reduction (which is what is meant by the implicit cost of the insurance) is likely to be fairly small. The basic idea is that the implicit cost of what Jane pays for her benefits (in the form of lower wages) is usually much lower than the explicit cost of what she would have to pay for life insurance if she had no firm benefits. Her second option in this case would be to receive zero units of insurance but at a higher salary than $10,000 — that is, $10,000 plus approximately what the employer pays for the insurance benefits. This pay raise, however, is likely to be less than the $6,000 that she would have to pay in order to re-establish her coverage of three units. That becomes a second point on the budget constraint. If she values the insurance benefits a lot, she is likely to take the original option, because that insurance is provided at a fairly low implicit cost. If she values the insurance benefits a little, she is likely to take the option of higher pay in lieu of benefits, as the extra income, while small, is worth more to her than the extra insurance coverage.

Firm-provided compulsory insurance is less expensive, as there is much less of an adverse selection problem.

3a. It is a common practice to impose a ceiling on payroll taxes. The rationale is that since there is a ceiling on the level of wages that are covered by unemployment insurance or old age insurance benefits (called maximum insurable earnings), there should be a commensurate ceiling on the earnings to which the contributions are applied. This means that after the employee has earned E-bar, then the tax rate on further hours is nil.

b. The marginal cost of hiring one more hour of labour is W (1 + t), if Wh < E-bar, which is the earnings ceiling, and W, if Wh > E-bar.

c. and d. This cost structure gives the firm the incentive to increase the number of hours worked by an individual once he/she has reached the threshold of E-bar. After this point, we expect to see longer hours, because if more workers are hired, the payroll taxes must be paid until the new hires have worked sufficient hours to earn E-bar. If the workers have not reached that threshold, the firm is indifferent between lengthening the workweek and adding new workers. Collecting payroll taxes on all earnings would remove the incentive to work the existing labour force longer hours at the expense of hiring new workers. The tax would then be neutral as far as the decision of hiring more workers versus working the existing labour force longer hours is concerned. Most labour economists would argue in favour of this proposal, as it should raise the level of employment.

5. We are given that the $MP_L = 10 - 0.5*L$. This means that the $VMP_L = P*MP_L = 10 (10 - 0.5*L) = 100 - 5*L$.

a. The firm selects the level of input where the $VMP_L = $ wage. Given the wage of $10, this works out to $L_0 = 18$ units. If the price of the output falls to $5, then the $VMP_L = 5 (10 - 0.5*L) = 50 - 2.5*L$. Given the wage of $10, this works out to $L_0 = 16$ units. This result makes sense; as the price of the output falls, so does the demand curve for labour.

b. Based on Equation 6.1 in the textbook, the firm selects the level of input where the $VMP_L = $ wage + H + T = $10 + $20 = $30. Since there is only one time period, the sums that appear in Equation 6.1 disappear, as does the (1 + r) term. This employer has to recuperate all the hiring and training costs in one period only. The equilibrium condition becomes $VMP_L = 100 - 5*L = $30, or L = 14 units. If the price of the output falls to $5, the equilibrium condition becomes $VMP_L = 50 - 2.5*L = $30, or L = 8 units.

c. If hiring costs were to fall, the employer would require a lower VMP_L schedule in order to employ the same number of workers. Alternatively, the VMP_L or labour demand schedule net of hiring and training costs would shift up. If hiring costs were to rise, the employer would require a higher VMP_L schedule in order to employ the same number of workers. Alternatively, the VMP_L, or labour demand schedule net of hiring and training cost would shift down (see Figure 6.2b). Occupations that involve high training and hiring costs would be expected to have lower layoff rates during recessions. This practice is called labour hoarding, and it occurs because firms are reluctant to lose their investment reflected in these costs, even if during the recession, the VMP_L is lower than the worker's wage.

Multiple Choice Questions

1. In the case of lower-paid, lesser-skilled employees, which of the following is likely to be the most important quasi-fixed labour cost?
   a) Payroll taxes, such as the CPP/QPP and unemployment insurance contributions
   b) Hiring and training costs
   c) Firing costs
   d) Health and pension benefits
   e) Hourly wages

2. A Royal Commission studying the issues involving part-time work recommended that firms provide a package of benefits to their part-time employees on a pro-rated basis. This means that if the individual works 20 hours per week, he/she will receive a benefits package that is half as costly as that of a full-time worker. What would be the likely effect of this law if part-timers currently have no benefits?
   a) For the part-timers, only the strictly variable labour costs would increase.
   b) For the part-timers, only the quasi-fixed labour costs would increase.
   c) For the part-timers, the labour total costs would increase.
   d) Employers would have an incentive to hire more part-time workers and reduce the hours of their existing part-time workers.
   e) None of the above.

3. A Royal Commission studying the issues involving part-time work recommended that firms provide a package of benefits to their part-time employees on a pro-rated basis. This means that if the individual works 20 hours per week, he/she will receive a benefits package that is half as costly as that of a full-time worker. What would be the likely effect of this law if part-timers currently have no benefits?
   a) Employers would alter the mix of their labour force such that full-timers comprise a larger share.
   b) Employers would alter the mix of their labour force such that full-timers comprise a smaller share.
   c) Employers would not alter the mix of their labour force, so the shares of each kind would not change.
   d) It would lower the cost of hiring a part-time worker relative to that of hiring a full-time worker.
   e) The quasi-fixed labour costs for both types of workers would be reduced.

4. In the United States, there has been some talk of obliging employers to provide health insurance benefits to their employees who currently do not have such coverage. What would be the likely effect of this policy?
   a) The working time of those already having health insurance benefits would increase, and the employment levels of those currently without health insurance benefits would increase.
   b) The working time of those already having health insurance benefits would increase, and the employment levels of those currently without health insurance benefits would decrease.
   c) The employment levels of those already having health insurance benefits would increase, and the working time of those currently without health insurance benefits would decrease.
   d) The working time of those already having health insurance benefits would decrease, and the employment levels of those currently without health insurance benefits would increase.
   e) There would be no change in the employment mix between these two groups of workers.

5. Quasi-fixed labour costs are defined as:
   a) Costs that decrease when the number of workers increases.
   b) Recruitment, hiring, and training costs.
   c) Labour costs that are associated with a fixed capital stock.
   d) Labour costs that increase with the number of workers employed but do not vary with the number of hours worked by the existing workers.
   e) Costs that increase only with the length of working time for the typical worker.

6. Labour hoarding is defined as:
   a) Employers retaining workers despite the fact that their marginal revenue product is below their wage.
   b) Employers retaining workers despite the fact that the discounted present value of their marginal revenue product is below the discounted present value of their wage.
   c) Laying off workers in response to a temporary drop in product demand.
   d) Employers adopting aggressive recruitment practices (headhunting) in order to hire employees away from competing firms.
   e) Hordes of labourers engaged in job-related action.

7. If quasi-fixed labour costs increase (which is indeed the case over the past 15 years), one would expect to see all of the following to occur *except* which?
   a) Increasing recourse to temporary/casual/part-time work.
   b) The costs of adjusting the labour force would increase.
   c) Over the business cycle, the swings in the total number of hours worked would increase relative to the swings in the number of employees.
   d) Greater recourse to overtime hours.
   e) None of the above.

8. If quasi-fixed labour costs increase (which is indeed the case over the past 15 years), one would expect to see all of the following to occur *except* which?
   a) The buffer zone between the employee's marginal revenue product and her wage increases.
   b) The costs of adjusting the labour force would decrease.
   c) Well-paid workers with full-time employment would be affected.
   d) Less recourse to overtime hours.
   e) Part-time workers would likely benefit the most.

9. Quasi-fixed labour costs have indeed risen greatly over the past 15 years in Canadian labour markets. Which component of quasi-fixed labour costs is primarily responsible for that development?
   a) Vacation pay and other pay for hours not worked
   b) Payroll taxes, such as CPP/QPP contributions
   c) Health care benefits
   d) Hiring and training costs
   e) Private pension benefits

10. A major point in the theory of dynamic labour demand is that:
    a) Labour markets clear very quickly whenever there is a change.
    b) The costs of labour force adjustment do not play a major role.
    c) It is more costly to adjust the number of employees than the number of hours worked.
    d) Unskilled labour is adjusted more slowly than skilled labour.
    e) None of the above.

Answers to Multiple Choice Questions

1. A   Lower-paid employees typically do not receive attractive health and pension benefits, so response D is wrong. Lesser-skilled employees typically do not receive much training, so response B is wrong. Response E is totally incorrect, as it is a totally variable cost.

2. C   Response A is totally wrong, as the quasi-fixed labour costs would rise a lot. Response B is almost correct, as the quasi-fixed labour costs would rise, but so would the total labour costs. For response D, there is less incentive to hire part-time workers and greater incentive to work them longer hours, if they have been hired.

3. A   There is less of an incentive to hire part-timers because they now involve quasi-fixed labour costs, albeit at a lower level than the full-timers. Response C is wrong because there has been a change in the relative costs of hiring the two types of labour. Response D is totally wrong, as the opposite would occur. Response E makes no sense.

4. B   This is the same idea that is raised in questions 2 and 3. The quasi-fixed labour costs of the affected workers would increase from a low level to a high level, making it more expensive to hire them relative to those workers who already have benefits. Those with full benefits may work longer hours.

5. D   Response B includes only a partial list of quasi-fixed labour costs. Response E is totally wrong, as it refers to variable labour costs. Response A makes no sense.

6. A   This is defined explicitly in the textbook on page 181. For response B, we would never expect an employer to retain the worker under those circumstances if all of the fixed costs have been factored in. The opposite of response C is true. For response D, labour hoarding refers only to workers on payroll. Response E is a sample of the author's sense of humour, for better or for worse.

7. E   Response A applies because hiring these workers usually doesn't involve high quasi-fixed labour costs. Responses B, C, and D are stated explicitly in the textbook in the section entitled "Quasi-Fixed Labour Costs."

8. D   Response E applies, provided that part-time workers do not receive high benefits. For response C, well-paid full-time workers would probably be affected, as it is now more expensive to employ them.

9. B

10. C   This definition is made explicit in the textbook on page 180. Responses A, B, and D are totally wrong, as the very opposite is true.

CHAPTER 7

Chapter Highlights

1. The Competitive Firm's Interaction with the Market

This chapter is essentially a continuation of Chapter 5, where four primary cases were mentioned: i) perfect competition in the product market and the labour market, ii) monopoly in the product market and monopsony in the labour market, iii) perfect competition in the product market and monopsony in the labour market, and iv) monopoly in the product market and perfect competition in the labour market. In that chapter, only the cases of perfect competition in the labour market were considered. In this chapter, the case of market power in the labour market is considered. This chapter also superimposes the supply curve with the demand curve in order to generate the equilibrium wage and employment level.

For case i), the supply curve of labour facing the individual firm is infinitely elastic at the going market wage. This is equivalent to saying that the firm is a "wage-taker." The market demand curve for labour is obtained as the horizontal summation of all of the individual firm demand curves. The market wage is equal to the firm wage, and it is determined by the intersection of the market demand curve and the market supply curve.

2. Imperfect Competition in the Product Market

This corresponds to case iv), which was covered in Chapter 5. There is no difference in the supply of labour between case i) and case iv). The only difference between these two cases lies in the structure of the demand curve. The labour demand curve when the firm is a monopolist in the output market is steeper than it is when the firm is a perfect competitor in the output market. The curve is also higher in the latter case. Although the demand curve in case iv) lies below the demand curve in case i), this does not necessarily imply that the wages paid by the monopolist will be lower. In practice, monopolists often are observed to pay higher than competitive wages (that is, higher than the going market wage), and the text mentions several possible explanations. The general conclusions reached in this comparison of perfect competition versus monopoly in the output market continue to apply to the intermediate cases of monopolistic competition and oligopoly in the output market. Firms that have market power (that is, as "price makers") in the output market may or may not behave like perfect competitors (that is, "wage takers") in the labour market.

3. Working with Supply and Demand

The purpose of this section is to work through exercises that are called comparative statics. We are given certain shifts in the labour supply and/or labour demand curve, and the objective is to determine the effects on equilibrium wages and employment levels. Given the values of the parameters of the two curves, one can determine the direction as well as the magnitudes of the changes in equilibrium wages and employment levels. The case that is illustrated, with linear supply-and-demand functions, is the easiest to deal with, as there are two parameters: the slope and the intercept term. This type of analysis is frequently applied to evaluate the impact of a change (usually an increase) in the payroll tax. To evaluate the incidence of a tax graphically, the labour demand curve shifts downward by the amount of the tax (assuming that it is a fixed-amount lump-sum tax applied to each employee). The incidence of tax refers to the proportion of the total levy that is paid by suppliers and demanders after the equilibrium wage has adjusted. The empirical evidence seems to indicate that most of these taxes are paid by workers in the form of lower wages than what would otherwise be the case. This fact implies that the disemployment effects of payroll taxes are minor.

4.   Monopsony in the Labour Market

This corresponds to cases ii) and iii). When the employer is an imperfect competitor in the labour market, we say that it is a monopsonist. This firm is a "wage-maker," or a wage setter in the labour market, as opposed to a "wage taker." This implies that the labour supply curve facing the individual firm is upward sloping. A pure monopsonist has the entire labour supply to itself. Once the supply curve slopes upward, a new variable is introduced into the analysis, and a new curve emerges: the marginal cost (MC) of labour curve. The MC of labour curve slopes upward and lies above the labour supply curve. To determine the equilibrium level of labour hired, set the MC of labour curve equal to the MRP or VMP curve. To determine the equilibrium value for the wage, find the wage on the labour supply curve that corresponds to that equilibrium employment level. Technically, there is no labour demand curve in monopsony; there is only the MRP curve or the VMP curve.

All other factors held constant, the equilibrium wage level and the equilibrium employment level are lower than the levels that would prevail if the labour market were competitive. Unlike the competitive equilibrium, all of the workers, even marginal workers, receive a wage that is lower than their MRP or VMP. The height of the labour supply curve represents the reservation wage of the marginal worker hired. All of the intramarginal workers receive wages higher than their reservation wage, but not as high as they would receive in a competitive labour market.

A monopsonist is most likely to arise in an instance where a single employer is large in relation to the labour market, so it employs a significant portion of the total supply of labour.

In the standard case of monopsony, all of the workers are paid the same wage. In the case of perfectly monopsonistic wage differentiation, every worker is paid his/her reservation wage, so therefore they all receive a different wage. In this case, the supply of labour coincides with the marginal cost of labour curve. The equilibrium level of employment is equal to the competitive level, but all workers except for marginal workers receive wages that are lower than the competitive level.

5.   Evidence of Monopsony

Although the evidence is not conclusive, there does appear to be evidence of monopsony in at least some particular labour markets. It is not likely to last in the long run, but it is a rather common phenomenon in the short run, as the labour supply curve that a monopsony faces can be upward sloping temporarily, even though in the long-run, it is likely to become flatter (more elastic).

Although monopsony in its pure form is rare, the monopsonist's choice is not. Many employers are faced with an upward-sloping supply curve for hiring a few more workers (at least in the short run). They have to pay a higher wage in order to recruit these workers, but they want to avoid having to pay a higher wage to their incumbent workers. It is common for employers to try to pay their employees wages that are differentiated according to their reservation wage. In other words, they would like to hire more workers at the going wage, but not if they have to grant a raise to all of their workers.

6. Minimum-Wage Legislation

This has long been a hot issue in labour economics, and it can be analysed by applying the supply-and-demand framework. Standard neo-classical theory (with a positively sloped labour supply curve and a negatively sloped labour demand curve) states that, in a competitive labour market, the implementation of a minimum wage exceeding the competitive wage will lead to a disemployment effect as the quantity demanded of labour falls. In addition, the quantity supplied of labour will rise, yielding a surplus in the labour market. If the demand for labour is elastic, the disemployment effect could be significant.

In the case of monopsony on the labour market, however, a paradox can arise. If the monopsony wage level is below the competitive wage level, then the equilibrium employment level will actually increase if a minimum wage is imposed, provided that the minimum wage does not exceed the competitive wage level. The derivation of this result is somewhat difficult, and it is explained in several different ways in the subsection entitled "Expected Impact: Monopsony in the Labour Market."

Putting the point concerning monopsony aside, the model of labour demand indicates that the minimum wage is likely to cause disemployment, or adverse employment, effects. This is because industries that hire low-wage labour and, hence, may be affected by the minimum wage tend to have fairly elastic demands for labour and operate in very competitive output markets. The impact is expected to fall disproportionately on the lower-skilled, inexperienced workers. Hundreds of empirical studies have been carried out in order to investigate the alleged disemployment effect, and the findings tend to point toward a minor disemployment effect. The minimum-wage law has a minor and probably negative effect on employment. While this finding supports the position of the proponents of the minimum-wage law, research has also indicated that the minimum-wage law is a poor instrument for fighting poverty.

Helpful Hints

- Always be careful to specify the degree of competition in the labour market, as well as the degree of competition in the output market. It is easy to confuse them and to omit the modifier of whether you are talking about the labour market or the output market.
- Be careful to distinguish between the supply of labour to the market and the supply to the individual firm. In the case of the pure monopsonist, they are the same.
- The hallmark of an imperfectly competitive labour market is the firm facing an upward-sloping supply of labour curve. This also brings about a marginal cost of labour curve, which lies above the labour supply curve. The underlying concepts are: a) to recruit marginal workers, a higher wage must be offered to the candidates; and b) all of the incumbent workers are thus awarded a raise; so c) the marginal labour cost of recruiting workers can be very high compared to what would occur if the labour market were perfectly competitive and the firm faced an infinitely elastic supply of labour.
- If the labour supply curve is horizontal (perfectly elastic), the marginal labour cost curve does exist, but it coincides with the labour supply curve, so there is no point in distinguishing them.
- The competitive equilibrium in the labour market is determined by the intersection of the labour demand and the labour supply curves for the entire market. That is the benchmark to which other cases, such as monopsony, are compared.

- If the labour market is competitive, it means that the firm is a "wage taker" and pays the going market wage. There is a floor on wages in this case, regardless of whether the firm is a perfect competitor or a monopolist in the output market.
- The subsection entitled "Concluding Observations on Non-Competitive Product Markets" is very informative, as it deals with the ambiguous question of the link between the equilibrium wage level and the degree of competition in the output market.
- In the section entitled "Working with Supply and Demand," the degree of competition in the output market does not matter, and we are assuming that the labour market is competitive.
- You should know the formula for the wage elasticity of labour demand by heart, or be able to derive it.
- To determine the equilibrium for the monopsony model, select the equilibrium employment level first. The next step is to drop vertically downward to the labour supply curve. That point yields the wage level that is consistent with hiring that many workers on the labour market.

Answers to Odd-Numbered End-of-Chapter Questions

1. Each demand curve would become steeper and, in most cases, less elastic. For these individual firms, nothing would happen to the wage levels in the short run due to the fact that they face infinitely elastic labour supply schedule. This means that the wage is supply-determined. For the entire labour market, one would expect a rotation of the aggregate labour demand curve that would bring about a fall in demand, hence a decrease in the equilibrium market wage and the equilibrium employment level. Since the labour supply curve facing each individual firm is perfectly elastic at the going market wage, each labour supply curve would thus decrease at the end of the exercise. The equilibrium market wage would decline, and thus the wage paid by each firm would decline.

3. The supply curve that we see in Figure 7.6 is pretty elastic. A less elastic supply curve cutting through S_m would be steeper. This latter supply curve would have a marginal cost of labour curve that is steeper and higher than the MC curve in Figure 7.6. This would generate an equilibrium wage-employment combination on the labour supply curve, which lies below S_m. The less elastic supply curve generates an equilibrium that is less favourable to the labour force. This result makes intuitive sense, as less elastically supplied labour is less responsive to wage changes (less likely to quit when the pay is cut and less likely to work more when the pay is raised) than is the case for elastically supplied labour.

5. Explain why a minimum wage increase, over a certain range, would lead to a monopsonist actually increasing employment. See the subsection entitled "Expected Impact: Monopsony in the Labour Market," which includes a paragraph explicitly answering this question.

   Given this possibility, could the monopsony argument be relied upon to negate the critics of minimum-wage legislation who argue that minimum wages will have an adverse employment effect and, hence, harm some of the very people they were designed to help? Yes, this model does counter the frequent critique that the minimum wage has an adverse employment effect. Note that it is applicable only for a certain range of the minimum wage, however, and it applies only in the case where the employer has monopsony power. If the minimum wage were to be raised substantially, it probably would cause an adverse employment effect. This would be the case if the minimum wage were to raised above the wage that would prevail in a competitive labour market (the intersection of VMP and S=AC in Figure 7.9)

Could minimum wages ever be applied selectively to monopsony situations? Could wage fixing via unionization be applied more selectively? Minimum wages and union wage setting work in the same fashion. The response was essentially given in the question above. The imposed wage has to be between the wage that the monopsonist would set and the wage that would prevail in the absence of market power (that is, the intersection of the supply and the VMP schedule). In the subsection mentioned above, the point is made that the sectors that are most likely to pay minimum wages are not those that are likely to have monopsony features.

Answers to Odd-Numbered End-of-Chapter Problems

1. This statement is true if the prevailing market wage is above the wage that would prevail in a competitive equilibrium. In a competitive equilibrium, there is no monopsonistic power in the labour market, and the equilibrium wage is determined by the intersection of total labour demand and total labour supply. On the other hand, if the prevailing market wage is below the wage that would prevail in a competitive equilibrium due to the exercising of monopsony power, then the statement is false. This is explained thoroughly in the subsection entitled "Expected Impact: Monopsony in the Labour Market," which includes an intuitive explanation, a formal exposition with graphical analysis, and an example with figures. Note that this somewhat tricky result — that the implementation of a minimum wage can actually raise the level of employment given a monopsony — applies to a particular range of wages. This range is between the monopsony wage and the competitive equilibrium wage. Since one would never observe a wage that is lower than a monopsony wage (except for the case of perfect wage differentiation), the case of a minimum wage below the monopsony wage is irrelevant.

3a. One would expect the value of a to be negative, in order to generate an inverse (negative) relationship between L^D and W, and the value of b to be positive, in order to generate a direct (positive) relationship between L^D and W. If a is equal to -1, for example, then $L^D = A / W$, and we have a negative relationship between L^D and W. If b is equal to 1, for example, then $L^S = BW$, and we have a positive relationship between L^S and W. The labour supply curve would be a linear function passing through the origin with a positive slope of $1 / B$ (assume that $B > 0$), and the labour demand curve would be the reciprocal function having the two axes, wage and the labour quantity, as asymptotes. It has a negative slope. More generally, the equilibrium condition is $Aw^a = Bw^b$, which solves algebraically to $w = (A / B)^{1/(b-a)}$

  b. Take the natural logarithm of both sides of those equations, using the basic axioms of logarithms. Plotting the log of the wage on the vertical axis and the log of the employment level on the horizontal axis, you should have a linear labour demand function with an intercept of A' and a slope (negative) of a, and a linear labour supply function with an intercept of B' and a slope (positive) of b. In order to solve for the equilibrium log wage level, set $l^D = l^S$, and solve for w. You should obtain $w = (B' - A') / (a - b)$. Substitute this value for w into either the original l^D or l^S equation to obtain $l = (B'a - A'b) / (a - b)$.

  c. Assuming that the tax is collected from firms, only the labour demand function changes. Replacing ln W with ln $[W(1 + t)]$, we obtain ln $W + $ ln $(1 + t) = $ ln $W + t$. The new labour demand function reads $l^D = A' + aw + at$. To determine equilibrium, set $l^D = l^S = A' + aw + at = B' + bw$. The equilibrium wage is $w = (B' - A' - at) / (a - b)$. This is the market wage as well as the take-home wage. Notice how it is lower than it was in Problem 3b. The firm pays this wage to its workers plus t to the government. The employment level is $(B'a - A'b - at^2) / (a - b)$. Notice how it is lower than it was in Problem 3b. The labour elasticity is denoted by a, and the supply elasticity is denoted by b. As the value of a increases, the equilibrium wage falls relative to the case of no tax (in the formula above, the numerator falls and the denominator rises), which implies that the share paid by the workers rises. The effect of an increase in the value of b is to decrease the denominator and thus to increase the ratio relative to the case with no tax, which implies that the share paid by the workers falls. If we set a = 0, the labour demand is totally inelastic, and the firm pays all of the tax as the market wage is unaffected. If we set b = 0, the labour supply is totally inelastic, and the workers pay all of the tax as their wages are docked by the full amount of t. In the long run, we expect the value of b to be quite low, implying that workers will bear an increasing share of the tax.

d. Assuming that the tax is collected from workers, only the labour supply function changes. Replacing ln W with ln [W(1 - t)], we obtain ln W + ln (1 - t) = ln W - t. The new labour supply function reads $l^S = B' + bw - bt$. To determine equilibrium, set $l^D = l^S = A' + aw = B' + bw - bt$. The equilibrium wage is w = (B' - A' - bt) / (a - b). This is the market wage, but it is not the take-home wage, because the workers have not paid their taxes yet. To obtain the take-home wage, subtract t from that expression, and you obtain (B' - A' - at) / (a - b), which is the same take-home pay as in Problem 3c.

5a. When the firm maximizes profits, it sets the VMP_L = wage, so the labour demand function becomes W = 30 - 2L. If you are ever in doubt as to which substitution to make, draw a quick sketch of your demand or supply curve in order to see if the slope is correct.

b. Rewrite the labour demand function as L = 15 - W / 2, and then multiply by 10 as the firms are all identical. Recall that the market demand curve is obtained by summing up the individual labour demand curves horizontally. This means that we multiply the abscissa (the L variable) by 10 to obtain the market demand curve L = 150 - 5W. To find the equilibrium, set the labour supply = labour demand in order to obtain W = 10 and $L^D = L^S = 100$.

c. The labour demand curve shifts upward by $3. Take the labour demand curve and rewrite it as W = 30 - L^D / 5. When it shifts upward by $3, the slope remains the same, but the intercept increases to 33, so the equation for the labour demand curve becomes W = 33 - L^D / 5, or L^D = 165 - 5W. Setting this equal to L^S gives an equilibrium wage of $11 and an equilibrium employment level of 110. The workers definitely benefit.

d. This would have the effect of shifting the labour supply curve down and to the right by $3. The equation for labour supply becomes W = -3 + L^S / 10. The equilibrium wage is now $8, but once workers collect their $3 bonus from the government, their take-home wage becomes $11, just like in Problem 5c. The equilibrium level of employment is 110. The opposition party is wrong, as the impact of the two policy measures on the labour market equilibrium is the same.

7. This statement is true. As mentioned in the "Helpful Hints" section presented above, there is not enough information to determine labour market outcomes in this statement. The subsection entitled "Concluding Observations on Non-Competitive Product Markets" deals with the ambiguous question of the link between the equilibrium wage level and the degree of competition in the output market. In general, we need information on demand conditions and supply conditions on the labour market. In practice, it seems as though employers having market power in the output market do tend to pay a wage premium, but there is no theoretical reason why this has to be so.

Multiple Choice Questions

1. Which of the following statements concerning labour supply is *false*?
    a) The individual worker's labour supply curve to a certain market may have a negatively sloped portion.
    b) The market labour supply curve is derived as the horizontal summation of all of the individual labour supply curves.
    c) The market labour supply curve is derived as the horizontal summation of all of the individual labour supply curves to the firms.
    d) If the labour market is perfectly competitive, the labour supply curve facing the individual firm is infinitely elastic at the going wage.
    e) If the labour market is perfectly competitive, the firm is a wage taker.

2. If there is market power on the supply side of the labour market, yet perfect competition on the demand side of the labour market, then the situation is characterized by which of the following?
    a) A labour union
    b) A monopsony
    c) A bilateral monopoly
    d) An oligopoly
    e) A free-market equilibrium

3. When one says that the labour market clears instantaneously, one means that:
    a) Wages and employment levels are quite flexible.
    b) The wage is equal to the marginal revenue product of the last worker at all times.
    c) The transactions wage is equal to the equilibrium wage.
    d) There is never an excess quantity demanded or an excess quantity supplied of labour.
    e) All of the above statements are true.

4. If a labour market is characterized by a situation of involuntary unemployment, then:
    a) There is an excess supply of labour at the going transactions wage.
    b) The market-clearing wage level involves some unemployment.
    c) There is an excess demand of labour at the going transactions wage.
    d) Jobs are being rationed at the market-clearing equilibrium wage.
    e) The going transactions wage is below the market-clearing equilibrium wage.

5. Which of the following would be an effect of the imposition of a payroll tax on a labour market that was in a state of free-market equilibrium? Assume that the tax is applied as a fixed amount per worker.
    a) The labour supply curve would shift to the right.
    b) The labour supply curve would shift to the left.
    c) The labour demand curve would shift to the right.
    d) The labour demand curve would shift to the left.
    e) Neither the demand curve nor the supply curve would shift.

6. Which of the following would be an effect of the imposition of a payroll tax on a labour market that was in a state of free-market equilibrium? Assume that the tax is applied as a fixed amount per worker.
    a) The more elastic the demand for labour, the greater the share paid by the employer.
    b) The more elastic the demand for labour, the less the share paid by the employer.
    c) The tax is borne by the employer because the government collects it from him/her.
    d) The tax is borne by the employees as their wages are reduced dollar for dollar by the amount of this tax.
    e) The more elastic the supply of labour, the greater the share paid by the employees.

7. Which of the following statements concerning payroll taxes is *false*?
    a) They are relatively easy to administer.
    b) They are relatively difficult to evade.
    c) It has been demonstrated by empirical research that they are "job killers."
    d) It has been demonstrated by empirical research that employees pay most of the tax.
    e) In the past 15 years, their level has increased considerably.

8. Consider Figure 7.5, which depicts a competitive labour market to which a payroll tax has been applied. This tax is a constant amount per worker and is levied on the firm. The share of this tax that is paid by the workers is given by line segment:
    a) CB
    b) DC
    c) DA
    d) BD
    e) None of the above, because workers assume none of this tax burden

9. Consider Figure 7.5, which depicts a competitive labour market to which a payroll tax has been applied. This tax is a constant amount per worker and is levied on the firm. The share of this tax that is paid by the employer is given by line segment:
    a) CB
    b) DC
    c) DA
    d) BD
    e) None of the above, because employers assume none of this tax burden

10. Consider Figure 7.5, which depicts a competitive labour market to which a payroll tax has been applied. This tax is a constant amount per worker and is levied on the firm. The amount of this tax that is remitted to the government by each worker is given by line segment:
    a) CB
    b) DC
    c) DA
    d) BD
    e) It does not appear on this graph

Labour Market Economics, Fifth Edition

11. Consider Figure 7.5, which depicts a competitive labour market to which a payroll tax has been applied. This tax is a constant amount per worker and is levied on the firm. The change in employment that results is given by which of the following distances?
    a)   There is no change in employment.
    b)   There is an increase in employment because the government spends the tax revenue, which creates jobs.
    c) $N'N_0$ (decline).
    d) $N'N_1$ (decline).
    e) N_1N_0 (decline).

12. When one says that the individual firm that hires labour in a perfectly competitive labour market is a wage taker, one means that:
    a)   The employer cannot affect the going market wage by altering the amount of labour that she hires.
    b)   The employer is motivated by profit maximization.
    c)   There is free entry for workers into the labour market.
    d)   The firm's demand curve for labour is infinitely elastic at the going market wage.
    e)   The market-clearing wage is determined by the intersection of the market labour supply curve and the market labour demand curve.

13. Which of the following statements concerning labour supply is *false*?
    a)   The individual worker's labour supply, the labour supply to the individual firm, and the market labour supply are all distinct.
    b)   The market labour supply is derived as the horizontal summation of all of the labour supply curves to individual firms within that industry.
    c)   The market labour supply is derived as the horizontal summation of all of the labour supply curves of individual workers within that industry.
    d)   If the labour market is perfectly competitive, the labour supply curve facing the individual firm is infinitely elastic at the going rate.
    e)   If the labour market is perfectly competitive, the firm is a wage taker.

14. What is the relationship between the long-run demand curve of labour and the short-run demand curve of labour?
    a)   There is no meaningful distinction between the two.
    b)   The short-run curve is more wage elastic than the long-run curve.
    c)   The long-run curve is more wage elastic than the short-run curve.
    d)   It depends on the wage elasticity of labour demand.
    e)   It depends on whether the firm is a wage taker or a wage setter.

15. Consider a perfectly competitive market for labour, the so-called market-clearing or neo-classical model. Assume that all jobs and all workers within the relevant market are homogeneous. Which of the following statements is *true*?
    a)   Wage differences are unlikely to persist in the long run due to labour mobility.
    b)   Wage differences cannot exist in the short run.
    c)   Wage differences are unlikely to persist in the long run due to adjustments in labour demand.
    d)   Firms have an incentive to pay higher than competitive wages.
    e)   Firms have an incentive to pay lower than competitive wages.

Answers to Multiple Choice Questions

1. C   It is the labour demand curve that is derived as the horizontal summation of all of the individual firms' labour demand curves. All of the other statements are true.
2. B   Even if the output market is competitive, if there is market power on the supply side of the labour market, there is a monopsony.
3. E   Market clearing means that there is no impediment to the wage reaching the equilibrium level.
4. A   Responses B and D contradict the definition of market-clearing wages. Responses C and E would produce a labour shortage (as opposed to a labour surplus), and we would expect wages to rise.
5. D   This point is made explicitly in the textbook (see Figure 7.5). In the case depicted here, the government collects the tax from the workers.
6. B   See the subsection entitled "Application: Incidence of a Unit Payroll Tax."
7. C   See Exhibit 7.1. Responses A and B are true statements that are made in the subsection entitled "Application: Incidence of a Unit Payroll Tax."
8. A   This is explained in the subsection entitled "Application: Incidence of a Unit Payroll Tax."
9. B   This is explained in the subsection entitled "Application: Incidence of a Unit Payroll Tax."
10. D   This is explained in the subsection entitled "Application: Incidence of a Unit Payroll Tax."
11. E   This is explained in the subsection entitled "Application: Incidence of a Unit Payroll Tax."
12. A   This point is made quite explicit in the "Chapter Highlights" section above. Response B is true, but that has nothing to do with the state of competition in the labour market. Response C is an assumption of a perfectly competitive labour market and not a result. Response D is false. Response E is true, but irrelevant.
13. B   The market labour supply curve is derived as the horizontal sum of all of the individual workers' labour supply curves, so response C is a correct statement. We never sum up the labour supply curves across firms.
14. C   Response D is too vague. Response A is totally wrong, while the opposite of response B is true. Response E applies to the labour supply conditions that the firm faces.
15. A   See the subsection entitled "Wages and Employment in a Competitive Labour Market" in Chapter 1.

CHAPTER 8

Chapter Highlights

1. Purposes of Wages and Wage Structures

This chapter marks the beginning of a new unit whose topic is wage structures. In the preceding chapter, the supply side of the labour markets was superimposed on the demand side in order to determine the *level* of wages in equilibrium. The basic idea in this unit is to analyse *relative* wages in equilibrium, which means a comparison of wages that prevail in one sector or in one occupation to those in another. There are a number of approaches that have been applied to explain wage differentials across individuals, sectors, or occupations. This chapter deals with only one of these approaches — the theory of compensating wages, or differentials.

2. Theory of Compensating Wages

The basic idea is that the wage structure, meaning the differentials or discrepancies between the wages paid to one category of labour relative to those paid to another, is based on the amenities and/or the disamenities that are associated with the two categories of labour. *Ceteris paribus,* if two jobs are totally equivalent with the exception that one has an amenity (disamenity) while the other does not, the first job should pay more (less).

For the graphical analysis of this chapter, all of the curves are drawn in wage-safety space. Wage is plotted on the vertical axis, and job safety, an amenity, is plotted on the horizontal axis.

The first graph is the firm's isoprofit curve, defined as the locus of all combinations of wages paid and job safety levels provided that generate equal profit to the firm. From the firm's perspective, they are both "bads" in the sense that they are costly to provide and diminish profitability. This implies that the curve has a negative slope. For the same reason, higher isoprofit curves reflect lower levels of profitability. The isoprofit curve also has a concave shape or curvature, much like the production possibilities frontier. This curvature indicates each firm's trade-off between the marginal expense of paying higher wages against the marginal expense of providing better working conditions. If the output market is competitive, then only one isoprofit curve matters, and that is the one that yields zero profits. Normally, different firms will have different job safety technologies, which means that, while their isoprofit curves will have negative slopes, they will have different positions, shapes, and slopes. Placing these isoprofit curves on the same graph, as far as the labour market is concerned, only the outer shell — called the offer envelope or the market envelope — matters because any wage-safety offer that a given firm has below this market envelope curve is dominated by another firm. The offer curve has a scalloped shape and is interpreted as a "menu" of wage-safety combinations that employers are willing to offer.

The second graph is the indifference curve of the workers, defined as the locus of all combinations of wages paid and job safety levels provided that generate equal utility to the worker. From the worker's perspective, they are both "goods" in the sense that they generate positive utility levels, which implies that the curve has a negative slope. For the same reason, higher indifference curves reflect higher levels of utility. The indifference curve also has a convex shape or curvature reflecting a diminishing rate of marginal utility between a wage increase and an improvement in job safety. Since not all workers have the same tastes toward higher wages versus greater job safety (that is, risk aversion), these curves will differ in their positions, shapes, and slopes (although they all have negative slopes).

An equilibrium wage-safety locus (a whole set of wage-safety outcomes) is generated by superimposing the indifference curves with the employer's offer curve and tracing out the points of intersection. This equilibrium line, which normally will not be a straight line, is generated by collecting the points of tangency between the market envelope curve and the indifference curves of many different workers. It is the result of the competing demand-side forces (the firms' technology for providing job safety) and supply-side forces (the workers' preferences for job safety). It is the slope of this equilibrium curve that is important, as it indicates the trade-off in the labour market between higher wages in exchange for lower job safety and vice versa. This trade-off is reflected in the negative slope of the curve. The underlying intuition is that firms and workers are heterogeneous. Workers will sort themselves into different firms, occupations, or industries on the basis of their willingness to accept risk in the form of a compensating wage differential. The labour market provides incentives such that workers who are the most risk averse will be matched with employers who can provide the extra margin of job safety more cheaply (that is, the safer environment). The least risk averse will be matched with employers who can provide the extra margin of job safety in a costly fashion (the more dangerous environment).

3.   Effect of Safety Regulation

In markets that are operating competitively, the effect of regulation may be perverse. A regulatory agency that requires both the firm and the employees to achieve a certain level of safety would make one or both parties worse off. Either profits could be higher, or the level of utility could be higher, or both. The basic idea is that some workers would voluntarily contract with employers to accept a certain level of risk of job safety at an agreed-upon wage differential to compensate them for that risk. The act of regulation risks undoing the matching of risk-averse individuals working for safer firms at lower wages and less risk-averse individuals working for less safe firms at higher wages. That point is premised, however, on all parties being well informed as to the level of job safety.

4.   Empirical Evidence on Compensating Wages

It is difficult to obtain empirical evidence of compensating differentials for desirable or undesirable working conditions because of the need to hold all other factors (such as the structure of the labour market or of the output market) that affect wages constant. In particular, in situations in which the employees have strong bargaining power, they can often extract higher wages without sacrificing job safety or working conditions. This is an example of the omitted variable bias problem. Ideally, in order to test for the existence of a compensating differential, one would have to find two occupations that are identical in all respects except for the level of job safety. There are other econometric problems as well, such as the difficulty in accurately measuring the risk of jobs. The literature seems to indicate that compensating wage premiums are paid for work hazards, but only for fairly dangerous (as opposed to inconvenient) ones.

5.   Policy Implications

As mentioned above, if the labour market is reasonably competitive, and if workers and firms are well informed about working conditions, economists are usually opposed to the setting of uniform standards on working conditions. This stems from the fact that workers have heterogeneous preferences (some of them may be willing to accept higher risk for higher wages) and firms have heterogeneous production technologies (for some firms, it is more expensive than it is for others to provide good working conditions).

Helpful Hints

- In order to understand the graphical analysis in this chapter, a firm grasp of intermediate micro-theory is required. On the other hand, if the goal is to grasp the basic concepts and intuition that are contained in this chapter, such preparation is not necessary. It is possible to understand the concepts, the central ideas, and the empiricism that appear in this chapter without a thorough knowledge of the graphs.
- As a quiz question, ask yourself why the isoprofit curves in Figure 8.1b cross and why the indifference curves in Figure 8.2b cross. This is because they belong to two different firms and two different workers, respectively. Isoprofit curves pertaining to the same firm cannot cross, and indifference curves pertaining to the same worker cannot cross.
- There is no one equilibrium point that prevails, so do not search for one point of intersection. Instead, search for the locus of points of intersection, which is the equilibrium relationship between wages and job safety. Given this curve, employers and employees basically decide for themselves where to locate along the market wage-safety locus.
- The subsection on alternative portrayal, which contains Figure 8.4, is difficult. The results are the same, but the graph has a different variable on the horizontal axis, which means that the curves have very different forms and slopes.
- The "Chapter Highlights" section above contains some discussion of the intuition underlying the theory of compensating differentials. These ideas are central in explaining why economists claim that excessive regulation can be counterproductive and that the optimal level of job-related risk is zero.
- There are a number of problems that are inherent in the empirical analysis of compensating differentials. The most important one is the unavoidable omitted variable bias problem. See the comments in the "Chapter Highlights" section above.
- Read the captions under Figures 8.1 to 8.3 carefully and be able to explain why each curve slopes the way it does and why it has a certain curvature.

Answers to Odd-Numbered End-of-Chapter Questions

1. For this question, note the structure of the cost function. Logically, there is a positive relationship between wages and total costs, as well as a positive relationship between job safety and total costs. In order to obtain the profits function, profits = total revenue (TR) - total cost (TC). The problem is simplified by the information that TR = 100.

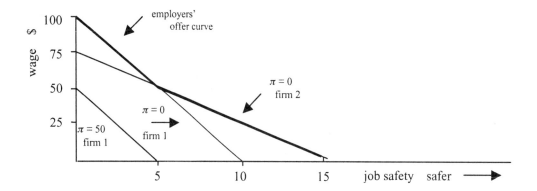

a. If profits = 0, which is the case in the long run if the output market is perfectly competitive, then the isoprofit function is W + 10S = 100, or in slope-intercept form, W = 100 - 10S. If profits = 50, then the isoprofit function is W + 10S = 50, or in slope-intercept form, W = 50 - 10S. These two functions are linear, which is a special case. Place W on the vertical axis and S on the horizontal axis. They both have a slope of –10, and they are parallel. Note that the lower isoprofit curve corresponds to higher profits, because at each level of safety, the corresponding wage is lower.

b. Profits = total revenue (TR) - total cost (TC) = 75 - W - 5S. If profits = 0, then the isoprofit function is 75 = W + 5S. Again, we have a linear function, but it is less steep, as its slope is -5. In slope-intercept form, it is W = 75 - 5S. Note that this firm is safer in that it can improve job safety more cheaply than the other firm can — at $5 per unit rather than $10 per unit. The two lines that correspond to the case of zero profits will intersect, and the outermost segment (sometimes called the outer shell) constitutes the offer curve for the group of employers.

3. First, consider the case of a point on isoprofit curve I_c to the right of E_c. Imagine an indifference curve cutting through that point. In this case, the worker is not on his/her highest possible indifference curve given some wage-safety combination along I_c, which would imply a tangency with I_c. It is possible to move counter-clockwise along I_c, which makes the firm neither better off nor any worse off, and it makes the worker better off as he/she reaches a higher indifference curve U_c. Next, consider the case of a point on indifference curve U_c to the right of E_c. Imagine an isoprofit curve cutting through that point. In this case, the firm is not on its lowest possible isoprofit curve given some wage-safety combination along U_c, which would imply a tangency with U_c. It is possible to move clockwise along U_c, which makes the worker neither better off nor any worse off, and it makes the firm better off as it reaches a lower isoprofit curve I_c. Using arguments of this nature, it can be shown that any point other than E_c can be dominated by E_c, and both parties are willing to choose that point.

5. If the workers have good quality information regarding the true level of job safety, then the perceived indifference curve U_p will correspond pretty closely to the actual indifference curve U_a. It should not have much of an effect on the isoprofit curve, as this point relates to the information regarding job safety rather than the cost of providing it. The higher the level of monitoring, and the more accurately that safety levels are reported, the more likely it is that both parties will reach the optimal level of safety E_0. Remember that this is premised upon a perfectly competitive labour market and a perfectly competitive output market.

Answers to Odd-Numbered End-of-Chapter Problems

1a. In responding to this question, be careful to distinguish between 0 (that is, zero) and O (that is, office jobs). In the F sector, the supply of labour is 0 for any wage below $6. At $6, the supply of labour is infinitely elastic from L = 0 to L = 100. For wage = $10, the supply of labour is infinitely elastic for L levels greater or equal to 100. For wages between $6 and $10, the quantity supplied of labour is 100. The graph is a step function, with a vertical segment for wages between $0 and $6, a horizontal segment for a wage of $6, a vertical segment for wages between $6 and $10 at 100, and a horizontal segment at wage = $10 until L = 200. In the O sector, the supply of labour is 0 for any wage below $6. At $6, the supply of labour is infinitely elastic from L = 0 to L = 100. For wage = $8, the supply of labour is infinitely elastic for L levels greater or equal to 100. For wages between $6 and $8, the quantity supplied of labour is 100. The graph is a step function, with a vertical segment for wages between $0 and $6 at L = 0, a horizontal segment for a wage of $6, a vertical segment for wages between $6 and $8 at L = 100, and a horizontal segment at wage = $8 until L = 200.

bi. Given these demand conditions, the equilibrium wage in the F sector is $10, while the equilibrium wage on the O sector is $6. The differential is thus $4.

ii. One hundred J workers in sector F are earning rents, because they are willing to work there for $6, but they receive $10.

iii. Fifty L workers working in sector F earn no rents, because they require $10 to work there. Fifty L workers working in sector O receive no rents, as they are willing to work there for $6. They also earn more than their outside opportunity in sector O, whose working conditions they like less anyway.

3a. In these diagrams, wage goes on the vertical axis, and paid vacations goes on the horizontal axis. Since they are both goods from the point of view of the worker, the indifference curves have a negative slope. This is because utility is increasing in both variables. Since they are both "bads" from the point of view of the firm, the isoprofit curves have a negative slope. This is because profits are decreasing in both variables. Although both curves have negative slopes, since the indifference curves have a convex curvature and the isoprofit curves have a concave curvature, there will be an equilibrium at the point of tangency. Going from the case of one firm and one worker to the entire market, we obtain a locus of combinations of wages and paid vacations that has a negative slope. Normally, it would not be a straight line, but it indicates a negative trade-off between the wage level and the length of vacations.

b. No, it would not necessarily invalidate that theory. Holding all other factors constant, one would expect a negative trade-off between the wage level and the length of vacations. Many other factors, such as the structure of the labour market or the structure of the product market, can influence both variables. For example, consider the case of a labour union (which implies imperfect competition in the labour market) that supplies labour to a monopolist. Often, the union can exercise its power in the labour market to raise the wage above the competitive level and simultaneously improve the vacation package. These gains are financed by lower profits earned by the employer, who (in the case of monopoly) does not operate under the zero-profit constraint. If two firms are totally identical in all respects pertaining to the labour market, one would expect the firm that pays higher wages to offer shorter vacations and vice versa.

c. The wage structure would probably be compressed, which means that the differentials would diminish. Those workers who were willing to trade off some of their vacation time in exchange for higher wages will earn less than before. Those workers who were willing to trade off some of their wages in exchange for shorter vacations will earn more than before. This outcome would be inefficient because some workers and firms are prevented from making mutually beneficial trades. It would be possible for the leisure-loving workers to be better off (hence, reach a higher indifference curve) without making their employer worse off, and for wage-loving workers to be better off without making their employer worse off.

5. This quote is indeed frequently evoked in order to justify the expenditure levels and the generous provisions of the unemployment insurance program (at least in the case of seasonal workers) in its current state. If special UI benefits in fishing or other very cyclical industries were eliminated, it is true that many workers who currently gain their livelihood from that industry would have to exit it. It is probably an exaggeration, however, to claim that nobody could earn a living in fishing under these circumstances. The most productive and/or successful fishermen would earn the most money from fishing, and that income would help tide them over during the off-season. A few fishermen would find work during the off-season, doing maintenance work or some other unrelated activity. In addition, those who cherish the lifestyle of fishing the most would be willing to accept lower wages (a negative compensating differential) than they could get elsewhere. That point certainly applies to university professors, who generally earn considerably less income than many other occupations requiring the same (or even less) level of education. They accept lower salaries in exchange for more favourable working conditions. All in all, we would likely see a much smaller fishery that employs only the most devoted and productive fisherman. As far as the opinion that "a culturally important way of life would be destroyed" is concerned, most economists would consider this to be a subjective, value-laden statement. Similar claims could be made to justify the subsidization of many activities, such as dairy farming, crop farming, publishing, theatre, cinema, and so on. One wonders where this group of subsidized economic activity would end.

7. This is a very good question. No, it certainly does not imply that the theory of compensating differentials is wrong in this case. There are at least two reasons why the theory has not been invalidated. First, there is the issue of reverse causality. As the quality-of-life index (QOLI) improves, according to the theory of compensating differentials, we would expect wages to fall, all other factors held constant ($beta > 0$). On the other hand, as wages increase, that implies that many of the inhabitants are high-income earners, and they are likely to purchase normal goods and services, including higher taxes to provide nice public services that are frequently associated with a high quality-of-life index. This force would act to raise the magnitude of beta, and maybe even produce a value for $beta > 0$. This two-way causality problem (wages affecting the quality of life and vice versa) means that a simple regression estimate of beta, the coefficient of the QOLI, is biased. Second, it is necessary to include control variables in the regression in order to capture as many of the other factors that influence wages as possible, such as the level of skill, education, and training of the city's labour force; the local cost of living; the degree of unionization; and the structure of the labour markets and output markets.

Multiple Choice Questions

1. The theory of compensating differentials was first elaborated by which famous economist?
   a) Keynes
   b) Marx
   c) Smith
   d) Ricardo
   e) Marshall

2. All of the following job attributes may give rise to a compensating differential *except* which attribute?
   a) Long commute time
   b) Adverse working conditions
   c) Economic rent
   d) Lengthy training and educational requirements
   e) Unstable employment patterns

3. Which of the following phrases applies to compensating differentials?
   a) They are solely a labour demand-side phenomenon.
   b) They are solely a supply demand-side phenomenon.
   c) They are both a labour demand-side and a labour supply-side phenomenon.
   d) They are neither a labour demand-side nor a labour supply-side phenomenon, as they are not elements of the neo-classical approach.
   e) They are neither a labour demand-side nor a labour supply-side phenomenon, as they are a strictly empirical phenomenon.

4. Within the compensating differential model, which of the following statements concerning isoprofit curves is *false*?
   a) They differ in shape and form across firms.
   b) The higher the position of the curve, the lower the profits.
   c) They reflect the technology of production.
   d) They are drawn in wage-employment space.
   e) They are drawn in wage-job attribute space.

5. Consider an indifference curve with wages on the vertical axis and job safety on the horizontal axis. Which of the following statements is *false*?
   a) These curves can never cross.
   b) These curves slope downwards.
   c) A steep curve reflects more risk-averse preferences.
   d) A shallow curve reflects less risk-averse preferences.
   e) The higher the curve, the better off the worker.

6. Consider the market equilibrium involving many firms and many individual workers. The relevant job attribute is job safety. Which of the following statements is *false*?
   a) There are many different equilibria with different wages and different levels of job safety, but there is a trade-off between them.
   b) Generally, the most risk-averse workers will pair up with the firms having the safest working conditions.
   c) Generally, the least risk-averse workers will pair up with the firms having the least safe working conditions.
   d) There is one equilibrium for all workers and firms with uniform wage and uniform working conditions.
   e) Because there is a compensating differential for workers who accept less favourable working conditions, marginal workers are indifferent between working at more dangerous firms and less dangerous firms.

7. All of the following statements are assumptions underlying the theory of compensating differentials *except* which statement?
   a) There is free entry and exit of workers and firms from this industry.
   b) There is an absence of market power on both the supply side and the demand side.
   c) There is perfect information.
   d) There are many different firms and workers with heterogeneous tastes and production technologies.
   e) In equilibrium, there is a trade-off between wages and favourable job attributes.

8. All of the following are problems involved with the empirical research on the topic of compensating differentials *except* which?
   a) One needs to take account of the process by which heterogeneous individuals choose jobs and occupations.
   b) It is difficult to isolate the effect of one characteristic on wages.
   c) It is difficult to measure certain job attributes that may give rise to compensating wage differentials.
   d) There are doubtless some instances in which the theory of compensating differentials does not apply.
   e) In cases in which the workers have strong bargaining power, they may enjoy high wages and generous benefits without having to compensate for them by accepting more adverse working conditions.

9. It has been observed that two workers, Mutt and Jeff, receive unequal wages. In particular, Mutt is paid more. All of the following are possible explanations *except* which?
   a) Jeff works for a monopsonist, but Mutt does not.
   b) Mutt receives a compensating differential associated with unfavourable working conditions, while Jeff does not.
   c) Mutt receives a compensating differential associated with favourable working conditions, while Jeff does not.
   d) Mutt receives a compensating differential associated with stringent job-training requirements, while Jeff does not.
   e) Mutt works for a very profitable firm, and Jeff does not.

10. There is much anecdotal evidence that poorly paid workers sometimes endure unfavourable working conditions. This does not necessarily invalidate the theory of compensating differentials. Why not?

   a) Sometimes it is observed that workers who enjoy attractive working conditions earn more than workers with unfavourable working conditions.
   b) Workers who endure adverse working conditions will earn more than workers with more favourable working conditions, *ceteris paribus,* but there are other factors pulling down the wages of workers who endure adverse working conditions.
   c) The theory of labour market segmentation holds that workers in the secondary labour market have little opportunity to obtain more attractive jobs in the primary labour market.
   d) Labour markets do not clear.
   e) None of the above.

Answers to Multiple Choice Questions

1. C   This is made quite explicit in the textbook.
2. C   Economic rent refers to a portion of the wage that exceeds the minimum level necessary to retain the worker. It is like a windfall, so it is the antithesis of a compensating differential. Responses A, B, and E refer to negative job attributes that might be associated with a negative differential. Response D is likely to give rise to a human-capital differential.
3. C   Since the preferences of the worker and the technology of production enter into the equilibrium wage-job attribute locus, both supply-side and demand-side forces are at work. Response D is totally wrong, as this is a very neo-classical approach. Response E is incorrect, as all of the theoretical development contained in this chapter indicates.
4. D   Responses A, B, C, and E are made clear in the textbook (the section entitled "The Theory of Compensating Differentials") as well as in the "Chapter Highlights" section above. For response D, the labour demand and supply curves appear in wage-employment space.
5. A   Responses B, C, D, and E are made clear in the textbook (the section entitled "The Theory of Compensating Differentials") as well as in the "Chapter Highlights" section above.
6. D   See the "Chapter Highlights" and "Helpful Hints" sections above. The basic idea behind compensating differentials is stated succinctly in response A. Responses B and C make intuitive sense.
7. C   There does not have to be perfect information, but the information has to be of fairly high quality.
8. D   Responses A, B, C, and E are mentioned in the section of the textbook entitled "Empirical Evidence on Compensating Wages." For response D, no economic theory is ever designed to be 100% valid in all circumstances such that there are no counter-examples at all. Theories are designed to be generalities that apply in most cases.
9. C   For response C, Mutt would be paid less within the theory of compensating differentials. All of the other responses refer to situations in which Mutt would earn more than Jeff, *ceteris paribus.*
10. B   Response B is made clear in the textbook as well as in the "Chapter Highlights" section above. Response A is a true statement, but it does not address the question asked.

CHAPTER 9

Chapter Highlights

This chapter shares a common theme with Chapter 8, namely the structure of wages. The preceding chapter dealt with the role of compensating differentials in determining the wage structure, and this chapter examines the role of human capital formation in determining the structure of wages.

1. Human Capital Theory

The essence of human capital theory is that workers and firms make investments in human resources in the form of education and training so as to raise productivity and earnings. This activity is considered to be an investment analogous to the investment in physical capital, because the costs are usually incurred up front, while the benefits are reaped gradually over time periods stretching far into the future. This theory operates in a cost-benefit framework, and it is crucial to consider opportunity costs of time spent while in training. As the old saying goes, "When you are learning, you are not earning."

2. Private Investment in Education

One of the central tenets of human capital theory is that wage premiums are paid not for the innate ability of a worker, but rather as payment to the worker for having invested in a certain type of training or educational program. The typical diagram that is employed appears in Figure 9.1, which is called an age-earnings profile. Age is the variable on the horizontal axis, and earnings is the variable on the vertical axis. For most individuals, these age-earnings profiles have a positive slope (reflecting positive wage returns to labour market *experience*) and a concave shape (reflecting diminishing marginal returns to *experience*). *Ceteris paribus,* the higher (lower) the level of human capital, the higher (lower) the placement of the age-earnings profile. According to human capital theory, the individual worker has some choice over his/her human capital investment decision and will choose the quantity of education that maximizes the net present value of lifetime earnings. This optimal choice occurs where the marginal cost of investing in human capital (in discounted present value terms) is equal to the marginal benefit of investing in human capital (in discounted present value terms). The primary implication is that we expect for human capital decisions to be made early in one's lifetime.

3. Education and Market Equilibrium

The market equilibrium always requires a supply side and a demand side. The workers supply human capital (basically, skills and know-how) through the process depicted in Figure 9.2, and these preferences are reflected in the indifference curves. The firms demand human capital because it raises the marginal revenue product of labour, and these preferences are reflected in the isoprofit curves. These two types of curves are superimposed in wage-years of education space. This market framework is very similar to the one presented in Chapter 8, the major difference being that the variable on the horizontal axis, years of education, is considered a "bad" in the sense that it is costly to obtain. The indifference curves slope upward because wages are a good and human capital attainment is a "bad." The isoprofit curves also slope upward because higher wages detract from profits while higher levels of human capital cause higher productivity levels, which in turn cause higher profits.

The equilibrium relationship is generated by the locus of tangencies between the two types of curves. Much like the model in Chapter 8, it is called a sorting equilibrium because employees with the strongest preferences for education are matched with the firms whose technology of production renders such employees the most valuable. Similarly, employees with the weakest preferences for education are matched with the firms whose technology of production renders such employees the most valuable. This relationship (depicted in Figure 9.3) is upward sloping and need not be linear. The positive slope indicates that workers having higher levels of human capital can expect to receive a positive compensating differential, *ceteris paribus.*

4. Education as a Filter

The filtering model of educational attainment is an alternative and competing approach to the human capital theory of educational attainment. According to this approach, firms do not value education for the direct impact that it has on the skill levels and, hence, marginal productivity of workers. Instead, they interpret the successful completion of a degree as a signal that a job candidate is, or can be moulded into, a highly productive employee. Employers in this model are assumed not to know the true productivity of workers prior to the time that they are hired, so there is a climate of imperfect information. Both the signalling approach and the human capital approach have the same implication, namely a positive relationship between years of education and earnings levels, but the underlying behavioural mechanisms are very different.

5. Empirical Evidence

There is an almost unanimous view that the empirical evidence indicates that there is a positive relationship between education and lifetime earnings; that is, as a general rule, education pays off in terms of higher earnings, *ceteris paribus.* Nevertheless, this positive relationship is subject to diminishing marginal returns. Age-earnings profiles based on real Canadian data appear in Figure 9.5. The form of the typical empirical earnings function specifies log wages as a linear function of the level of schooling, the level of potential experience, and the level of potential experience squared. The estimated coefficient of the variable giving the years of education can be interpreted as the annual rate of return in percentage terms. The estimated returns to education for women tend to be a bit higher than they are for men.

There are at least two major challenges involved in estimating this equation. The first is called ability bias, which refers to the possibility that people who are more highly educated also tend to be those with the greatest inherent ability. If this applies, the returns to education are overestimated (that is, an upward bias). Assuming that wages are determined by marginal productivity, only a portion of the higher wage reflects higher educational attainment; the other portion reflects the higher innate ability. In order to resolve this obstacle, one has to fully control for the innate ability of workers. Recent empirical research, however, seems to indicate that ability bias does not play a strong role. A more serious econometric problem may be measurement error, which refers to the fact that the data for the years of education variable are often somewhat inaccurate. If this applies, the returns to education are underestimated (that is, a downward bias) for reasons that are beyond the scope of this textbook.

A very hot topic in recent research in labour economics is the increased returns to education that have been realized since the early 1980s in the U.S. contributed to a greater degree of inequality of the distribution of earnings. Most of the widening inequality, however, has been generated by increases in the "returns to unobserved skill," which means that the empirical research in its present state cannot explain it. In Canada during the 1990s, it is primarily the returns to labour market experience that have increased. Clearly, labour markets in both countries have experienced a profound evolution in wage structure, which creates a fertile field for empirical research into the underlying causes, which may include declines in the rate of unionization, declines in the minimum wage, changes in international trade patterns, major changes in information technology, and high levels of immigration.

6. Training

Training is another form of human capital that is distinct from education. Most jobs involve some form of training, either on the job or through a vocational program. There are two basic types of human capital associated with training: general and specific. General training is training that can be used in various firms, not just the firm providing the training. Specific training has no value to an employer other than the one who provides it. Like educational attainment, job training has its costs and benefits. We expect that general training will be financed entirely by the worker, while the cost of specific training will typically be shared between the firm and the worker. This theory can be applied to explain differences in the rate of earnings growth, the quit rate, and the layoff rate across industries and occupations.

It is somewhat difficult to evaluate government-sponsored training programs for displaced workers and disadvantaged workers for a number of reasons. It is necessary to estimate the counterfactual earnings of participants — what they would have earned without having participated in the training program. The general approach taken to evaluate programs is to calculate the earnings of the group of participants (called the "treatment group") before and after they have participated in the training program, and then to compare this difference to the same quantity (the before and after earnings) of a "control group" of workers who did not participate in the training program but are otherwise quite similar to the treatment group.

Helpful Hints

- Human capital theory has demand-side elements as well as supply-side elements, but the latter typically receive more attention.
- Regarding the age-earnings profile, do not confuse movement along a curve with displacement of a curve. The profile refers to one individual's earnings as he/she ages. As we move from left to right, the curve indicates how the yearly earnings evolve as he/she advances through his/her career. Two different profiles can be used to compare the career paths of two different individuals or various scenarios for the same individual who decides how much and what type of training or education to receive.
- Do not confuse the age-earnings profile (Figure 9.1), which deals with the earnings over time for one or several individuals, with the diagram for education and the market equilibrium (Figure 9.3), which shows the equilibrium locus of potential combinations of wage levels and years of education. While they both have the same vertical axis, they mean very different things.
- The age-earnings profile depicted in Figure 9.1 is a somewhat difficult model to grasp, but it is the key to understanding this entire chapter. You should also work through the equations on pages 248–249 of the textbook and understand the link between that diagram and these equations.
- The optimization approach involving the internal rate of return (shown in Figure 9.2b) is an alternative to the marginal cost-marginal benefit approach (shown in Figure 9.2a). They are mathematically equivalent, but conceptually, the internal rate of return approach is more difficult.
- There is no one equilibrium point that prevails in Figure 9.3, so do not search for one point of

intersection. Instead, search for the locus of points of intersection, which is the equilibrium relationship between wages and years of education. Given this curve, employers and employees basically decide for themselves where to locate along the market wage-years of education locus.

- The diagram for the signalling approach, Figure 9.4, is difficult. The intuition that underlies this approach is easier than the mathematical and graphical representation.

- You should know the expression for the rate of return to education, or the growth rate of earnings. It is given as the change in *wages* observed between two periods divided by the initial value of wages, which is a *level*. The units of the numerator are dollars, as are the units for the denominator, and these give rise to a percentage.

- Many students will find the information presented in Table 9.2 to be interesting. You should know how to interpret these coefficients. They all refer to wages in percentage terms. A positive (negative) coefficient means that an increase in that particular variable causes higher (lower) earnings, *ceteris paribus*. Note how the returns to experience are not constant; they diminish as experience is accumulated. For highly experienced workers, the returns may actually turn negative, which sometimes induces workers to retire.

- For the sections dealing with changes in the returns to education over time and the trend towards widening inequality of income, think in terms of shifts in the supply and demand for labour in the aggregate supply-and-demand framework. There are two grades of labour, with markets for "skilled" and "unskilled" labour.

- The graphs in Figure 9.7, which are called wage-experience profiles, may look complicated, but think of them in intuitive terms. There is a logical relationship between the wage, the value of the marginal product, and the fashion in which the cost of the training is distributed between the two parties.

Answers to Odd-Numbered End-of-Chapter Questions

1. In the broadest sense, capital is defined as something that is used to make something else and is thus not consumed (like a raw material or an intermediate input would be) in the production process. Capital does depreciate (wear out), however, as it is used, and thus it loses value over time if it is not maintained. Because capital is used as a means to an end, it is expected to generate a flow of economic returns in the future. Since there is no such thing as a free good, these returns are associated with a cost, which is usually in the form of an upfront investment. One usually expects to recoup the initial cost of the investment only gradually.

    In theory and often in practice, human capital meets all of these conditions. It is used to produce a flow of goods and/or services from the worker, from which both parties benefit. Workers don't necessarily want the training and/or education as an end in and of itself. They expect it to pay off in the form of higher earnings in the future. In order to create the human capital, a substantial upfront investment must be made, both in terms of explicit costs of training and education and in terms of implicit costs, such the trainees' time.

3. One can assume that the training involved is specific to the firm, otherwise the employer would not pay at all. The basic approach is to consider the costs and benefits from the firm's perspective with and without the training program. What wage stream is paid to the worker with and without the training? What is the marginal product stream of the worker with and without the training? Are there any explicit costs that the employer must incur, such as paying the instructor and diverting her efforts and attention from her normal duties? Worker morale may improve, but that is hard to evaluate quantitatively. It is important to know how long the training period will last.

Finally, an important factor is the probability of losing a worker (particularly through a quit) who has undergone the training. See the discussion surrounding Figures 9.7b and 9.7c.

5. This question overlaps with the previous question. The argument in favour of government subsidies in order to correct for a socially suboptimal level of human-resource development (typically, this means job training) is the following: When there are positive externalities to training and education activities, the providers (either the employer or a firm contracted to provide the training) and the trainees do not capture all of the benefits that it bestows on others. These benefits that others receive are external to their decision of how much time and money to invest in the training activities. They will thus tend to underinvest in training from a social point of view, as the marginal social benefit exceeds the marginal private benefit. They only respond to the latter.

    The indirect nature of on-the-job training, where it is difficult to assess exactly how much each worker contributes and benefits, makes it more likely that there is an underinvestment in training from a social point of view. One instance where there is widespread agreement for a major government role is in training laid-off and disadvantaged workers. A modern industrialized economy is typically subjected to changes in demand patterns and technology, which generate structural unemployment and underemployment. These phenomena generate high social and economic costs, and it seems pretty clear that private interests, such as firms and charities, do not have the economic resources (and sometimes they do not have the incentive) to provide job-training programs and counselling to these workers. See page 278.

7. The "virtues" of these different channels for providing training and education are not treated explicitly in the textbook, so this discussion is a bit broader. What follows is a brief contrast between them. On-the-job training (OJT) is likely to generate human capital that is quite specific to the firm. This is sometimes referred to as vocational training. The cost of providing it is typically shared between the employer and the worker. It is often informal in nature, meaning that there is not a diploma or certification. More discussion of its traits is found on pages 275–278. The decision for investment in OJT is made by both parties, and it is one of the primary factors determining the bond between the employer and the worker. The process of providing and financing the training is governed by the mechanisms illustrated in Figure 9.7. In many cases, we expect the parties to arrive at some agreement to provide at least some degree of OJT. Although there are some difficulties in assessing and assigning the costs and benefits of OJT, they are easier to evaluate than is the case in institutional education.

    Institutional training and education is likely to generate general human capital. This is more broadly applicable than specific human capital. It involves the development of skills, such as numeracy, literacy, and computer literacy, that can be applied to a wide variety of functions, as well as knowledge, such as civics, history, literature, and so on, that is deemed useful in Canadian society. The decision process for how much to invest in institutional training is the human capital investment decision, which is made primarily by the worker. The employer is expected to contribute nothing. This mechanism is described in a fair amount of detail on pages 246–253. There are several reasons to believe that without government intervention, the level of investment in institutional education is likely to be suboptimal. There are tremendous barriers to accessing it, in large part due to its high costs and imperfect capital markets. The returns to education are tougher to assess than is the case for OJT. Furthermore, whereas the economic function of OJT seems to be pretty clear (to directly enhance the MRP of the worker), the exact role of institutional education is less clear. That is the basic idea behind the conflicting interpretations of investment in education as a form of human capital or as a signalling device. Each of these stories yields different policy prescriptions for the government and makes efficiency analysis — are we overinvesting or underinvesting? — more complex.

Answers to Odd-Numbered End-of Chapter Problems

1. The benefits of the university degree are the higher earnings that you will receive for the ten years after you leave the university. In periods 5 through 15, you will receive $4,000 more per year. This stream of payments must be discounted by the market rate of interest. In present discounted value terms, we have

$$\sum_{i=5}^{15} \frac{4000}{(1.05)^i}$$

The costs are all incurred between periods 1 through 4. The explicit costs are $700 in each of those four years. To these, it is necessary to add the implicit costs of the $6,000 in foregone earnings in each year. The total costs in each year are $6,700. This stream of costs can be converted to a single figure for costs by applying the discounted present value formula. The expression for the total costs is

$$\frac{6,700}{1.05} + \frac{6,700}{1.05^2} + \frac{6,700}{1.05^3} + \frac{6,700}{1.05^4}$$

Calculate the discounted present value of the total costs. If they exceed the present discounted value of the benefits, do not make the investment.

See Figure 9.1.

3. In order to solve a problem like this, the first step is to list the payouts in each period for the two options. Starting with the high-school-only option, in each period the payout is Y_H. For the university option, the earnings are $5,000, but the explicit costs of the option are $5,000. This means that the net benefit, or payout, for that option in the first time period is zero. In the second time period, we are given a payout of Y_U. In order for her to attend the university, the discounted present value of the net benefit of attending university (summed up over periods 1 and 2) has to exceed the discounted present value of the net benefit of attending high school only (summed up over periods 1 and 2). The mathematical expression is

$$Y_H + \frac{Y_H}{1+R} < \frac{Y_U}{1+R}$$

Multiplying the first term by $(1 + r) / (1 + r)$, we obtain a common denominator. Since this denominator must be positive, the sign does not change direction, and we obtain the following inequality:

$$Y_H (1+R) + Y_H < Y_U$$

This simplifies to the sought-after result. The higher the interest rate, the less likely she is to select the university option, *ceteris paribus,* because the higher income levels that she would earn in the future are more steeply discounted. In other words, the higher the interest rate, the more valuable the option of receiving money today, relative to the option of receiving money tomorrow. Given a declining interest rate, that is the option that pays more money early in the time frame and also costs less at the beginning.

5. As in Problem 3, the first step is to list the payouts in each period for the three options. Grant is currently in time period 0.

	Time Period 1	Time Period 2	Time Period 3
A) Hotel	20000	20000	20000
B) Human resources	-5000	50000	50000
C) Art history	-10000	-10000	90000

The next step is to calculate the discounted present value of each of these three options. In order to do so, an interest rate of 10% is assumed, but any other positive value for the interest rate could be assumed. For option A, we have

$$\frac{20,000}{1.1} + \frac{20,000}{1.1^2} + \frac{20,000}{1.1^3} = 51,062$$

For option B, we have

$$\frac{-5,000}{1.1} + \frac{50,000}{1.1^2} + \frac{50,000}{1.1^3} = 77,655$$

For option C, we have

$$\frac{-10,000}{1.1} + \frac{-10,000}{1.1^2} + \frac{90,000}{1.1^3} = 56,270$$

a) In purely pecuniary terms, he should select option B.
b) The implicit consumption value that he places on that career option is its value ($56,270) relative to the value of the highest foregone alternative, which is $77,655.
c) The offspring of wealthy parents, or those with outside income, are more likely to be able to afford the high opportunity cost of option C.
d) If society deems that there is a high social value for the services of art historians, and this social value exceeds the private value, then the market is probably failing to produce a sufficient number of them, and a case may be made for subsidized tuition. Note, however, that it is costly for either the private sector or the public sector to train them due to the length of the training process, and this training process has an opportunity cost. On the other hand, if the private value coincides with the social value, we would expect those with the

Labour Market Economics, Fifth Edition

strongest preferences for studying art history would be willing to accept the relatively low value of that option. For option C, the low relative value is not due to really low salaries, but the fact that the training period is relatively long. Generally, subsidized tuition would not be warranted, as the marginal cost of educating one more art historian may well exceed his/her marginal productivity as an art historian.

7a. No, this statement is fallacious, because it offers no estimate of the counterfactual earnings, that is, what earnings would be had the women not participated in the training program. As it stands, this very simple analysis takes no account of any of the other variables that could have been acting over this period to influence the earnings of this group. The *ceteris paribus* condition is not satisfied. For program evaluation purposes, this is typically done by comparing the wage growth rate of the treatment group with that of a control group, and the control group has to be selected such that it resembles the treatment group as closely as possible when it comes to education and training levels, innate ability, motivation, and other factors that affect marginal productivity. Unfortunately, some of these traits are difficult to observe, as workers typically do not wear signs indicating that they are lazy, conscientious, intelligent, dumb, strong, weak, cooperative, abrasive, and so on.

b. Yes, this information would constitute a small step in the right direction. Over the period that the program was operating, the rate of wage growth for full-year, full-time female workers was +8.6%. While this group is not an appropriate control group, because the women in this group are not disadvantaged and are well integrated into the labour force (that is, the training program is not designed for women with their work experiences), the approach is valid. We want to estimate what the wage growth rate would have been for disadvantaged women who did not participate in the program. The 8.6% figure may be interpreted as a reasonable estimate of an upper bound for that figure. The researcher obtains an increase of 50% for annual earnings for the treatment group, which far exceeds the rate of wage growth for working women on average. That probably is meaningful, although one should also take account of the number of hours that the women in the treatment group worked before and after going through the training program.

Multiple Choice Questions

1. All of the following are elements in the decision concerning the optimal level of human capital investment *except* which?
   a) The higher wages that generally result from education
   b) Explicit expenses for tuition and books
   c) Foregone earnings while attending school and training
   d) The utility and enjoyment that one may derive from the educational process
   e) The discount rate

2. An individual should invest in a certain educational program if:
   a) The internal rate of return is positive.
   b) The internal rate of return exceeds the discount rate.
   c) The discounted present value of the costs of the investment exceeds the discounted present value of the benefits.
   d) The income streams that will flow from the educational program are higher than those that would be earned without the degree.
   e) None of the above.

3. What is the typical shape of age-earnings profiles?
   a) They slope positively as workers become older, due to on-the-job training, but at a decreasing rate because workers become less productive after they have reached a certain age.
   b) They slope positively as earnings increase with age, due to on-the-job training, but at a decreasing rate because of diminishing marginal returns to experience.
   c) They slope positively as earnings increase with age, due to on-the-job training, but at a constant rate because of the durability of their training.
   d) They slope positively as earnings increase with age, due to on-the-job training, but they tend to level out very quickly for most workers as they learn their occupations quickly.
   e) They are actually quite flat for most workers.

4. Age-earnings profiles for university-educated individuals tend to be steeper than those of individuals who have completed only secondary school. According to the human capital model, this difference is due to the fact that:
   a) University graduates typically have a greater capacity to learn a wider variety of skills and are thus more likely to obtain on-the-job training.
   b) The steepening reflects greater incentive for individuals to invest in a college education.
   c) University graduates tend to acquire skills whose value does not diminish over time.
   d) University graduates are more likely to be covered under collective bargaining agreements, which accord significant wage increases in accordance with seniority.
   e) All of the above.

5. What is a prominent implication of human capital theory?
   a) Education should be subsidized by the government.
   b) Investments in human capital are likely to be made early in one's lifetime.
   c) The discounted present value of the benefits of the investment exceed the discounted present value of the costs.
   d) The internal rate of return exceeds the discount rate.
   e) Employees differ in their preferences for education because of factors such as differences in tastes for acquiring knowledge, learning ability, and the discount rate.

6. Which of the following statements is *false*?
   a) The signalling theory is an alternative to the theory of human capital in interpreting the acquisition of education and training.
   b) Imperfect information is a major element in the signalling approach.
   c) In the signalling approach, education has no direct role in affecting productivity.
   d) In the signalling approach, employers believe that there is an indirect but positive relationship between education and productivity.
   e) All of the above statements are true.

7. An important assumption of the signalling approach is that:
   a) More able workers have a lower cost of acquiring education and thus are more apt to sort themselves into educational programs.
   b) More educated workers tend to earn higher wages and salaries as they are more productive.
   c) Workers with skills and education are more valuable to employers because these skills make them more productive.
   d) Low-ability workers have a strong incentive to obtain more education and training to compensate for their weakness.
   e) Major investments in education are likely to be carried out early in one's career.

8. Which of the following statements concerning the human capital model is *false*?
   a) It can be used as a tool to evaluate policy, such as subsidizing higher education.
   b) One would expect highly educated workers to earn higher wages, *ceteris paribus*.
   c) The level of education of an individual is determined primarily by sociological factors.
   d) The level of education of an individual is determined primarily by his/her optimal choice in weighing the costs against the benefits.
   e) The approach that economists use to analyse decisions to invest in physical capital — comparing the upfront costs with the stream of benefits in the future — can be applied to the decision to obtain education.

9. Consider the human capital approach in the context of training expenses. Which of the following statements is *false*?
   a) The employee is expected to pay for general human capital accumulation.
   b) The employee may quit her job if the employer has paid for the training involved with specific human capital.
   c) Both parties will generally pay for the training involved with specific human capital.
   d) The employer may fire the worker if the employee has paid for all of the training involved with specific human capital.
   e) All of the above statements are true.

10. Which of the following statements concerning the empirical research regarding the rate of return on education is *false*?
    a) Rates of return to education generally decline with the amount of education already obtained.
    b) The marginal rate of return from completing high school is high.
    c) Earnings tend to decline slightly for workers in their late 50s.
    d) There is a wide dispersion in the rates of return to education among holders of university degrees.
    e) The salary differential between those with and without university degrees is low for younger workers, so in many cases it is not worthwhile for them to obtain a university degree.

11. Which of the following most closely describes a human capital earnings function?
    a) The dependent variable is the log of wages, and the independent variables are age and schooling.
    b) The dependent variable is the log of wages, and the independent variables are schooling and experience.
    c) The dependent variable is the log of wages, and the independent variables are schooling, experience, and the discount rate.
    d) The dependent variable is the log of wages, and the independent variables are schooling, experience, and experience squared.
    e) None of the above.

12. Which of the following statements concerning the human capital earnings function is *false*?
    a) The rate of return to schooling for women is lower than it is for men.
    b) The rate of return to experience is higher for men than it is for women.
    c) A negative coefficient for the experience-squared variable indicates diminishing returns to experience.
    d) A positive coefficient for the experience variable indicates positive returns to experience.
    e) The form and the variables that are included in the estimating equation are based on the human capital model.

13. What is meant by ability bias, and what is its significance?
    a) Individuals have different innate abilities, and the more able are more likely to obtain higher levels of education. This tends to lead to an overestimate of rate of return on education.
    b) Individuals have different innate abilities, and the more able are more likely to obtain higher levels of education. This tends to lead to an underestimate of rate of return on education.
    c) Individuals have different levels and qualities of education, and these are measured with error. This tends to lead to an overestimate of the rate of return on education.
    d) Individuals have different levels and qualities of education, and these are measured with error. This tends to lead to an underestimate of rate of return on education.
    e) None of the above.

14. What was observed to occur to the returns to education during the past 30 years?
    a) From the early- to late-1970s, the greatest increases in earnings were received by groups with the most education.
    b) The monetary returns to higher education declined during the 1980s.
    c) During the 1980s, the greatest increases in earnings were received by groups with the most education.
    d) The monetary returns to education declined in the 1980s.
    e) No clear trends are discernible over this period, as the earnings gap between the university educated and the non-university educated remained relatively constant.

15. What is thought to be behind the growing polarization of incomes observed in North America?
    a) A decline in the demand for unskilled labour, due in part to skill-biased technological change
    b) An increase in the supply of university educated and highly trained skilled workers
    c) A decline in the supply of lesser skilled workers
    d) A decline in the demand for skilled labour, due to increased foreign competition
    e) None of the above

Answers to Multiple Choice Questions

1. D   This is made explicit in the section of the textbook entitled "Investment in Private Education." Although many people do derive utility from the educational process, it does not enter into the human capital model.

2. B   The opposite of response C is correct. Response D does not take costs into account. Response A is incorrect because one has to compare the rate of return from investing in human capital with the rate of return from investing in other ventures.

3. B   Response A is almost correct. If workers actually become less productive, there is a negative slope. Responses C, D, and E are pretty similar and are incorrect because these profiles slope upwards.

4. A   Response B is a true statement, but does not address the question. Responses C and D are totally false.

5. B   Responses C and D are true statements if the individual elects to invest in human capital, but they are essentially premises of the human capital model. Response E is also an assumption.

6. E   All of the points in responses A, B, C, and D are made explicit in the textbook in the subsection on signalling.

7. A   Responses B and C are totally wrong, as it refers to the human capital model. The opposite of response D applies. Response E is an implication of human capital approach.

8. C   Many people would claim that response C is true, but it is not a tenet of the human capital approach. Most of the other points were made explicit in the textbook in the section in which the model is developed.

9. D   Responses A and C are made explicit in the textbook. Response B is true, as the employee has not paid for her training. Response D is correct, as the employer has no incentive to make this choice.

10. E   Most of these points are made explicit in the textbook in the subsection on the empirical returns to education. Response E is false, because the differential widens considerably as workers age.

11. D   This equation appears in the textbook.

12. A   The very opposite of response A is true. The remaining statements are true.

13. A   Response A is made explicit in the textbook in the subsection on ability bias. Response D is a true statement, but that problem is not the ability-bias problem.

14. C   This point is made explicit in the textbook in the subsection on the empirical returns to education. The other statements are false.

15. A   Response D may apply if one were talking about unskilled labour. Responses B and C would tend to reduce earnings inequality.

CHAPTER 10

Chapter Highlights

This chapter shares a theme with the preceding two chapters, namely its focus on the structure of wages, which involves a comparison of wage levels across two workers or groups of workers and an explanation of the cause of the differential. Chapter 8 dealt with the role of hedonic traits of jobs and occupations, meaning the amenities or disamenities attached to them, in generating wage differentials, *ceteris paribus*. Chapter 9 dealt mostly with the role of human capital in generating wage differentials, *ceteris paribus*. Even after taking account of these important factors, however, the labour market is rife with wage differentials.

1. Explorations with the 1996 Census

We use the same equation to analyse earnings that was used in the preceding chapter, namely the earnings function specified in Equation 10.1. The natural logarithm of earnings is a linear function of the level of education, the level of labour market experience, the level of labour market experience squared, and an additive term to capture unobservable or random factors that influence wages. The interpretation of any of the coefficients is the percentage change in wages that is generated by a unit change in any of those three variables. This equation is augmented by a series of additive terms, which in this chapter reflect different industries, occupations, or geographical regions. The interpretation of any of the coefficients (represented by gammas in Equation 10.2) is the percentage change in wages that is associated with a given industry, occupation, or geographical region, holding fixed the level of education, the level of labour market experience, the level of labour market experience squared, and all other factors except for that particular industry, occupation, or region in question. Estimates generated from such an earnings function (with actual 1996 data from the Canadian labour market) are presented in Table 10.1.

2. Theoretical Issues

Suppose that one is confronted with a wage differential to explain, and it seems as though human capital considerations do not explain all of the wage differential. The textbook mentions a four-point checklist of factors that could be relevant:

1. The non-pecuniary aspects of a job — the amenities and the disamenities — that can generate compensating differentials.
2. Immobility of labour flows between sectors typically undermines the degree of competition that exists in a labour market, which will often lead to prevailing wages that are not equilibrium wages. A market-clearing wage is the equilibrium wage obtained when quantity supplied equals quantity demanded. A disequilibrium wage is the opposite of a market-clearing wage, and it is typically associated with some sort of market power, that is, a non-competitive feature of the labour market.
3. The time frame. If a disequilibrium wage emerges, if there is mobility of labour across sectors or industries, then a competitive wage is expected to prevail in the long run.

4. Unobserved heterogeneity, which can arise when the data do not measure the level of skills and ability very accurately. In this case, two wages of different workers may differ because they have different marginal productivity levels, but according to the data that we have (that is, education and experience), they appear identical.

3. Occupational Wage Structures

The analytical tool for this entire chapter is the elementary supply-and-demand framework, as illustrated in Figure 10.1. Given the basic determinants of occupational supply and demand, the theory of competitive labour markets predicts that the forces of supply and demand will ensure an equal present value of net advantage at the margin (that is, the last few workers hired) across occupations in the long run. If a wage differential exists after one has adjusted for the non-pecuniary aspects, the human capital requirements, and the innate ability required of the two occupations, we expect an adjustment process called arbitrage to occur. Workers at the margin will move from jobs of low net advantage to jobs of high net advantage. If this process does not occur in the long run, then we suspect that non-competitive forces, such as barriers to entry into occupations, are at work. The degree of the adjustment from the short run to the long run (if it occurs) is governed by the elasticity of supply of labour for the occupation that has the higher net advantage. The wage elasticity of labour supply in the short run is usually less than it is in the long run.

4. Regional Wage Structures and Geographical Mobility

The same basic approach is applied to wage differentials across geographical regions. Regional wage disparities are marked in Canada, but they have diminished somewhat over time. Given the basic determinants of regional supply and demand, the theory of competitive markets predicts that the forces of supply and demand will ensure an equal present value of net advantage at the margin in the long run across regions. If a wage differential exists after one has adjusted for the non-pecuniary aspects and the human capital requirements of jobs in a certain region, we expect an adjustment process to occur. Workers at the margin will migrate from jobs of low net advantage in low-wage regions to jobs of high net advantage in higher wage regions. If this process does not occur in the long run, then we suspect that non-competitive forces, such as subsidies and income transfers to workers and firms in the low-wage areas, or barriers to migration, such as inadequate housing in high-wage areas, are at work. The choice of geographical migration is analysed much like the decision to invest in human capital.

5. Inter-Industry Wage Differentials

This subsection deals with average wages within an industry. This wage will reflect a combination of factors, including the occupational composition and characteristics of the labour force, the size of the typical firm in a sector, and the geographical location of the sector. As a consequence, pure inter-industry wage differentials (holding all other factors that can influence relative wages constant) are difficult to measure. There is substantial overlap between wage differentials attributable to region, occupation, industry, and characteristics of the labour force. A pure inter-industry wage differential reflects the premium that a worker in one sector of the economy receives, relative to an otherwise identical worker employed in another sector of the economy. The same basic approach is followed in analysing the nature of inter-industry wage differentials. One examines the non-pecuniary characteristics of the industries, the effects of short-run demand changes (that is, wage premiums that are expected to dissipate over time), and non-competitive factors.

The structure of wages across industries, holding all other factors constant, is remarkably constant over time. Often they are caused by rents earned by firms that have monopoly power in the output market. A portion of these rents is shared with the workers, often in response to union pressure. An alternative explanation to persistent wage differentials across sectors is the efficiency wage theory. According to this hypothesis, firms voluntarily pay workers a wage that exceeds the going market wage (that is, the competitive wage) in order to elicit more effort from the workers. The workers thus receive a rent in addition to the wage that is required to compensate them for the non-pecuniary aspects of the job, including the human capital requirements. These efficiency wages can improve morale and reduce turnover, shirking, and absenteeism. Although firms that pay efficiency wages pay more than they have to in order to recruit workers, these wage levels are consistent with profit-maximizing behaviour and will not be competed away in the long run.

Although this theory is fairly popular among labour economists, it is not easy to prove its existence empirically. This problem is due in part to the challenges that are ever-present in empirical work: statistically controlling for all of the other factors that simultaneously affect wages, and specifying factors that affect wages but are unobservable. Most of the existing studies indicate that pure inter-industry wage differentials exist, although it is much more difficult to determine whether they are due to the payment of efficiency wages or the sharing of monopoly profits between the firm and the union.

6. Inter-Firm Wage Differentials and Firm Size

It is an empirical regularity that, *ceteris paribus,* larger firms tend to pay higher wages than smaller firms. It is much more difficult to determine the economic reasons behind this phenomenon. The basic problem in determining the nature of this effect is that many other factors that can influence wage differentials are correlated with firm size. In other words, the wage premium paid by larger firms arises because larger firms are more likely to have wage-enhancing characteristics. For example, larger firms are more likely to be unionized than smaller firms, so what looks like a wage premium associated with firm size is actually a union premium. Occupational premiums or inter-industry wage differentials can also be confounded with firm-size differentials. To make matters more complicated, sometimes these factors that are correlated with firm size are unobservable. For example, some economists believe that larger firms are more likely to hire workers of higher innate ability. What looks like a firm-size premium would actually reflect the higher marginal productivity of better quality workers.

7. Public-Sector/Private-Sector Wage Differentials

This is a particular type of inter-industry wage differential. The basic question of this subsection is the extent to which public-sector employers pay higher wages than private-sector employers, *ceteris paribus.* Recent empirical evidence suggests that public-sector workers may earn a premium of 9%, and this applies particularly to lower-skilled workers and female workers. Most of the discussion in the textbook involves these other factors that are supposed to be held constant in analysing the wage gap between the public sector and the private one. The textbook discusses a rather long list of potential influences on wages in this context, such as short-run adjustments to shifts in labour demand, non-competitive factors such as monopsony power, non-pecuniary factors such as job security, and an elasticity of labour demand that is generally considered to be inelastic. Because public-sector employers do not operate in markets and are in a position to compel payment of taxes, there is the potential for public-sector unions to extract high rents from the governments that employ them.

Helpful Hints

- The basic question for this chapter is relative wages, or the wage structure. Be prepared to analyse the reasons why Mutt may earn more than Jeff, or vice versa. Always think in terms of the effect of a certain variable on the wage structure, *holding all other factors constant.*
- The baseline case to which any wage is compared is typically the competitive wage, which means the equilibrium wage level that exists where the supply curve for labour intersects with the demand curve.
- The graphical analysis for this chapter is not difficult — it is the simple supply-and-demand framework. Typically, the graphs, representing the supply-and-demand relationships for two different occupations, sectors, or geographical regions, are placed adjacent to each other.
- The empirical analysis contained in this chapter is somewhat difficult. You should be able to replicate the earnings function and be able to interpret the economic meaning of the coefficients. Review the challenges that researchers face in conducting empirical analysis. They are mentioned above in the "Chapter Highlights" section.
- Know how to read and interpret the figures in Table 10.1.
- Here is the basic conceptual approach to take. First, consider what one would expect the relative wage between the given jobs to be if the labour market were competitive. It should reflect the compensating differentials for non-pecuniary factors and for the human capital requirements of the two jobs. If there still appears to a differential, or a net advantage, then one may expect for it be competed away in the long run if there is free entry into the favoured job. If no adjustment occurs in the long run, and the differential persists, one may search for non-competitive factors.
- A rather simple criterion that can be applied in order to assess if workers in a particular occupation, sector, or region are "overpaid" is whether one observes a long queue of workers waiting to accept such jobs when they are offered.

Answers to Odd-Numbered End-of-Chapter Questions

1. There are many factors that influence labour supply, such as labour market information (concerning outside opportunities), mobility, training requirements, working conditions, immigration and demographic factors, and the general state of the macroeconomy. Retail sales clerks or fast-food workers have an elastic supply schedule. If wages were to be increased, a lot of people would enter, because usually the training requirements are not that heavy. Medical doctors have an inelastic supply schedule because it takes a long time to train them, and their training is very specific. If wages were to be increased, the quantity supplied would not respond for a few years. The skill differential would narrow if both occupations were to experience a similar increase in demand for their services. In both cases, there is upward pressure on the wage, but in the occupation with the elastic (flatter) supply curve, more of this increase is absorbed through an increase in the quantity of labour demanded. In an occupation with inelastic labour supply, more of the increase is absorbed through an increase in the equilibrium wage.

3. The issue in this question is the negative externalities that are imposed on a city's current residents in the face of rapid growth through migration. These externalities include increased pollution, traffic, and congestion; strained public services and infrastructure; and, above all, high housing prices. If newly arrived, migrating workers are charged for the external costs that are imposed on the long-time residents, the externality is addressed, and the city has a better chance of reaching its optimal size. The statement in the question assumes that these costs are not internalized. In that case, one would not want wage levels in the overcrowded area to rise in

order to compensate for the higher cost of living and other disamenities associated with urban congestion. In the subsection on inter-regional wage differentials, the textbook suggests that governments implement many policies that have an unintended side effect of reducing migration. Since migration is the force that would bring about wage adjustments (in this case, one may want the non-urban wage to rise, relative to the urban wage), dampening migration will not help alleviate congestion. One factor that the textbook does not mention is local urban-development policies. There could well be government policies that encourage suburban sprawl, which have the effect of reducing the costs of migration. If migrants to an overcrowded city are not charged the full cost of their contribution to urban disamenities, then there is less upward pressure on wages.

5. One possible explanation is the efficiency wage effect. It is thought that, in larger firms, the technology of production is likely to be capital intensive, which often makes it costly to monitor directly the productivity of the individual workers. Larger firms tend to operate by team production techniques, and it is difficult to assess the contribution (or lack thereof) of production by individual workers. An efficiency wage is one mechanism that may be used to deter shirking behaviour and to elicit high effort levels from the workers. The key to assessing the importance of efficiency wages is first to fully account for the roles of other determinants of wage structures: non-pecuniary differences in the nature of jobs (especially working conditions), short-run demand changes, and non-competitive factors (such as labour unions). After adjusting for those factors, if the wage still appears to be higher than the going wage in other sectors, it is possible that an efficiency premium is being paid. The textbook gives reasons for which of those wage-increasing factors above may be positively correlated with firm size. An important point is that it is a challenge to distinguish empirically between a wage premium that is due to a combination of those other factors and one that is attributable to an efficiency wage premium.

7. There is an element of truth to this statement, and some of the debate in the scientific literature has revolved around this point. According to some analysts, it is the public sector that ought to serve as a model for the wage and employment practices of the private sector, and not the other way around. Observers from the institutionalist and dual labour market camps are likely to take this position, although they reject the paradigm of a competitive labour market driven by supply-and-demand forces. They claim that those forces should not be permitted to determine wages at all because they do not generate "just" and equitable outcomes. They also claim that non-economic constraints and market imperfections are the rule rather than the exception.

The confines of this question appear to suggest that the competitive labour market is the ideal one. It follows that labour markets in the private sector should serve as a benchmark, provided that they are relatively free from imperfections such as discrimination, barriers to entry and mobility into certain occupations and firms, and unequal bargaining power (a labour union on the supply side or a monopsony on the demand side). Unfortunately, this ideal is not always obtained in the real world, and when it is, it is not always easy to measure the going, perfectly competitive market wage. For this reason, when labour economists try to examine public-sector wages, they are forced to rely on imperfect benchmarks for the going private-sector wage holding education levels, skill levels, and certain non-pecuniary aspects of the jobs (for example, working conditions) constant. Indeed, great care must be taken in researching the question of whether public-sector wages (or wages in just about any sector) are too high. One has to control for many factors that may not be easy to assess, and one has to find some point of comparison (a benchmark). One indicator of whether public-sector wages are too "high" or "low" is the turnover behaviour of its labour force. If quits are very rare, and there is a long queue of workers waiting for any job opening, wages are probably above the competitive level. If quits are very frequent, and there is no queue of workers waiting for job openings, wages are probably below the competitive level.

Answers to Odd-Numbered End-of-Chapter Problems

1. This claim essentially says that no worker is lucky to have the opportunity to work in a certain industry. In other words, there is no net advantage associated with any industry. If workers in sector A earn more than they do in sector B, and all of the conditions of perfectly competitive labour markets are satisfied (no barriers to entry, perfect information regarding going wages and working conditions, and no market power exercised by either firms or workers), then it must be due to some compensating differential for an adverse non-pecuniary aspect of the job, an efficiency wage, or the superior quality or qualifications of workers in that industry. There is one camp of labour economists who believe that often what appears to be an industrial wage premium (for example, janitors at school boards earn more than janitors in commercial office buildings, or retail clerks at Ontario's beer stores earn more than their counterparts at Zellers) is actually due to an unobserved quality differential. According to this story, the clerks at Brewer's Retail and the janitors at public school boards are more skilled and have a higher level of responsibility. Under these conditions, their higher pay is not a rent. The subsection on the empirical evidence regarding inter-industry wage differentials argues against the proposition contained in the question. According to that position, a pure inter-industry wage premium can exist, and it is probably caused in some cases by efficiency wages and in other cases by the sharing of monopoly profits with the workers.

3. First of all, there must be a very solid barrier to mobility in the two sectors, otherwise the highly skilled workers in the low-wage industry, who are totally identical to those in the high-wage industry, would migrate to the high-wage industry. During a recession, all of the unskilled workers earn $5.00. The skilled labourer earns $10.00 in one sector and $20.00 in the other. We are told that each sector employs the same number of skilled workers, so the average wage must be $15.00. This means that the differential is 3 to 1 (that is, 200%). During an expansion, the average wage for the skilled workers is still $15.00, while the average wage for the unskilled workers is $10.00. The skilled-to-unskilled differential has narrowed from 200% to 50%. As the question states, the inter-occupational wage differential contracted during the expansion. This occurred because the unskilled labour is supplied more elastically (both in this question and in the real world). When times are good, they gain disproportionately. During a recession, the workers in the low-wage industry earn an average of $7.50, as they are equally divided between the skilled workers earning $10.00 and the unskilled workers earning $5.00. The workers in the high-wage industry average $12.50. This differential works out to 67%. During an expansion, the workers in the high-wage industry earn an average of $17.50, while the workers in the low-wage industry continue to earn an average of $7.50. This works out to a differential of 133%. The inter-industry differential widened as the high-wage sector changed its wage structure, while the low-wage sector did not.

5. This statement is true. If there were no non-competitive factors, no discrepancies between the two sectors in short-run demand conditions, no differences in conditions giving rise to efficiency wages, and identical labour supplies in the two sectors (especially education, skill requirements, and non-pecuniary factors), then the differing elasticities of demand for labour would not

generate a wage differential. If higher wages were being paid in the public sector, *ceteris paribus,* then workers in the private sector would be lured to the public sector. This migration would continue, and the relative supplies of labour would adjust such that the wage differential between the public sector and the private sector would erode.

7. The graphical analysis would consist of a supply-and-demand graph for veterinarians and another one for pharmacists. Suppose that the supply curves are similar due to comparable human capital requirements and relatively equal numbers of individuals with a strong preference toward working in those two professions. Originally, the demand curves were in a similar position as well. The demand curve for pharmacists has shifted to the right recently and is currently positioned far above the demand curve for veterinarians. In the short run, this creates a substantial $20,000 salary premium for pharmacists. This differential will persist for several years, but the green pastures in pharmacy work are likely to attract new entrants into the profession. One could argue that after a lengthy adjustment period (we are told that it takes six years to train a new pharmacist), the short-run supply curve will shift to the right, and we will reach a new equilibrium salary for that occupation in which the $20,000 premium is eroded. All three of these equilibria — the original one, the short-run equilibrium that occurs after the demand for pharmacists shifts to the right, and the final equilibrium after all entry has occurred — lie on the long-run supply curve of pharmacists, which is flatter and more elastic than either of the two short-run supply curves.

Multiple Choice Questions

1. Which of the following conditions may yield a non-competitive industry wage differential whereby workers in industry A are paid more than the workers in industry B?
    a) Less desirable working conditions in industry A.
    b) More able workers in industry A than in industry B.
    c) Industry A tends to locate in less populated regions than industry B.
    d) Monopoly profits exist in the output market of industry A, yet there are zero profits in the output market of industry B.
    e) Higher levels of human capital required in industry A.

2. Which of the following conditions may yield a non-competitive industry wage differential whereby workers in industry A are paid more than the workers in industry B?
    a) Less stable working patterns in industry A, with a threat of layoffs.
    b) Efficiency wages are paid in industry B.
    c) Efficiency wages are paid in industry A.
    d) Unobserved heterogeneity — workers in industry A are more conscientious.
    e) The cost of living is higher in the regions in which industry A locates.

3. Which of the following conditions may yield any inter-industry wage differential whereby workers in industry A are paid more than the workers in industry B?
    a) The workers in industry A are unionized.
    b) Efficiency wages are paid in industry B.
    c) The human capital requirements are greater in industry B.
    d) The workers in industry B earn rents.
    e) The workers in industry A are employed by a monopsonist, while those in industry B are employed by a firm that is a competitor in the input market.

4. Which of the following statements concerning cross-industrial wage differentials is *false*?
   a) There is no evidence in the Canadian studies that they exist.
   b) There is not total agreement as to whether the wage differentials are pure or whether they reflect productivity differentials that are not fully controlled for.
   c) They are more likely to occur in industries that are unionized.
   d) We observe in practice that low-wage industries often have unfavourable working conditions.
   e) They are relatively stable over time.

5. What factor could not lead to an inter-occupational wage differential whereby workers in occupation A earned more than workers in occupation B?
   a) A barrier to entry in occupation A
   b) Differences in the non-pecuniary aspects of the two occupations
   c) Differences in the human capital requirements for the two occupations
   d) Rents accruing to workers endowed with certain talent
   e) None of the above

6. In the efficiency wage model of wage determination,
   a) The worker is paid her marginal revenue product.
   b) The worker is paid less than her marginal revenue product as wages are docked for training expenses.
   c) The worker is paid less than her marginal revenue product if the firm is making losses.
   d) The worker is paid more than her marginal revenue product in order to elicit more effort.
   e) The worker is paid more than her marginal revenue product because she is fully trained.

7. Consider the case of inter-industry wage differentials. For example, it so happens that wages in the beer and petroleum industries are higher than in most other sectors, given the occupation. The very neo-classical (competitive market-clearing) interpretation of this premium would be:
   a) Unobserved heterogeneity among workers. These industries hire more productive workers.
   b) An efficiency wage mechanism. These industries pay higher wages in order to elicit more effort.
   c) A compensating differentials mechanism. Workers in these industries are paid more in order to compensate them for less stable working conditions.
   d) A short run increase in labour demand.
   e) A market power mechanism. These workers are represented by a strong union.

8. Wage structures across markets are analysed along several different dimensions. Which of the following dimensions show wage differentials that do not tend to endure over the long run?
   a) By different occupations
   b) By different regions
   c) By immigrant versus native-born status
   d) By different industries
   e) By the public sector versus the private sector

9. All other factors held constant, workers in certain industries tend to earn negative or positive premiums, relative to workers in other industries. In which of the following industries do wages tend to be the lowest?
   a) Manufacturing
   b) Communication and utilities
   c) Finance and insurance
   d) Construction
   e) Accommodation/food/beverages

10. All other factors held constant, workers in certain regions tend to earn negative or positive premiums, relative to workers in other regions. In which of the following regions do wages tend to be the lowest?
    a) The Atlantic Provinces
    b) Quebec
    c) Ontario
    d) Manitoba and Saskatchewan
    e) Alberta

11. All other factors held constant, workers in certain occupations tend to earn negative or positive premiums, relative to workers in other occupations. In which of the following occupations do wages tend to be the lowest?
    a) Farming and horticultural
    b) Managerial and administrative
    c) Teaching
    d) Health care
    e) Natural sciences/engineering

12. Suppose that we observe that workers in one industry earn substantially more than workers in another industry. Assume that these workers all possess identical human capital. Which of the following factors would not be a possible explanation for the pay disparity?
    a) The non-pecuniary aspects of the jobs differ
    b) Immobility of workers across the two industries
    c) Disequilibrium in the short run due to adjustment costs
    d) Unobserved heterogeneity of workers reflecting innate differences in productivity
    e) Differing wage elasticities of labour demand

13. The theory of the equality of net advantage of all occupations at the margin in the long run says that after controlling (adjusting) for human capital and non-pecuniary factors, workers in the two occupations should not envy each other. Why not?
    a) Barriers to entry, such as a union, will prevent people from entering the desirable occupation.
    b) The law of diminishing marginal returns applies.
    c) In the long run, workers entering and exiting from occupations would erode the premium.
    d) Certain workers collect economic rents.
    e) The wage elasticity of demand is inelastic.

14. Assume that the demand for certain types of workers rises suddenly. In the short run, one would expect their wages to rise considerably. The long-run adjustment to this new short-run equilibrium is likely to take the longest, and wage premiums are likely to endure the longest, given that:
   a) Barriers to entry are low.
   b) The wage elasticity of supply is low.
   c) The wage elasticity of demand is low.
   d) The wage elasticity of supply is high.
   e) The wage elasticity of demand is high.

15. With all other factors held constant, which of the following statements concerning migration behaviour is *false*?
   a) Younger workers are expected to migrate more than older workers.
   b) Migration is more likely to occur out of higher unemployment areas.
   c) Migration is more likely to occur during recoveries than during recessions.
   d) Migration is more likely to occur from Quebec than from other provinces.
   e) Migration is more likely to be observed when the distances are long.

Answers to Multiple Choice Questions

1. D   For responses A, B, and E, workers in industry A would earn more, *ceteris paribus,* but it would be due to a competitive labour market. The opposite of response C is likely to be true.
2. C   For responses A, D, and E, workers in industry A would earn more, *ceteris paribus,* but it would be due to a competitive labour market. The opposite of response B is likely to be true.
3. A   For all of the other responses, workers in industry B are likely to earn more, *ceteris paribus.*
4. A   The negation of the statement in response A is made explicit in the textbook. Responses B, C, and E are stated explicitly in the subsection on inter-industry wage differentials.
5. E   Responses A, B, C, and D could all lead to the outcome described in the question. Responses A and D are made explicit in the textbook, while responses B and C are emphasized in the "Chapter Highlights" section above.
6. D   See the subsection in the textbook that treats efficiency wages. Response D is also stated explicitly in the "Chapter Highlights" section above.
7. A   For response B, an efficiency wage is above the competitive level. Response C is a sensible answer, but in the real world, these industries are characterized by very high job security. Response D refers to a short-run equilibrium, and the premium would not be expected to persist in the long run if the market were totally competitive. Response E is the antithesis of a competitive labour market equilibrium.
8. C   All of the other responses were mentioned in the textbook. Wage differentials compared across those dimensions have tended to be pretty stable over recent decades.
9. E   See the subsection in the textbook that deals with inter-industry wage differentials.
10. A   See the subsection in the textbook that deals with inter-regional wage differentials.
11. A   See the subsection in the textbook that deals with inter-occupational wage differentials.
12. E   Responses A, B, C, and D are made explicit in the "Chapter Highlights" section presented above. For response E, wage elasticities are relevant for how employers respond to a change in the wage rate.

13. C   If the condition in response A applies, this theory does not hold. Responses B and E are totally irrelevant. For response D, if certain workers do collect economic rents, they are very fortunate, as rents are competed away if the labour market is competitive.

14. B   For responses C and E, it is the wage elasticity of supply that is relevant for entry into an industry or an occupation. The opposite of response A applies. Response B is made explicit in the textbook.

15. E   See the subsection in the textbook that deals with migration.

CHAPTER 11

Chapter Highlights

There are three facets of the economics of immigration that are dealt with in this chapter. First, there is the economic performance of immigrants compared to native-born Canadians, usually defined in terms of wage outcomes. Second, there is the impact of immigration activity on the labour market outcomes of the native-born population. Finally, there is an evaluation of government policy towards immigration.

1. A Profile of Immigration to Canada

Immigration levels to Canada have been fairly high by historical standards and high compared to many other industrialized countries since the mid-1980s. For instance, in 1996, as a result of the three decades of immigration activity, about 17% of all Canadian residents were born outside Canada, compared to approximately 9% of the residents in the U.S. Most immigrants settle in large urban areas.

2. The Policy Environment

Governments have two major ways to affect immigration policy. They can decide on the number of immigrants they accept over a period of time, and they can decide who among the set of potential applicants is admitted. All immigrants are considered to be of the assessed classes or the non-assessed classes, each of which has a different set of criteria for selection. The applications of the former are judged primarily on their specific skills as they relate to the labour market, and these skills are evaluated on a point system that is supposed to be objective. The applications of the latter are assessed according to their family ties to Canadian residents (in the case of the family class) and their personal histories (in the case of the refugee class). In recent years, the share of the assessed classes has gained somewhat, relative to the share of the non-assessed classes.

3. The Impact of Immigrants on the Labour Market

This is an important policy question, as many Canadians fear that the immigrants in the labour market either depress their wages or make it more difficult to gain employment. The starting point for an economic analysis is the simple supply-and-demand model of the aggregate labour market, as depicted in Figure 11.4. The entry of immigrants to the labour market causes the supply of labour to shift to the right, and *ceteris paribus,* the equilibrium wage falls. However, the immigration activity also causes a rise in the population, and for that and other reasons, the demand for labour is likely to expand as well, placing upward pressure on the wage that may well offset the initial supply-side effect.

There are major challenges involved in empirically assessing the impact of immigration on the labour market. One problem involves determining whether the scope of the labour market over which the immigration flows may or may not have an effect. Another problem is quite common in empirical analysis: The counterfactual case is not observed, that is, what labour market conditions would prevail in the absence of immigration. A related issue is that immigrants do not arrive randomly in a particular labour market. They are likely to be attracted to areas with good labour market conditions. This is an example of the econometric problem of simultaneity: Labour market conditions can affect immigration activity, but immigration activity can affect labour market conditions. The two effects are confounded, which makes estimation unreliable and will likely lead to an understatement of adverse labour market consequences, if they exist at all. The remedy is to include variables in the analysis that can predict immigration activity but are independent of the labour market conditions. The existing evidence suggests that the link between immigration and labour market outcomes is weak, but in the U.S., immigration patterns have had some negative impact on the employment and wages of low-skilled natives.

4. Economic Assimilation

Most of the economic research about immigration has dealt with this issue, in part because it is easier to analyse. The idea is to track the earnings and employment experiences of immigrants after their arrival in Canada. The entry effect is defined as the level of earnings relative to their native counterparts upon their arrival in Canada, and this is usually negative. It can be thought of as a starting point. The process by which the labour market performance of immigrants eventually matches or even exceeds those of their native-born counterparts — in essence, overcoming the negative entry effect — is called economic assimilation. It can be thought of as "catch-up." As the immigrant spends more time in Canada, his/her earnings should also rise. Assimilation refers to the difference in the returns to age/experience by the immigrant and the comparable native, which is usually measured as a function of years since migration. If immigrants do experience assimilation, it implies that their returns to age/experience in the Canadian labour market exceed those of the native-born Canadian workers. These variables are graphed in Figure 11.5, which contain the age-earnings profiles of the immigrant worker and the native-born worker. The entry effect is represented by the difference in the intercepts. The assimilation effects are depicted by the difference in the heights (the wage coordinate) of the two profiles. The cohort effect refers to an effect of the age-earnings profile that is associated with a group of immigrants that arrived at a particular point in time.

Empirical research indicates that more recent cohorts of immigrants are not assimilating as rapidly as earlier cohorts of immigrants, which is due to worsening entry effects for new immigrants, although there is not a consensus. The evidence on economic assimilation suggests that assimilation rates are low, unless the immigrants arrive when the economy is booming.

5. Immigrant Outcomes and Public Policy

This section deals with the point system. There is some debate as to whether this policy actually meets its objective of selecting more highly educated and skilled workers. An analyst named Georges Borjas believes that the primary effect of the point system is to tilt immigration to Canada away from source countries that provide, on average, low-skilled workers. A very key policy variable is the mix of the flow of new immigrants between the assessed and the non-assessed classes. The class of the immigrant is a fairly accurate predictor of the economic success of immigrants, as the assessed classes fare better.

6. The Impact of Immigration on Source Countries

Currently, Canada is influenced by out-migration and by in-migration. The emigration of highly skilled Canadians to the U.S. is a source of concern because they have high marginal products. It is the occupational composition of the emigrants rather than their number that is a source of concern, and some analysts have linked this exodus to Canada's tax rates.

Helpful Hints

- The primary analytical tool of this chapter is the age-earnings profile, which is applied to the topic of immigration. The core consists of three distinct influences on the age-earnings profile: cohort effects, entry effects, and assimilation effects.
- The hardest part of this chapter is probably the material illustrated in Figure 11.6. This diagram does not illustrate the assimilation effect per se. Instead, it shows how wage growth attributed to assimilation can or cannot be estimated by a cross-section of data. The basic point is that if the earlier and the later cohort of immigrants had the same entry effect, then wage growth of the earlier cohort is depicted accurately by the difference in the heights (the wage coordinate) of the two profiles. This is the situation depicted in Figure 11.6a, points B to D. On the other hand, if the entry effects of two cohorts are not the same (as in Figure 11.6b), then there is a cohort entry effect at work. Wage growth attributable to assimilation is not depicted by the difference in the heights of the two profiles, because in this case it confounds an assimilation effect (the catch-up) and the entry effect associated with a given cohort. To estimate the entire assimilation effect, we take the age-earnings profile of a cohort of immigrants and compare it to the age-earnings profile of their native counterparts.
- Do not confuse the two central questions that are addressed in this chapter. First, there is the economic performance of immigrants *compared* to native-born Canadians. All of the material involving the age-earnings profiles, with assimilation, cohort, and entry effects, falls under this category. Second, there is the *impact* of immigration activity on the labour market outcomes of the native-born population. All of the material involving the supply-and-demand models of the labour market for skilled or unskilled labour falls into this category. This is not an exercise in comparison. It is an exercise in comparative statics in which the effects of changes in one variable (immigration flow) on other economic variables (wages and employment outcomes for natives) are modelled.
- See Exhibit 11.2 for a good illustration of how labour economists treat empirical issues such as the effect of immigration on the labour market. The article mentioned in this exhibit employs the "differences-in-differences" approach, which may give you an idea of not only the empirical challenges that are frequently faced but also how they are dealt with.

Answers to Odd-Numbered End-of-Chapter Questions

1. Does not apply

3a. Carefully define economic assimilation in the context of a human capital earnings function. This is treated in Figure 11.5. Essentially, it means that after controlling for the standard, observable variables that tend to influence earnings, such as education and experience, the earnings levels of immigrants reach parity with those of native-born Canadians. In other words, it is wage gains to experience spent in the host country, above and beyond the gains to experience observed for natives. The interpretation of this economic phenomenon is that immigrants are expected to enter the Canadian labour market with some disadvantages compared to native-born Canadians, as reflected in the so-called entry effect. This may be thought of as the entry disadvantage or penalty. As time passes, however, they may experience greater returns to experience, permitting them to catch up in terms of earnings.

   b. Outline some of the empirical difficulties encountered in estimating earnings assimilation. This is illustrated on Figure 11.6. It is necessary to understand what is meant by the term cohort. A cohort is an unchanging group of workers (the same people) that is followed over time as they age. The baby boom group is an example. They were born between 1946 and 1964, which means that in 2001 this generation is between 55 and 37 years old. The labour market outcomes of this cohort can then be compared to another cohort, such as the so-called "generation X." The underlying problem is certain unobservable factors that determine earnings. It is possible that there is a deterioration or perhaps an improvement in the assimilation process over time. In order to accurately assess it, one needs to evaluate both the entry effect (how far behind immigrants are when they first arrive) and the assimilation effect (how much faster, if at all, immigrants' earnings grow over time). More specifically, there is evidence to believe that the "quality" of immigrant has deteriorated, on average, in both the United States and Canada. This refers to their ability to realize labour market outcomes on a par with native-born workers. As the average skill and education level of immigrants falls over time, relative to their native counterparts, the entry effect will increase. This implies that recent immigrants (for example, those who entered in 1995) will be starting their work careers at a lower level of earnings than immigrants in the past (for example, those who entered in 1990). If one compares the 1995 earnings of the first group to those of the second group (the first group has five more years in Canada), this figure will overestimate assimilation because there are two factors determining the difference in their earnings levels in 1995: assimilation (the growth in earnings) and the entry effect. Recall that the latest cohort of immigrants started at a lower level of earnings than did the preceding cohort. Think of a race in which one wants to measure the speed of two participants. At the finish line, one cannot conclude who ran faster unless the participants start at the same place. The first step to addressing this problem is to have data on the same group of cohorts at several points in time. The quasi-panel approach that is mentioned in the textbook is somewhat difficult to grasp.

c. How can evidence on assimilation patterns of immigrants in Canada and the U.S. be used to evaluate the impact of Canadian immigration policy? Many but not all economists believe that the immigrant selection process should be improved. The criteria could be weighted more heavily toward the immigrant's suitability for the Canadian labour market. An even more controversial recommendation advanced by some is that the level of immigration should be reduced, or at least weighted more heavily to the assessed classes.

5. One has to compare outcomes across cities in order to analyse the phenomenon, so these data do hold some promise. A totally fallacious analysis would proceed as follows. One would correlate the percentage of foreign-born workers as a share of the labour force in each area with the average wage level in each area. If the correlation is negative, one would conclude, erroneously, that the immigration has adverse effects on native-born workers. This faulty analysis ignores the *ceteris paribus* condition. One has to account for as many other factors that affect labour market outcomes in these cities as possible. More specifically, the nature of the problem is the simultaneity, or joint determination, of immigration flows and labour market conditions. Immigration flows and labour market conditions influence each other in a two-way causal fashion. We seek to evaluate the magnitude of a one-way effect: how immigration flows affect the equilibrium wage levels. The difference-in-differences approach explained in the textbook is more appropriate but still has its shortfalls. The best way to proceed is to attempt to analyse an instance in which a wave of immigration was determined by political forces rather than economic forces. If the immigration is driven by factors unrelated to the labour market conditions, then we know that it is the immigration activity that may affect the labour market conditions rather than the other way around.

There is another approach favoured by Borjas, Freeman, and Katz that is discussed in the textbook, in which the unit of analysis is not the geographical unit (CMA) but rather a particular grade of labour. This approach would not use data like that presented in Figure 11.2.

7. This is discussed at the end of the chapter. Although the textbook makes the point that this phenomenon affects developing countries the most, it also affects Canada to some degree. This is most visible in the health care and software industries. Generally, the education of doctors and software engineers at Canadian universities is very highly subsidized and significantly less costly to the student than is the case in the United States. For a variety of reasons, doctors, nurses, engineers, finance specialists, software professionals, and university professors are much more highly paid in the United States, and they are tempted to emigrate from Canada. Reinforcing this trend is the higher level of taxation in Canada. It is extremely difficult to combat this trend, which harms the Canadian health care system, the software industry, and ultimately the economy. Some analysts suggest that this is an argument for lower taxes in Canada. Ironically, a number of decades ago, Canada benefited enormously from a brain drain from the United Kingdom. A similar counterpart is also observed in the realm of professional sports, which one may call the "brawn drain." It is driven by the same economic forces.

Answers to Odd-Numbered End-of-Chapter Problems

1. There are two cohorts: immigrants who arrived during the period 1981–1985 and immigrants who arrived during the period 1986–1990. They reflect two different groups of people. The entry effect for the first cohort cannot be evaluated from the table, as we do not know how much the native-born workers were earning at any time during the period 1981–1985. The latest cohort of immigrants enters with a disadvantage (an entry effect is thought to be negative) of $8,000 ($40,000 - $32,000). Note that between 1990 and 1995, the earnings of native-born Canadians grows slowly. This may be interpreted as the general growth of earnings in the economy, which should affect all groups (natives and immigrants alike) in the same fashion. The 1986–1990 group of immigrants had a negative entry effect of $8,000 in 1990 and reduced the gap, relative to native-born Canadians, to $5,000 in 1995 ($41,000 - $36,000), so they did assimilate somewhat because their earnings grew more quickly than those of native-born Canadians.

We cannot analyse the assimilation rates for the earlier cohort without making an assumption regarding their entry effect. If we were to try, compare the earnings of the 1981–1985 cohort in 1990, after they have been in the country for five years (point B in Figure 11.6) to the earnings of later immigrants in 1990 (point D). If the initial earnings of the earlier cohort are the same (an entry effect of $8,000 below the native born), we can conclude that the earlier cohort assimilated to the tune of $6,000 ($38,000 - 32,000). We know for certain that the earlier cohort did not assimilate at all between 1990 and 1995, as they gained no ground on the native-born Canadians.

The main point is that assimilation rates will typically vary across cohorts (here we have two cohorts, or waves, of immigrants) and/or across periods of time for the same cohort (for example, the 1981–1985 group between 1985 and 1990 and the same group between 1991 and 1995).

3. Note that there was a global effect of earnings losses between 1990 and 1995 that affected all cohorts of immigrants as well as native born.

a. Entry effects are easy to calculate. Working from one cross-section of data (corresponding to the year of entry), simply subtract the earnings of native Canadians to the earnings of the newly arrived immigrant cohort. This gives $25,653 - $38,002 = $-12,349.

b. Working from one cross-section of data and comparing the earnings of the two cohorts, we have $37,593 - $32,233 = $5,360. One may erroneously attribute this discrepancy to wage growth associated with assimilation of the 1981–1985 cohort. Projecting this growth to the earnings of the 1986–1990 cohort in 1995, we would add $5,360 to $32,233 in order to obtain $37,593. This is equivalent to projecting the distance from point B to point D in Figure 11.6a to point E.

c. What is confusing about these figures is that the labour market deteriorated greatly for everyone between 1990 and 1995, and the earnings of all cohorts were on a downward trajectory (or fell greatly and then started rising). We are told that the true earnings in 1995 were $29,960, so our estimate is way off. In order to measure the wage growth that is attributable to assimilation, follow the path of the 1986–1990 cohort from 1990 to 1995, and one obtains $29,960 - $32,233 = $-2,273. This corresponds to the movement from point D to point E in Figure 11.6. Due to the global trends, this cohort did not lose ground, relative to native workers, as their earnings fell by $4,836 over the same period. The latest cohort of immigrants actually gained ground, relative to the native-born workers, so they did assimilate to the tune of about $2,500. The lesson learned is that you have to consider a) the entry effect, b) the rate of growth of earnings of the immigrant cohort, and c) the rate of growth of earnings of the native-born workers in order to fully assess assimilation.

5. The easiest way to address this problem is to calculate the discounted present value of the discrepancy in the values of the two jobs. The job in the U.S. pays $25,000 more, and this stream of payments is augmented by 6% each year for a period extending 40 years into the future. In the following year, for example, the discrepancy is $26,500, while in the year following that, it is $28,090. Applying the formula for calculating DPV, the first three terms are $25,000 + 26,500 / 1.05 + 28,090 / (1.05)^2$. If we add up all 40 terms, we would have the amount by which the lifetime earnings in the U.S. exceed the lifetime earnings in Canada. Taking only pecuniary factors into consideration, the value of the Canadian job is the negative of that figure. Non-pecuniary factors, such as family ties, working conditions, or geographical preference, may weigh in the other direction, however, encouraging this person to remain in Canada. He/she may have a partner with a good career in Canada, which would constitute a pecuniary factor weighing against migration. There may also be very high mobility costs. If so, we would expect this person to move sooner rather than later in his/her career.

Multiple Choice Questions

1. Which of the following classes of immigrants is subject to assessment of their applications?
   a) The family class.
   b) The refugee class.
   c) The independent class.
   d) The Canadian–born class.
   e) All classes of refugees are assessed prior to obtaining permanent resident status.

Labour Market Economics, Fifth Edition

2. Which of the following classes of immigrants comprises the largest single group of immigrants during the 1990s?
   a) The family class.
   b) The refugee class.
   c) The independent class.
   d) The Canadian–born class.
   e) The groups vary in size from year to year.

3. Consider the simple supply-and-demand framework for the labour market. What is the most likely impact of a wave of immigration into this market?
   a) An increase in the supply of labour
   b) An increase in the demand for labour
   c) An decrease in the supply of labour
   d) An decrease in the demand for labour
   e) An increase in the supply of labour and an increase in the demand for labour

4. What have the empirical studies concerning the impact of immigration on the labour market tended to show?
   a) Immigrants tend to displace native-born Canadians in the job market.
   b) Immigrants have little adverse impact on the labour market outcomes of native-born workers, except perhaps the case of the lowest-skilled workers.
   c) To a significant extent, immigrants accept the positions that native-born Canadians refuse to perform.
   d) Immigrants tend to depress the wage levels of native workers, but they do not tend to displace them.
   e) Immigrants only fill voids in labour markets where jobs are going begging.

5. In the context of immigration, what is meant by the term assimilation?
   a) Wage gains by immigrants that are above and beyond those normally attributed to experience
   b) The positive selection of immigrants, whereby only those most likely to succeed in the host country immigrate there
   c) Wage gains by immigrants at the same rate as native workers, which is attributable to economic growth
   d) Wage gains by immigrants at a slower rate than native workers, which is attributable to the entry effect
   e) Immigrants displacing natives in the labour market

6. In the context of immigration, what is meant by the term cohort effect?
   a) It is similar to the entry effect, whereby immigrants earn less than similarly qualified natives upon arrival to the host country
   b) An effect on earnings that is particular to a certain group of immigrants who arrived in the host country over the same period
   c) An effect on earnings that affects all workers over a certain time period
   d) Wage gains by immigrants that are above and beyond those normally attributed to experience
   e) None of the above

7. What has the recent research on the wage growth patterns of immigrants tended to show?
   a) The rates of assimilation are increasing over time.
   b) The entry position of immigrants relative to native workers has been declining over time.
   c) The point system has no impact on the source countries.
   d) The class composition of the immigrants has no impact on their wage outcomes.
   e) Immigration to Canada offsets the negative impact of the brain drain to the United States.

8. In the Canadian context, the term "brain drain" typically refers to:
   a) Immigration of highly skilled workers to Canada.
   b) The composition of the inflow of immigrants among the various classes.
   c) Emigration of highly skilled workers from Canada.
   d) The assimilation of newer cohorts of immigrants into the Canadian labour force.
   e) Workers who have obviously lost their minds.

9. Which of the following statements regarding the emigration of workers from Canada is *false*?
   a) The phenomenon is a new development of the late-1990s.
   b) It often involves workers from the health care and engineering professions.
   c) Some analysts recommend that tax rates should be reduced in light of this problem.
   d) The number of permanent emigrants is somewhere between 20,000 and 40,000 per year.
   e) It represents a loss of income and production for the Canadian economy.

10. Approximately how many immigrants are legally received by Canada in a typical year during the late-1990s or the early-2000 years?
   a) 100,000
   b) 1,000,000
   c) 200,000
   d) 500,000
   e) The intake varies greatly from year to year.

Answers to Multiple Choice Problems

1. C   This is stated explicitly in the textbook in the section entitled "The Policy Environment."
2. D   This is stated explicitly in the textbook in the section entitled "The Policy Environment."
3. A   See the discussion regarding Figure 11.4. A rightward shift in the supply curve is likely in the long run.
4. B   See the discussion concerning the empirical analysis in the section entitled "The Impact on Immigrants on the Labour Market."
5. A   This definition is stated explicitly on pages 328–329 in the textbook.
6. B   This definition is stated explicitly on pages 328–331 in the textbook.
7. E   See the discussion concerning the empirical analysis in the section entitled "Economic Assimilation," pages 332–335.
8. C   See the section in the textbook entitled "The Impact of Immigration on Source Countries."
9. A   It is stated on pages 338–340 in the textbook that this rate has been higher in the past. Response E is totally wrong.
10. C   This is stated explicitly in the textbook in the section entitled "A Profile of Immigration to Canada."

CHAPTER 12

This chapter shares a common theme with the three preceding ones, namely the structure of wages. Not everyone earns the same wage, and so the underlying objective is to explain the nature of wage differentials. In this chapter, the relevant factors are the observable traits of gender and race. Wage levels do differ systematically between men and women, and this may well be due in part to discrimination in the labour market. The existence of a wage differential between the two groups, however, is not necessarily prima facie evidence of discrimination.

1.   Discrimination: Reasons and Sources

According to pure neo-classical labour market theory, discrimination (either through hiring, promotion, or compensation policies) against any group is not rational because it is inconsistent with profit-maximizing behaviour on the part of firms. Any firm that deviates from strictly profit-maximizing behaviour is doing its stockholders a disservice. We expect that workers are paid according to their marginal revenue products. Nevertheless, it can and does occur in labour markets, and an analysis is based on the source. There are generally three types: employer preferences, co-worker preferences, and customer preferences for the favoured group and against the unfavoured group.

2.   Theories of Labour Market Discrimination

There are several alternative theories. Demand theories of discrimination are centred around an equilibrium in which the demand for female labour is lower than the demand for male labour, given that their marginal productivity is equal. The demand curve for male workers would be higher. The wages will deviate from the marginal revenue product by a wedge that can be represented mathematically as a multiplicative coefficient. A supply-side theory called the crowding hypothesis is widely applied. Females tend to be segregated into female-type occupations, which causes the supply of labour in these occupations to expand, depressing the equilibrium wage. According to this approach, workers are paid their marginal products. The dual labour market theory is fairly similar to the crowding hypothesis. There are two separate and distinct labour markets: the primary sector with attractive jobs and the secondary sector with less attractive jobs. Men tend to be employed in the primary sector, but women may not have easy access to employment there and may be directed to the secondary labour market.

In non-competitive labour markets, labour market discrimination is more likely to occur. Consider a firm that pays a wage higher than the going equilibrium wage, such as an efficiency wage. In this instance, there is a queue of workers that desire the jobs, so rationing occurs. There is a greater latitude for the hiring decision to be affected by nepotism or discrimination. This rationing process may favour males, and if so, the end result is a wage gap attributable to discrimination. Recall that in the efficiency wage model, firms do maximize profits, so in this case, labour market discrimination is consistent with profit maximization. Recall that in the efficiency wage model, however, workers are not paid according to their marginal products.

A crucial point is raised in the subsection entitled "Productivity Differences: Choice or Discrimination." Because of their dual role in the household and in the labour market, women traditionally have a shorter expected length of participation in the labour market. This implies that many women have a reduced benefit period from which to recoup the costs of human capital formation. Women make various decisions with respect to education, training, hours of work, working conditions, and occupational choice that incorporate factors such as child-bearing and raising and household production. Many of them are less likely to acquire continuous labour market experience, which usually leads to lower wages, *ceteris paribus*. Women with young children have a much higher absenteeism rate than men. The key question is the following: Do these choices, which have negative repercussions for the age-earnings profile, reflect voluntary preferences or discriminatory constraints? If the former applies, the case for the existence of discrimination is weakened.

3. Evidence on Male-Female Earnings Differentials

This section deals with the empirical evidence and measuring discrimination. The raw wage differential, which does not adjust for any explanatory factor except for whether the worker is full-time or part-time, is about 0.3, or a ratio of 70%. The gap of 0.3 refers to the difference between the male wage and the female wage divided by the male wage. The ratio figure is the female wage divided by the male wage. Wage differentials can also be adjusted for factors such as age, education, race, labour market experience, marital status, city size, region, absenteeism, and number of children.

A key analytical tool is the Oaxaca decomposition. The basic objective is to estimate the following counter-factual: What would women earn if they had the same set of productive characteristics as men? It is based on a human capital earnings function. The total raw wage differential between men and women is decomposed into an element due to productivity characteristics and discrimination. In the absence of discrimination, pay differences should arise from differences in the *productive characteristics*, and not from differences in the *returns* to these characteristics. The former is called the explained portion (associated with the observable traits), while the latter is called the unexplained portion (associated with the coefficients of the observable traits in the earnings function). It is illustrated graphically in Figure 12.2.

Using industries and sectors as explanatory variables in the Oaxaca decomposition is problematic because they may be outcome variables rather than wage-determining variables. In other words, these are not necessarily pre-market characteristics and may therefore be the result of discrimination rather than a factor influencing a productive characteristic that in turn generates wages. Wage differences arising from differences in the occupational distributions of men and women are thought to contribute to the overall wage gap, but a number of recent Canadian studies find that the occupational segregation of women into lower-paying jobs does not explain a large portion of the gap.

Even after controlling for a wide range of wage-determining variables using the Oaxaca procedure, a pure wage gap appears to remain that is attributable to discrimination. The gap is narrowed considerably after controlling for the effect of these other determinants of wages, but a residual gap appears to remain.

4. Policies to Combat Sex Discrimination

There are essentially three approaches: conventional equal pay legislation, pay equity (comparable worth), and equal employment opportunity legislation.

The idea behind pay equity policies is to go beyond the conventional approach of awarding equal pay for equal work, awarding equal pay for different work that is assessed to be of equal value. A female-dominated occupation that is relatively low paid may be assessed to be of equal value to a male-dominated occupation that is relatively well paid. A classic example is the male truck driver compared to the female secretary. It can be problematic to evaluate the value of the work performed by one group of workers (that is, male dominated) to the value of the work performed by another (that is, female dominated). The jobs are first separated into the male-dominated and the female-dominated ones, and then the wage determining factors are considered. The job types are evaluated on a scale according to human capital factors, working conditions, and other pecuniary and non-pecuniary features. Female occupations are compared to male occupations that are judged to have the same number of points. The key point is the distinction between economic and administrative concepts of value. According to the former, wages are determined by the marginal revenue product of labour at the point of intersection of the labour supply and labour demand curves. Wages should be determined by the forces of supply and demand without intervention. According to the latter, the variables that the free market uses to determine wages (such as human capital and working conditions) do matter, but the market should not be allowed to determine the rate at which these wage-determining characteristics are remunerated. The comparable-value framework is complicated to implement, and many of the detailed technical and administrative issues are treated in the textbook.

Affirmative action or employment equity legislation is designed to prevent discrimination in recruiting, hiring, promotion, and firing. It is concerned with the allocation of jobs and has nothing to do with pay levels. These policies do not affect wages directly.

5.   Impact of Policy Initiatives

The existing empirical evidence on the impact of conventional equal pay policies indicates that they have not had any impact on closing the male-female earnings gap. Comparable-worth policies have been applied in only a few cases, mostly in the public sector. They seem to have some impact on closing the gap, but simulations of the potential economy-wide impact of comparable worth in the U.S. have estimated that it would close only a small portion of the gap. If pay equity or comparable-worth policies were to be implemented on fairly large scale, there is the possibility that employment growth would be weaker. This is true to the extent that the demand for labour in female-dominated occupations is elastic. An evaluative analysis of this topic based on the case of Ontario is described in Exhibit 12.15.

Helpful Hints

- A major concept that underlies the analysis in this chapter is the critical distinction between wage-determining attributes, such as the length of job market experience or the level of education, and the rate at which these attributes are remunerated. When the returns (in the form of wage increases) to human capital are lower for women than for men, there may be a case for discrimination. You can think of the first element as the qualifications that a worker has and the job description, and the second element as the pay scale.
- It is helpful to go over the pay equity example in Figure 12.3.
- The Oaxaca equation is a useful tool that can be applied to analyse just about any situation in which the remuneration system of one group of workers is thought to be different than that for another group of workers. These equations are not as intimidating as they first appear. You should try working through them.

- The textbook contains a lot of institutional detail about the various types of anti-discrimination policies. In order to avoid confusion, pay attention to the outline in the textbook and the "Chapter Highlights" section above.

Answers to Odd-Numbered End-of-Chapter Questions

1.   This statement is false. There is at least one model of labour market discrimination that is totally neo-classical and includes a discriminatory wage equilibrium. The crowding hypothesis works by shifting the supply of female labour down and to the right for many industries and/or occupations that are female dominated. One moves down and along the demand curve as this expansion in supply occurs, which means that the women workers are paid the marginal revenue product of their labour. Their wage is less than the wages of equally qualified males, because the male-dominated occupations and industries are not subject to this supply push.

3.   The answer is no. Some observers claim that most of the wage differential between men and women can be attributed to productivity differences. According to this perspective, women tend to have lower marginal productivity levels because men tend to have higher rates of labour force attachment and somewhat higher levels of training and education. Higher wages for men are justifiable on this basis. The central thrust of the counter-argument is that a worker's marginal productivity level is not always determined by the choices of the worker (such as how much human capital to obtain) and his/her natural endowment (such as innate characteristics or talent). The human capital decision (which in women's cases is sometimes affected by child-bearing activities) may be a matter of rational, individual choice, or it may also be a result of discriminatory social practices. It is true that, on average, women have higher turnover and absenteeism rates than men do, and this is often tied to household responsibilities. The next question is why does this practice emerge? Do women have equal opportunities to acquire human capital, the degree of labour force attachment, or the level of experience that many employers require in order to pay high wages? Some observers would say no. This point is analogous to the "Which came first? The chicken or the egg?" phenomenon.

5.   For policy purposes, does it matter if the reason for discrimination is prejudice, erroneous information (systemic discrimination), or job security? Yes, it matters. For the case of prejudice, one possible policy response is to alter preferences and attitudes. For the job security factor, equal opportunity of employment policies designed to increase the number of openings for women may be warranted in some cases, as the discrimination is tied to occupational segregation. The proponents of employment equity and comparable worth/pay equity claim that it is an effective instrument to combat erroneous information that gives rise to discrimination. Direct control and regulation are viewed by some as the most effective way to compel employers to hire targeted groups, whether employers intentionally discriminate or not. For the erroneous information type of discrimination, sometimes employers engage in systemic discrimination because they believe that female workers will be absent frequently. Policies to facilitate female employment may be the most productive. An illustration would be improving day-care services and the flexibility of hours, which would help meet the needs of female employees and the needs of their employers (less absenteeism). This is the type of policy measure that gains the most favour among economists.

     Does it matter if the main source of discrimination is employers, co-workers, or customers? Yes, it does, and the latter is the most difficult to combat. One can initiate employment equity proceedings against a firm whose owners or workers are alleged to engage in discriminatory employment practices, but one cannot take any kind of action against customers who discriminate. Facilitating policies are probably the least controversial method of combating discrimination, but they are ineffective against the source of customer prejudice.

7. See the subsections entitled "Scope of Equal Value Initiatives," "Design Features of Comparable Worth," "Pay Equity Example," and "Comparable Worth and Pay Equity." One important factor is that comparisons can be made only within the same employer. It is for this reason that, in practice, pay equity initiatives have been carried out only for very large employers such as the federal government and Bell Canada. It is also a complex and costly system to administer. One has to define what constitutes a male-dominated occupation and a female-dominated one, the job evaluation procedure for calculating the values of jobs, the procedure for linking the job evaluation point scores to the rates of pay of jobs, and the procedure for adjusting the pay in undervalued jobs. This procedure can be very contentious when applied. When the pay equity award is made, it must be financed by the employer, who (depending on the wage elasticity of labour demand) is likely to reduce his/her quantity demanded of labour for the lower-valued occupation.

9. This statement is true. The whole concept of comparable worth is antithetical to a market (supply-and-demand) framework. The contrast between these two underlying paradigms and philosophies is nicely explained in the textbook. Within the comparable-worth framework, there is a role for market forces, to the extent that compensating differentials are allowed for adverse working conditions, and differentials are allowed for educational attainment and skill acquisition. Overall, however, the equal value concept rejects the notion that market forces should be the prime determinant of the value and hence the pay levels of jobs. According to this perspective, market forces are the cause of occupational segregation, labour market crowding, and the systematic undervaluation of female-dominated jobs. The primacy of market forces is rejected in that the value and, hence, the remuneration of a job are not deemed to be low simply because there is an abundance of labour willing to do the work, or because there is little demand for that type of labour. Those market forces are not judged to produce acceptable outcomes. This is in contrast to the economic emphasis on the forces of supply and demand to determine the value and remuneration of a job. Note also the distinction between the administrative concept of value (used in comparable worth) and the economic concept of value (used in the free market).

11. One may expect discrimination (in one form or another) to be more prevalent in the private sector and the non-union sector than in the public or in the union sector. The textbook does not give reasons, but *within* the union sector, there is a much wider scope for administered wage-setting mechanisms as opposed to purely market-determined wage outcomes. (This does not exclude the possibility that unions can contribute to discrimination *between* union and non-union workers by excluding the latter from choice jobs.) This contrast between administered wages and market-based wages is important. In two places, the textbook mentions that in Australia, where the wages for a majority of the labour force are determined by wage tribunals, gender differentials are much narrower than in Canada, where the wages of most of the labour force are determined by market forces.

All of the various remedies, listed in the next question, are probably easier to implement in the public sector for several reasons. First of all, public-sector employers tend to be larger in size, which facilitates the implementation of most of the possible remedies. Second, it is the government that drafts the anti-discriminatory measures, and it has the authority to enforce them and sanction unlawful behaviour. It should thus set an example for private-sector employers to follow, and indeed this has occurred. The summary of the history of these various measures indicates that they typically applied only to the public sector during earlier phases.

13. This point is explained explicitly in the corresponding subsection of the textbook. According to the policy-capturing approach, the pricing mechanism for male-dominated occupations is applied to the female-dominated occupations. This procedure is seen to respect, for the most part, the market forces that operate in male-dominated occupations. The pricing mechanism for the job evaluation points — educational requirements, working conditions, and other non-pecuniary factors — is respected and extended to female-dominated jobs. This is viewed as a rational outcome, because the market forces are respected and perhaps even strengthened if the female-dominated occupations are subject to non-competitive forces. It is also viewed as an equitable outcome, as the same rules apply to both sets of occupations. This analysis, however, is based on a premise that the job evaluation procedure is very sound and thorough. It is reasonable to expect employers to always resist pay equity programs, as they will always raise labour costs considerably. This is because they require that parity be achieved by raising the wages of females rather than lowering the wages of males. See the response to Question 9 for a similar discussion.

Answers to Odd-Numbered End-of-Chapter Problems

1a. The job evaluation score is supposed to capture many of the job attributes, including the level of human capital required and the various amenities and disamenities, such as working conditions, the level of experience, and so on. Whether you are a man or a woman in a female-dominated occupation, your pay is estimated by the equation for Y_f. This equation generates estimates of actual pay based on averages. It does not predict the exact level of pay for everyone who works in that occupation. Simply insert the value of 200 into that equation to yield $4,000 + 80 (200) = $20,000$.

b. The idea behind pay equity is that anyone, man or woman, who works in a female-dominated occupation should earn a wage based on the pay scale (with its rates per year of experience, per educational degree, and so on) of the male-dominated occupation. The pay scale is described by the equation for Y_m. Each point awarded by the job evaluator is worth $100 in pay rather than $80 in pay, and the amount of pay associated with zero points (sometimes called the baseline case) has been raised from $4,000 to $5,000. The calculation is $5,000 + 100 (200) = $25,000$. The magnitude of the pay equity award is $5,000. Geometrically, this is represented by a vertical movement up to the higher pay line.

3a. The profit function is expressed as total revenue minus total cost. For simplicity, in this case we assume that labour is the only factor of production and that it is totally variable. This function is maximized with respect to L_F, the amount of female labour hired, and L_M, the amount of male labour hired. The labour demand function for men is $MRP_M = W_M (1 - d_M)$ and for women is $MRP_F = W_F (1 + d_F)$. Compare these equations to the normal equilibrium condition in which the marginal revenue product is equal to the wage. The impact of the discrimination parameter d_F is to drive a wedge between the MRP of women and the wage rate in equilibrium, which will lower the demand curve for women. The impact of the nepotism parameter d_M is to narrow the distance between the MRP of women and the wage rate in equilibrium, which will raise the demand curve for men.

b. By equating MRP_M and MRP_F, we can replace them by MRP. Using the equation above and applying transitivity, $MRP = W_M(1 - d_M) = W_F(1 + d_F)$, or $W_M(1 - 0.1) = W_F(1 + 0.1)$, or $W_F / W_M = 0.9 / 1.1$.

c. Employers are willing to hire females, provided that their MRP exceeds their wage by 10% or more. Women have to more than pay their way by a factor of 1.1 (instead of 1.0). Employers are willing to hire males, provided that their MRP is at least 90% of their wage. Male workers do not have to pay all of their way — only by a factor of 0.9 (instead of 1.0). Discrimination has its limits; this is not a case of discrimination at all costs. Even though the employer prefers male workers, if their productivity falls below that 0.9 threshold, they will not be hired. Even though the employer has a grudge against female workers, if their productivity rises above that 1.1 threshold, they will be hired.

Multiple Choice Questions

Questions 1 and 2 refer to the following earnings function for male workers. On average, males earn $54,000 while females earn $32,000. Although this discrepancy smacks of discrimination, we are going to perform a wage decomposition analysis in order to verify that women are suffering from discrimination in the labour market.

$$WAGE_{male} = 10000 + 3000 * EXPERIENCE_{male} + 2000 * EDUCATION_{male}$$

1. If the average male worker has eight years of experience and ten years of education, then the average male earnings are predicted to be which of the following?
   a) $37,000
   b) $54,000
   c) $43,000
   d) $46,000
   e) None of the above

2. If the average female worker has six years of experience and eight years of education, then we can conclude that:
   a) Women earn $22,000 less than men do, *ceteris paribus,* and women suffer from discrimination.
   b) Women actually earn more than men do, *ceteris paribus,* and women do not suffer from discrimination.
   c) Women have reached earnings parity with men, *ceteris paribus,* and women suffer from discrimination.
   d) Women earn $5,000 less than men do, *ceteris paribus,* and women suffer from discrimination.
   e) Women earn $13,000 less than men do, *ceteris paribus,* and women suffer from discrimination.

3. All of the following are different theories of discrimination *except* which?
   a) Demand theories of discrimination, whereby employers prefer to hire males, *ceteris paribus*
   b) Supply theories of discrimination, such as the crowding hypothesis
   c) Non-competitive theories of discrimination, stemming from unionization and other barriers to entry
   d) Non-competitive theories of discrimination, such as monopsonistic labour markets
   e) Human capital theories of discrimination, whereby some women are paid less because they have less education than their male co-workers

4. Without adjusting for any factor that is thought to affect earnings, full-time, full-year female workers earn what percentage of male earnings?
   a) About 70%, which is higher than the ratio 20 years ago
   b) About 70%, which is similar to the ratio 20 years ago
   c) About 70%, which is lower than the ratio 20 years ago
   d) About 60%, which is higher than the ratio 20 years ago
   e) About 80%, which is lower than the ratio 20 years ago

5. Which of the following components of the Oaxaca decomposition is indicative of labour market discrimination?
   a) The raw wage gap
   b) The component attributable to differences in the endowments of wage-determining characteristics
   c) The component attributable to differences in the economic returns to wage-determining characteristics
   d) Both components mentioned in responses b and c
   e) The component attributable to the elasticity in labour supply

6. Consider the graph of earnings functions in Figure 12.2. The top graph reflects the earnings function for males, while the bottom one reflects the earnings function for females. Which of the following segments reflects differences in the wage-determining characteristics between men and women?
   a) AB
   b) $X_F X_M$
   c) BC
   d) DC
   e) $Ln\ Y^M Ln\ Y^F$

7. Consider the graph of earnings functions in Figure 12.2. The top graph reflects the earnings function for males, while the bottom one reflects the earnings function for females. Which of the following segments the component of the wage differential that is unexplained, and thus indicative of discrimination?
   a) AB
   b) $X_F X_M$
   c) BC
   d) DC
   e) $Ln\ Y^M Ln\ Y^F$

8. Consider the graph of earnings functions in Figure 12.2. The top graph reflects the earnings function for males, while the bottom one reflects the earnings function for females. Which of the following segments reflects the component in the wage gap that is attributable to differences in the pre-market wage-determining characteristics between men and women?
   a) AB
   b) $X_F X_M$
   c) BC
   d) DC
   e) $Ln\ Y^M Ln\ Y^F$

9. Consider the graph of earnings functions in Figure 12.2. The top graph reflects the earnings function for males, while the bottom one reflects the earnings function for females. What is the significance of a steeper slope for the male earnings function?
   a) Men earn higher wages than women.
   b) Discrimination exists in the labour market.
   c) Men receive a higher rate of return to their productive characteristics than women.
   d) If both men and women had very low levels of productive characteristics, men would still earn more than women.
   e) Men have higher levels of productive characteristics than women.

10. The empirical research on male-female differentials has tended to show that:
   a) Even after controlling for a wide range of wage-determining variables using the Oaxaca procedure, a pure wage gap appears to remain, which is attributable to discrimination.
   b) After controlling for a wide range of wage-determining variables using the Oaxaca procedure, no pure wage gap appears to remain, which suggests that there is not much discrimination.
   c) Wage differences arising from differences in the occupational distribution between males and females are not an important contributor to the overall wage gap.
   d) The wage gap adjusted for differences in the wage-determining characteristics is larger than the raw, overall wage gap between men and women.
   e) None of the above.

Answers to Multiple Choice Questions

1. B   Insert the given numbers into the equation.
2. E   Insert the given numbers into the equation and obtain predicted earnings of $44,000 for men. Compare that figure to the actual earnings for women.
3. E   This is made explicit in the subsection of the textbook dealing with theories of discrimination. If statement E were to apply, the wage differential would not be attributed to discrimination.
4. A   See the section in the textbook that presents the data on the male-female wage gap.
5. C   This point is made explicitly in the textbook. See the discussion that accompanies the equations in the subsection entitled "Measuring Discrimination."
6. C   The horizontal distance indicates the differences between men and women for attributes such as education or experience.
7. A   This is made explicit in the discussion surrounding this graph in the textbook. Discrimination has to be measured holding the productive attributes fixed.

8. E   This is made explicit in the discussion surrounding this graph in the textbook. These figures are indicated on the vertical axis.

9. C   The slope of any earnings function indicates the rate at which wages change in response to changes in productive attributes such as education.

10. A   This is made explicit in the textbook in the subsection entitled "Empirical Results on Male-Female Differentials." Response D makes no sense. Response C is not a bad response, as some recent Canadian research has suggested that it may be true.

CHAPTER 13

The basic theme of this chapter is that there are many different mechanisms for compensating workers that deviate from the spot-market mechanism, whereby the worker is paid a wage equal to his/her instantaneous marginal revenue product. That is the purely neo-classical, supply-and-demand model of wage determination. Whereas we were examining different models of wage determination (that is, what is the wage *level*?), in this chapter we examine *how* the compensation is paid (that is, what is the pay practice?) Generally, the forces of labour market supply and demand still play an important role, but there are constraints imposed such that at most points in time, the marginal revenue product is not equal to the wage.

1. Agency Theory and Efficiency Wage Theory

The major underlying concept for the design of efficient compensation mechanisms is that the employment relationship is a principal-agent one. Principals are the employers who hire employees (the agents) to work assiduously for the firm and in the firm's best interests.

Due to the existence of asymmetric information, sometimes workers have incentives to cheat and shirk. Asymmetric information refers to the fact that the agents have better information than the principals do regarding how hard and efficiently they are working. If workers can be monitored easily, then there is not much of a principal-agent issue. It is in instances in which monitoring is costly that alternative compensation schemes are most likely to emerge. For all of these alternative compensation schemes, over the long run, the expected value of the total marginal revenue product, summed up over the length of the employment relationship, equals the expected value of the wage, summed up over the length of the employment relationship. The optimal compensation system is one that elicits the maximum effort from workers over the course of the employment relationship and prevents either party from severing the employment relationship before the contract is supposed to expire. It thus shares a theme with the efficiency wage approach; namely that the wage can affect the marginal revenue product in addition to the normal relationship of the marginal revenue product determining the wage.

2. Economics of Superstars

The main point of this section is that rather small differences in skill and talent level (that is, human capital) can generate very large and magnified differences in the marginal revenue product and compensation. This is particularly true when the product of the workers can be reproduced and very widely diffused to customers.

3. Salaries as Tournament Prizes

This theme is related to the economics of superstars. Rather small differences in skill level (that is, human capital) can generate very large and magnified differences in compensation, resulting in a tremendous degree of inequality in the distribution of the payroll. In this case, however, the pay does not appear to be tied directly to marginal revenue product of the executive. The basic idea beyond rank-order tournament compensation is that the winner takes almost all of the prize money (that is, the compensation), and all of the other workers receive only their marginal revenue product. This type of compensation mechanism can incite fierce competition among managers and does not necessarily foster cooperation in the workplace.

4. Efficient Pay Equality, Teams, and Employee Cooperation

While it is widely accepted that there is a trade-off between the equality of pay and efficiency, there is also a trade-off with the degree of inequality of pay if the degree of inequality is high. In other words, there is an optimal degree of pay inequality. Some dispersion in pay is required in order to provide an incentive to perform well and advance the hierarchy, but too much inequality may be inefficient if it fosters resentment and discourages cooperative behaviour and teamwork. If workers can affect each other's output (that is, there are cross-marginal product effects), the optimal degree of inequality is lower than what would otherwise be the case. The "1/N" problem is related to the free rider problem in the economics of public goods. It refers to the case of a workplace team, in which the workers are paid equal shares of the marginal revenue product of the entire team. In this completely egalitarian compensation scheme, workers may have incentive to free ride and not work as diligently as they would if they were paid their own individual marginal revenue product.

A number of promotion and personnel practices are analysed from an economics point of view. Under the "up-or-out" institutional rule, for example, if an employee fails to be promoted within a specified period of time, he or she is fired. This seemingly harsh and abrupt practice can be explained as a truth elicitation device. In a climate of asymmetric information, employers may have a better idea than employees regarding his/her marginal revenue product and the firm's ability to pay. This rule can have the effect of encouraging the employer to truthfully reveal private information on these points and, hence, to build trust. They can also compel managers to make hard and unpleasant (but sometimes appropriate) decisions to dismiss mediocre employees.

Many workers are compensated according to piece rates rather than by the hour. This mechanism gives the worker a strong incentive to produce, but it is necessary that the output be readily monitored so that payment can be based on output. Once again, the element of asymmetric information between the employer and the employee plays a role. Sometimes the quality of the product is difficult to monitor, which reduces the efficiency of a piece-rate system. Furthermore, if the amount of input cannot be ascertained easily, it can be difficult to set an appropriate rate. In that case, per-hour compensation may be more appropriate. Piece-rate systems vary considerably according to the characteristics of the product or service, as well as by the nature of the workplace and the technology of production.

5. Executive Compensation

This is an application of the rank-order tournament approach. The executive is often paid far more than his/her marginal revenue product, and part of the compensation package is a prize — not necessarily to recruit the best executive that money can buy, but rather to recruit the top-flight executive that is a suitable match for the corporation.

6. Deferred Wages

This refers to a long-term employment contract in which much of the worker's compensation is received toward the end of his/her career. It is in sharp contrast to the piece-rate system. Typically, workers are paid a wage that is below their marginal revenue product during the early stages of the career and then are paid a wage that is above their marginal revenue product during the later stages of the career. Firms have an incentive to fire workers towards the end of their career, so these contracts have to be designed to discourage such opportunistic behaviour. The basic idea is that these pay practices amount to the worker posting a bond, which discourages quitting and gives strong incentives not to shirk (and risk being fired). The earnings profile is shown in Figure 13.1. Workers may find this arrangement attractive as it constitutes a form of forced saving in the earlier part of their careers.

7. Rationale for Mandatory Retirement

The rationale for this practice is that the deferred compensation contract has reached its break-even point. The worker has been fully compensated for the wage losses that he/she experienced during the earlier period of the career. If the employment relationship were to continue, the employee would receive a wage greatly in excess of his/her marginal revenue product, which would render the lifetime compensation higher than the lifetime marginal productivity. That would be a big loss for the firm. One alternative to mandatory retirement is for the firm to retain the worker at the end of the contract, but to renegotiate the wage level such that it equals the marginal revenue product. The textbook discusses in detail the interface between the economic aspects and the legal aspects of mandatory retirement, as it can be interpreted as a form of age discrimination.

Helpful Hints

- Asymmetric information can cut both ways. The employer knows more about the financial condition of the firm than the worker does, and the employer also generally knows more about the worker's marginal revenue product to the firm. The employee knows better than the firm how diligently and efficiently that he/she is working. In other words, the employee often knows more about the level of inputs that are being used.
- Figure 13.1 is the only diagram in the chapter, and these earnings profiles are not too difficult. The key variable is the discrepancy between the instantaneous value of the marginal revenue product and the wage.
- Here is the crucial link between some of the elements of this chapter. Any employment relationship can be characterized as a principal-agent one, because the principal is paying the agent to work on his or her behalf. If there is asymmetric information about how well the agent is doing his/her job, and/or monitoring costs are high, shirking and unsatisfactory performance are possible. In this case, the very simplest pay mechanism, called the spot labour market, breaks down, and we are likely to see an alternative form of contract between the principal and the agent.
- Employers as well as employees can behave opportunistically. Firms are tempted to lay off workers as soon as their marginal revenue product is lower than the wage, thereby reneging on a contract involving deferred compensation.
- One of the primary objectives of this chapter is to explain the economic rationale for compensation practices that we do see in the real world, such as up-or-out personnel policies. Be prepared to provide verbal, intuitive explanations to questions such as, "Under what conditions are we likely to witness mandatory retirement as a major feature of the compensation system?"
- The fundamental trade-off for this chapter involves incentives. Greater incentives always generate greater inequality in the compensation; but provided that they are designed to stimulate output, they are efficient.

Answers to Odd-Numbered End-of-Chapter Questions

1. The two topics are related, but they are not identical. Efficiency wages fall within a framework of the principal-agent situation, in which employers (principals) hire agents (workers) to act in their interests (to contribute to profit maximization). The central thrust of efficiency wage models is that the wage influences the level of marginal productivity on a continual basis. The primary goal is to deter shirking and elicit conscientious work effort. The time frame for deferred-wage contracts is much longer, sometimes over a 40-year horizon. The goal is to encourage long-term bonding between the employer and the employee, especially in instances where there is a lot of training involved. The emphasis is not so much on deterring shirking, but on deterring quitting. In contrast to the efficiency wage model, the wage is generally independent of the marginal revenue product.

The pros and the cons of the efficiency wage mechanism are not discussed in this chapter. For the deferred compensation mechanism, one of the challenges is to avoid opportunistic behaviour on the part of employers and employees. In the latter part of her career, the employee is paid more than her MRP. It is during this phase, when the deferred compensation is being paid, that the employer has an incentive to dismiss the worker. On the other hand, at a very late stage of her career, after the deferred compensation has been paid, the employee may behave opportunistically by refusing to retire.

3. It would be optimal to have a pay structure involving some degree of wage compression if the technology of production hinged on a lot of cooperative teamwork, and it was difficult to measure the marginal revenue products of the individual workers. Another way to state this is that the cross-marginal products of the workers are positive and significant. A very large degree of pay dispersion can spawn feelings of resentment and unfairness. Often the co-workers wonder why somebody received a huge raise, questioning whether it was based on merit or on politics. In some workplaces where workers are somewhat risk-averse and have some sentiments of solidarity (belonging to a team), *some* degree of wage compression is valued by employees and can boost the morale of the labour force.

5. See the subsection entitled "Up-or-Out Rules." This is a human-resource management policy in which employees are evaluated at a specified point in their career and are either promoted to a higher position or terminated. These rules are common in universities and law firms. They are logical only in a climate of imperfect information. Both parties know that the employer has a better idea of the employee's marginal revenue product. Given this situation, an employer has the option of paying valuable employees less than their marginal revenue product for long periods of time, provided that the employee does not quit. The employer can say that I am paying you as much as you are worth to me, while bluffing with deliberate understatements of this amount. Up-or-out rules can force the employer to reveal the true value of the marginal revenue product of the employee, as they must fish or cut bait. The idea is that they have a strong disincentive to fire a competent employee that outweighs the incentive that they have to pay him/her a wage lower than the true value of the marginal revenue product.

The disadvantages are not discussed much in the textbook. One disadvantage is that the stakes are quite high (that is, either a worker is fired or he/she has very long-term job security), and if an error has been made by the firm, these decisions are irreversible. Another disadvantage is that after the promotion has taken place, the employee has much less incentive to perform well, and agency problems may emerge. We all know of weak university professors who were granted tenure. The entire career can rest on a one-time decision.

7. This statement is probably not true. They may have an incentive to carry out layoffs, but bankruptcy is a very serious matter that would make it much more difficult to raise financial capital in the future. If the demand conditions were substantially worse than they were when the contracts were implemented, the firm would be better off attempting to renegotiate its long-term contracts with its employees. If they are successful in persuading the employees that the demand conditions have changed for the worse, they can then avoid the negative reputational effects that would have occurred had they reneged on their contracts.

9. This question overlaps a bit with Question #8. The topic of the likely impact of banning mandatory retirement is treated in detail at the end of the chapter. An important point is that if the convention of mandatory retirement is abolished, then one can expect other economic side effects to occur, and some of them will be unintended. Since it is built into certain employment relationships — often under the consent of both parties — there must have been efficiency gains involved. To disband early retirement does involve trade-offs. One would expect to see shorter-term contracts with bonuses as opposed to longer-term contracts with deferred wages. There is a strong trend toward early retirement and voluntary buyouts. Under such a mechanism, instead of the employee being forced to retire, he/she is induced to do so with an extra payment. The result is the same as the case of mandatory retirement, but the worker is now better off and the firm is worse off than would be the case with mandatory retirement. The wage profile would likely tilt downwards, such that the wages of older workers with more seniority will fall and the wages of younger workers would rise. Ironically, the wage cuts for older workers would likely provoke protests of age discrimination, despite the fact that the instigating factor — the abolition of the convention of mandatory retirement — occurred because of protests of age discrimination.

The textbook describes another half-dozen or so events that one may expect to occur as a response to the abolition of mandatory retirement. Some of them involve pension schemes, which are intricately linked to the timing of retirement and the normal age-earnings profile. One must not conclude that it would cause economic turmoil — only that there are trade-offs involved. Furthermore, the longer the elapsed time from the point of abolition, the longer workers and firms would have to adjust and try other alternatives to deferred compensation with mandatory retirement.

11. This statement is true. It is unclear why executive compensation is much higher in the U.S. than in any other country, and why the pay of executives compared to average earnings of North American workers has risen substantially over the past 15 years or so. In order to explain that fact, one would take the discussion of the factors that are thought to influence executive compensation and search for a *change* in those factors over this period. One may point to the increased globalization and worldwide integration of product and capital markets, or perhaps to the incredible development of information technology that has occurred in this period (these two factors are themselves related), but that is only a conjecture. They have yet to be linked directly to exploding executive compensation.

There is a subsection in the textbook that treats the factors that are thought to influence the level of executive compensation. One factor is related to the point concerning the compensation of superstars. The act of compensating an executive is thought to be governed by a tournament prize process. In colloquial terms, the winner takes almost all, even if she is only slightly better than the runner-up. Finding the very best matched executive can mean a huge difference for the bottom line of a firm, so paying an extra million dollars or so is economically rational. Small differences in innate productivity can be magnified incredibly in the distribution of compensation in instances where the added productivity positively influences the productivity of many workers at a large firm. The textbook also discusses an alternative perspective, which suggests that, to a certain extent, executive compensation is determined by a "good-old-boy" network, whereby corporate executives engage in mutual back-scratching by determining each other's salaries. This perspective does not imply that the tournament prize story is wrong — only that it is often applied in situations rife with conflicts of interest. In other words, the system of executive compensation needs more checks and balances. The textbook also talks about the downside of excessive compensation. For instance, it can harm labour relations as well as a firm's image.

Answers to Odd-Numbered End-of-Chapter Problems

1. In all four cases, the profile for the value of marginal product (VMP) would assume a negative slope for high levels of seniority. There would be a dip in that curve over the final quarter or so of the career. For cases b and d, the wage profile coincides with the VMP profile. For cases a and b, the wage profile would probably retain its shape, but it would shift down a little bit as the worker's lifetime VMP has declined.

3a. The variables on the vertical axis are the wage (W) and the marginal revenue product (MRP), while the variable on the horizontal axis is time spent working with the firm (T). It is a linear function starting from the origin, and it has a slope of 0.67. The equation of the wage profile, which is a ray from the origin, is $W = 2/3 \, T$. The MRP function is a horizontal line at $10. The vertical difference between the two lines is the discrepancy between the wage and the MRP.

  b. Yes, this wage profile, which is a bonding mechanism, can persist, as it is economically feasible provided that there is mandatory retirement.

  c. To calculate the break-even point, simply set the wage equal to the marginal revenue product, $(2/3) \, T = 10$, or $T = 15$. For the first 15 years of service, the worker is paid less than his/her MRP, but at this point, he/she is being paid exactly in accordance with the value that he/she contributes to the firm's revenues.

  d. We can appeal to the constant slope of the wage-profile equation in order to respond to this question. Due to symmetry, the first 15 years of the employment relationship are the mirror image of the second 15 years of it. Each year, the worker receives a raise of $0.67. For the last 15 years of service, the worker is paid more than his/her MRP. After 30 years of service, he/she is paid $20, and he/she has recuperated all of the lost wages stemming from the earlier part of the career. After 30 years of service, total MRP is $300 (for each of the standard hours worked over the course of the career), and it can be shown that the total remuneration received (for each of the standard hours worked over the course of the career) is also $300. If you know calculus, evaluate the definite integral of the function $2/3 \, T$ with respect to T as T goes from 0 to 30. If you do not know calculus, the sum of the function $2/3 \, T$ as T goes from 0 to 30 can be evaluated easily using a spreadsheet program. (All of these calculations are based on hourly pay. To convert to annual pay, multiply by 2,000.)

  e. Simply add a career spanning 30 years to that age of 35 to obtain a mandatory retirement age of 65.

f. A positive discount rate implies that workers place a lower value on the compensation received in later years and a higher value of the compensation received in earlier years. The employers would prefer the wage profile of deferred compensation even more, given a positive discount rate, because they are paying the wages. There would be pressure to prolong the active career so that workers could benefit from the high-pay periods a bit longer. That implies later retirement.

g. The employer would likely obtain a very unfavourable reputation and would have trouble recruiting new workers. Even those workers remaining with the firm would probably mistrust the employer, and thus would be less likely to work conscientiously. Since the purpose of the profile is to elicit honesty and sincere effort on the part of employees, the move undermines the economic rationale.

h. You would have to compensate them for the total, cumulative amount by which their wages were below their marginal revenue product. The total MRP was $10*2,000 hours*15 years = $300,000. Now turn to the calculation of the total wage bill. If you know calculus, evaluate the definite integral of the function 2 / 3 T with respect to T as T goes from 0 to 15. If you do not know calculus, the sum of the function 2 / 3 T as T goes from 0 to 15 can be evaluated easily using a spreadsheet program. The amount is $75. All of these calculations are based on hourly pay. To convert to annual pay, multiply by 2,000. The total wage bill is $75*2,000 = $150,000. The amount of the severance package should be $150,000.

i. This question is related to Problem 3h. Carry out the calculations for years 29 and 30 of the contract. In the final year (year 30), he/she is supposed to be paid $20. In the penultimate year of the contract (year 29), he/she was supposed to be paid 2 / 3 * 29 = or $19.33. Since the arbitrator deems that the compensation need only cover the wage loss (we assume that the person can obtain work elsewhere at a rate of $10 per hour) and not the total wage stipulated in the contract, the hourly wage loss in the first year is $9.33 and during the last year is $10. Multiply by 2,000 in order to obtain the annual amounts. The amount is $38,666.

j. The total amount of deferred compensation that these workers have coming to them is ten times the value of the package described in Problem 3h. If the firm continues to operate as normal, it will incur those costs. If it goes bankrupt, it will incur costs of a different nature as well as legal costs. If the costs of declaring bankruptcy are evaluated to be lower, then this firm has a purely pecuniary incentive to do so.

5. The textbook mentions that one difficulty that is involved in the implementation of piece-rate systems is potential quality control problems. Ideally, there should be accurate measures of output quantity (usually this occurs) as well as output quality (this is more problematic). In this particular case, the inputs often are not monitored at all. The physician is paid a fixed amount regardless of the amount of time and supplies that she has put forth. Technological change can often improve productivity and, hence, reduce per-unit costs, which would result in a higher profit margin per unit for the physician. Since it is usually economically desirable to have competitive markets, the piece rate should be driven down such that the rate of return for the worker is not supernormal. In this case, many medical providers, such as radiologists, end up collecting economic rents, while other specialists, such as obstetricians, tend to earn lower salaries than many other specialists do. Any attempt by the provincial health insurance administrations or the private health insurance companies to realign these payment schedules in order to reflect technological advances and other reductions in per-unit costs is vigorously opposed by those interests who stand to lose. Given this type of technology of production for which inputs are not easily monitored, it may be more economically efficient to pay hourly wages.

Multiple Choice Questions

1. All of the following are examples of principal-agent problems *except* which?
   a) Workers shirking on the job
   b) Corporate executives not making decisions that will maximize profits
   c) Government officials accepting bribes
   d) Firms knowing the product market conditions better than workers do
   e) Managers not introducing innovative production techniques

2. The stratospheric pay of superstars in sports, entertainment, and corporate management is best explained by which model of age determination?
   a) Efficiency wage theory
   b) Monopsony theory
   c) Marginal revenue product theory
   d) Rank-order tournament theory
   e) Principal agent theory

3. Consider the four figures of Figure 13.1, which represent wage-seniority profiles. Which one refers to a compensation mechanism governed by a spot market that clears instantaneously?
   a) A
   b) B
   c) C
   d) D
   e) None of the above

4. Consider the four figures of Figure 13.1, which represent wage-seniority profiles. Which one refers to a compensation mechanism governed by a deferred-wage contract with no company-specific training?
   a) A
   b) B
   c) C
   d) D
   e) None of the above

5. All of the following statements are rationales for deferred-compensation mechanisms *except* which statement?
   a) The worker pays a bond in the early stage of her career that ensures loyalty and conscientious effort.
   b) Such compensation reduces the need for constant monitoring of workers' output.
   c) Such compensation allows the employer to adjust wages and employment levels quickly in response to changes in market conditions.
   d) Such compensation may reduce excessive turnover and help firms recoup their quasi-fixed hiring and training costs.
   e) Such compensation may provide workers with a stake in the long-term financial condition of the firm.

6. A possible economic rationale for the practice of mandatory retirement is:
   a) When the worker reaches that stage of his/her career, the discounted present value of the marginal revenue product throughout his/her career is equal to the discounted present value of the compensation throughout his/her career.
   b) Senior workers tend to be less productive than junior workers.
   c) The rank-order tournament pay system has run its course.
   d) The worker's marginal revenue product now exceeds the wage.
   e) None of the above.

7. A difficulty involved in the implementation of piece-rate systems of remuneration is:
   a) Monitoring the quantity of output produced.
   b) Monitoring the quantity of the inputs and the average costs of production.
   c) The worker has an incentive to shirk.
   d) The employer has an incentive to pay a rate that is too low.
   e) None of the above.

8. A difficulty in the implementation of piece-rate systems of remuneration is:
   a) Monitoring the quantity of output produced.
   b) Monitoring the quality of output produced.
   c) The worker has an incentive to shirk.
   d) The employer has an incentive to pay a rate that is too low.
   e) None of the above.

9. An advantage of the piece-rate systems of remuneration is:
   a) There are no elements of uncertainty or imperfect information that can interfere with efficient pay systems.
   b) Employers are more likely to turn a profit.
   c) The cost of monitoring the quantity of output is low.
   d) It is often carried out as part of a deferred-compensation system.
   e) Labour relations between the workers and the employer are improved.

10. What is a disadvantage of a compressed or egalitarian pay structure?
    a) They tend to foster excessive rivalry and competition among employees, thereby undermining teamwork.
    b) They tend to foster cooperative teamwork such that one worker's efforts are aimed to raise the output of his/her co-workers.
    c) It is easy for the employer to assess each member's marginal product.
    d) They tend to encourage free riding and shirking on the part of some employees.
    e) There is no deferred-compensation mechanism.

Answers to Multiple Choice Questions

1. D Response D is a case of asymmetric information, but it does not involve a flawed arrangement between two parties in which the agent fails to act in the interests of the principal. All other responses involve such "fail-to-deliver" type of behaviour.
2. D This is made quite explicit in the textbook. See the subsection on "Salaries as Tournament Prizes."

3. B In the age-earnings profile, there is only one line, as the profile for marginal revenue product coincides with the profile for the wage.

4. A With company-specific training, the wage is above the marginal revenue product at the early stages of the career, as the employer pays for some of the training. At the middle stage of the career, the wage is below the marginal revenue product, as the employee pays for some of the training. At the end of the career, the wage is above the marginal revenue product, in order to tie the employee to the employer, much like a pure deferred-wage mechanism.

5. C Response C refers to the spot-market mechanism, in which the wage is always equal to the marginal revenue product.

6. A Anyone who selects response B could find themselves facing a law suit. For response C, unlike deferred-compensation mechanisms, rank-order pay mechanisms do not have a time dimension, so there is no break-even point. For response D, the opposite is true.

7. B Responses A and C are the primary advantages of that type of pay mechanism. Response D is wrong, because an employer who tries to pay a subcompetitive wage will not be able to recruit any workers.

8. B See Question # 7 for an explanation of the incorrect responses.

9. C Response A is false. Response B would apply only in certain circumstances. Response E may apply, but that is not the primary motivation for piece-rate systems. Response D is totally incorrect, as a piece-rate system resembles a spot market.

10. D The opposites of responses A and C are true. Response B is a true statement, but that is an advantage. Response E may or may not apply, but it is irrelevant.

CHAPTER 14

Chapter Highlights

This chapter contains a lot of institutional information on labour unions, which play a fairly important role in determining wage and employment levels in Canadian labour markets. This information serves as a useful background leading into Chapter 15, which deals directly with models of union behaviour and their effects on the labour market. The central question of this chapter involves the variables that have an influence on the likelihood of a worker being unionized. Under what conditions are they likely to exist, and for what reasons?

1. Unions and Collective Bargaining in Canada

A key indicator of union presence is the union density rate, which is typically defined as the percentage of the civilian labour force, either aggregate or by sector, that is either a union member or is covered by a collective agreement specifying wage and employment conditions. This term is interchangeable with the unionization rate or the incidence of unionization. Much of the remaining material in this chapter deals with variation in this rate between countries, industries, geographical regions, demographic traits (for example, gender and age), and occupations. In the late 1990s, approximately 33% of non-agricultural, non-military Canadian workers were covered by a collective agreement.

2. The Legal Framework

This subsection consists of a very brief history of the laws pertaining to union formation and activity, such as how they become certified, how they can bargain (for example, do they have monopoly rights to represent the group of workers), and how strikes are conducted. (For example, can management replace strikers? How much advance notice must be given? How much support must the union leadership have in order to call a strike?)

3. Factors Influencing Union Growth and Influence

The greatest waves of growth in union membership in Canada took place during the years 1940–1950 and 1965–1975.

The rate of growth has not been even, and it has declined slightly since the mid-1980s. Table 14.2 demonstrates the differences in union density across countries. Due to enormous differences in union institutions between countries, great care must be taken in comparing these figures. The union density for coverage by a collective agreement (the second measure of unionization) is probably a more meaningful statistic. In many nations, these rates have declined in recent decades. One interesting development is the fact that the union density in the United States was once on par with Canada, but in the late 1990s, the Canadian rate was double the rate in the United States. This unionization "gap" between the two countries has been the focus of some economic research. There are a number of possible explanations, and the findings suggest that the differences between Canada and the United States in the legal regime governing unions and collective bargaining play an important role in explaining the decline in the U.S. union movement. Another trend that has attracted much attention is the precipitous decline in the unionization rate in the United States since the 1970s.

Data on union density is widely available, and there is wide variation across several different categorization schemes, as demonstrated in Table 14.3. In many cases, these differences can be explained by economic variables, namely the demand for and the supply of union representation and services. On the demand side, the employees are the principal actors. They consider the net costs of becoming unionized. On the supply side, the principal actors are the providers of union services (that is, the union officials and administrators) and the firms. Administering the collective agreements covering existing union members and organizing newly unionized groups of workers generates costs. Unions have to allocate their scarce resources to those activities that are expected to yield the greatest return. Since unions can have multiple objectives, and since the interests of the members are sometimes diverse, this is quite a challenge for unions. These operating costs are influenced by the legal framework surrounding collective bargaining (are they "union-friendly" or "union-hostile"?) and the actions of firms.

4. Empirical Evidence

This subsection deals with a large body of empirical research whose objective is to explain which workers are unionized and which ones are not. The data typically identify the union status of a worker so that union status can be observed. Nevertheless, in practice it is difficult to discern whether union status is driven primarily by supply-side or demand-side forces. The textbook outlines six types of factors:

i)   Social attitudes towards unions and collective bargaining can be interpreted as a supply-side or a demand-side factor.
ii) The legislative framework governing unionization and collective bargaining can also be interpreted as a supply-side or a demand-side factor.
iii) Other economic and social legislation can be interpreted as a demand-side factor.
iv) Aggregate economic conditions.
v)   Industry and enterprise characteristics.
vi) Traits of individual workers.

Much is known about factor v, which includes the firm-size effect, the effect of industrial concentration, and the capital intensity effect. The greater the average firm size, the higher the concentration of the industry, and/or the greater the capital intensity of the production process, the higher the unionization level. Because of the importance of all three of these effects when analysing union density, it is necessary to adjust for the industrial structure of the labour market. For both supply-side and demand-side factors, union density tends to be higher in capital-intensive industries such as manufacturing and utilities than in many service industries, with the notable exception of the public service. The following is an example of the industrial composition effect: Because the composition of aggregate output has shifted from manufacturing activity to service activity, and the former is much more heavily unionized, union density has declined in recent decades.

Factor vi refers not to firm or sector characteristics, but to attributes of the individual workers themselves, such as the degree of labour force attachment, the stage of the worker's career, and whether the worker is white-collar or blue-collar.

Helpful Hints

- The central thrust of this chapter is predicting the circumstances under which a worker or a group of workers is likely to be represented by a labour union.
- Do not totally ignore the treatment of the historical evolution of labour law, as there may be a multiple choice or short answer question pertaining to it on the examination.
- It is unnecessary to memorize the numbers in Table 14.3. Some of the more salient patterns are that union density tends to be highest for middle-aged workers, similar for men and women, highest in Quebec and lowest in Alberta (among the large provinces), higher for full-time workers than for part-time workers, much higher in the public sector than in the private sector, much higher in large firms than in small firms, and increases with job tenure.
- It is very important to distinguish between firm attributes and individual attributes in analysing differences in union-density rates.
- There are no graphs to master in this chapter. The only model is the simple supply-and-demand model, but it is somewhat difficult to apply in this context. One has to avoid confusing the supply-side effects and the demand-side effects.

Answers to Odd-Numbered End-of-Chapter Questions

1. This is a very interesting economic puzzle, in particular because of the relatively similar industrial composition and economic systems of the two countries. The factors that may explain a decline in unionization for any country — in particular, the shift from a manufacturing-based economy to a service-based economy and from larger employers to smaller employers — apply to each country. Structural differences probably tell part of the story. In Canada, the public sector and the natural-resource sectors account for proportionally greater components of the economy, and they are particularly susceptible to unionization in both countries. According to the Riddell [1993] reference, social attitudes towards unions, as measured in public-opinion polls, are fairly similar in both countries. In both countries, they have a lot less public credibility than was the case 30 years ago. The consensus seems to be that there is a different legal regime governing unions and collective bargaining in the two countries. See Exhibit 14.1 in the text that deals with this issue. While this point is valid, it still begs the issue as to why the industrial relations institutions that prevail in Canada are more favourable toward unions than is the case in the United States. Presumably, these laws are at least in part a reflection of popular opinion.

3. There are actually a number of measures of union density, which depend in part on the country that is being studied. The union structure for the United Kingdom, Canada, United States, and Australia are similar, and it is sometimes called the British model. On the other hand, the union structures in continental Europe are quite different from the British model, as well as from each other. In particular, the French system is so unique that some would argue that it is misleading to compare the unionization rate in France with that for any country. Just about the only feature that all these unions operating in different countries have in common is that they represent, in one fashion or another, with or without much effective power, the interests of workers. They always serve as spokespersons for the interests of workers, although not all workers agree that they serve this function adequately. Union-density rates in North America typically refer to workers who are explicit members of a union and who pay union dues. Their employment packages are the subject of collective bargaining between one employer and one union. In some cases, however, workers who are not technically union members are covered by collective agreements. They should probably be considered unionized from an economic perspective. The best indicator is the

percentage of workers that are covered by a collective agreement. This finer point illustrates a broader concept: Union activity has economic effects for non-unionized workers as well.

5. The approach is to go through the list of explanatory factors and determine whether each variable evolved differently across the provinces. The social attitudes towards unions and collective bargaining are probably more favourable in Ontario, Quebec, and British Columbia than they are in Alberta, for example. As far as federal legislation is concerned, the legislative framework governing unionization and collective bargaining is the same for all provinces, so that variable cannot have an effect. On the other hand, parts of the labour code do vary by province as well. The NDP government in Ontario modified the legislative framework governing unionization and collective bargaining in the early 1990s in order to favour unionization, but upon election, the next government (the Tories) repealed these acts. To the extent that the legislative framework governing unionization and collective bargaining is more favourable toward union activity in certain provinces, it could partially explain why unionization is higher in some provinces than in others. The aggregate economic conditions do vary across provinces, and the fact that the economies of the Atlantic Provinces are typically weaker may partially explain why unionization rates are lower there.

The provincial pattern of unionization rates is primarily a function of industrial structure and firm characteristics. For reasons that were already mentioned, unionization tends to be much higher in manufacturing and mining sectors than in agriculture and service sectors. These sectors are more prevalent in Quebec, Ontario, and British Columbia. On the other hand, public-sector employment is both significant and unionized in most provinces, so interprovincial differences in unionization are not likely to be due to factors tied to public-sector employment. Finally, personal characteristics are not likely to vary significantly across provinces to the extent that they could cause major differences in unionization. The age and gender distributions of provinces are fairly similar.

Answers to Odd-Numbered End-of-Chapter Problems

1. This statement is probably true. What is most important for answering this question, however, is whether you understand the theory and apply it correctly in this context. What are the primary factors that are thought to influence the pattern of unionization across countries, industries, regions, and occupations? In the textbook, this theory is laid out in terms of the demand for and supply of unionization. The demand for union representation emanates from employees and depends on the expected benefits and costs of union representation. The supply of union representation emanates from the organization and contract-administration activities of unions. In short, this means the set-up costs and the day-to-day costs of operating a union. The pattern of unionization is probably driven more by differences in supply-side factors than by differences in demand-side factors. In other words, almost all workers are likely to be interested in the benefits of union representation, such as higher wages in many cases. On the other hand, the feasibility of union organization differs greatly across firms.

Most of the factors that are discussed at some length in the textbook fit into a supply-and-demand framework. Both the supply side and the demand side can be influenced by social attitudes towards unions and collective bargaining. This qualitative factor is hard to observe and measure, and thus hard to analyse empirically. The same applies to the legislative framework governing unionization and collective bargaining, which is also an important factor. The effect of aggregate economic conditions is one of the more straightforward factors to analyse. Empirically, the industry and enterprise characteristics are the most powerful explanatory factors. Like the variable of aggregate economic conditions, they can often be observed, and thus empirical analysis is feasible. Finally, see the subsection in the textbook dealing with the role played by personal characteristics.

3. One cannot answer this question with certainty unless one is given the full set of explanatory variables. Based on the graph in Figure 14.1, one would guess that if one were to extrapolate the trend from 1920–1960 to 1998, it is likely that union growth would be overestimated. It is unlikely that the tremendous decline in unionization in the United States would be captured by Ashenfelter and Pencavel's equation. What variables would they have had to include in their equation in order to capture this decline? In order to forecast correctly, one needs to include the correct set of explanatory variables. Use the list of supply-side and demand-side variables. One also has to have a reasonably accurate forecast of the values of the explanatory variables. In the case of the United States, this would require an accurate forecast of the changes that occurred in the legislative framework governing union activity and the significant structural changes that occurred in the economy. See Exhibit 14.1 in the textbook.

Multiple Choice Questions

1. In the late 1990s, approximately what percentage of the Canadian labour force was unionized?
    a) 15%
    b) 27%
    c) 33%
    d) 43%
    e) 51%

2. Which of the following statements concerning unionization in Canada is *false*?
    a) It is much higher in the public sector than in the private sector.
    b) Compared to other industrialized countries, Canada has a fairly high rate of unionization.
    c) Unionization is highest in blue-collar occupations such as forestry, mining, and construction.
    d) The likelihood of being unionized increases sharply with age until workers reach their mid-50s.
    e) The rate of unionization in Canada has been fairly stable since the 1950s.

3. All of the following factors have been associated with a marked decline in the rate of unionization in the United States since the early 1970s *except* which factor?
    a) Several deep recessions
    b) Differences in the legal regime governing collective bargaining, union certification and decertification, mandatory membership in the union, and so on
    c) Restructuring of the composition of economic activity away from the manufacturing sector toward the services sector
    d) The growth of services to workers that are provided by non-union entities, such as employment protection and grievance procedure by non-union employers
    e) A deterioration of the image of organized labour in the eyes of the public, weakening their political clout

4. Which of the following statements is *false*?
   a) The demand for union representation emanates from employees and depends on the expected benefits and costs of unionization.
   b) The supply of union representation emanates from the organization and contract-administration activities of union leaders and their staff.
   c) Most of the tremendous gap that exists between the unionization rates in Canada and the United States can be attributed to demand-side factors.
   d) Most of the tremendous drop that occurred in the unionization rate in the United States since the early 1970s can be attributed to demand-side factors.
   e) In both the United States and Canada, it appears as though public opinion is less favourable toward unions than it was 30 years ago.

5. Empirical studies have found that union density tends be high in all of the following situations *except* which?
   a) Industries with large firms
   b) Industries that are more concentrated
   c) Industries with capital-intensive production processes
   d) Industries with more hazardous jobs
   e) Industries that are export-oriented

6. Empirical studies have found that unionization tends to be most likely for workers having all of the following characteristics *except* which?
   a) Female workers
   b) Full-time workers
   c) Middle-aged workers
   d) Workers near the lower end of the wage distribution
   e) Workers in urban areas

7. Recent empirical studies in Canada have indicated that the most important factor in determining whether an individual is unionized is:
   a) The personal characteristics of the worker.
   b) The firm characteristics.
   c) Aggregate economic conditions.
   d) The legislative framework governing unionization and collective bargaining.
   e) None of the above.

8. All of the following are demand-side factors that could affect the outcome of whether a group of workers is organized *except* which factor?
   a) The benefits that workers perceive they can obtain if they are organized
   b) The costs that workers perceive they have to incur if they are organized
   c) The costs of organizing the work unit and administering the collective agreements
   d) The greater employment security that unionized workers typically receive
   e) All of the above are demand-side factors

9. All of the following are supply-side factors that could affect the outcome of whether a group of workers is organized *except* which factor?
    a) The degree of employer resistance to unionization and union activities
    b) The legislative framework governing unionization and collective bargaining
    c) The costs of organizing the work unit and administering the collective agreements
    d) The state of public opinion regarding unionization and union activities
    e) The benefits that workers perceive they can obtain if they are organized

10. There was a significant growth in union density in Canada between 1965 and 1975. What is the likely source of this development?
    a) The climate for organizing workers became much more favourable due to legislative changes.
    b) There was rapid growth in the public sector, which tends to be heavily unionized.
    c) The economy was booming over most of this period.
    d) Union density in the U.S. was falling.
    e) Social attitudes were leaning towards increased militancy.

Answers to Multiple Choice Questions

1. C   See Figure 14.1.
2. B   This information is stated explicitly in the textbook. See the subsection entitled "Factors Influencing Union Growth and Incidence."
3. A   See Exhibit 14.1, which mentions the role of the structural factors but not the cyclical ones.
4. C   The textbook (Exhibit 14.1) indicates that supply-side factors, such as the legal regime governing unions and collective bargaining, are likely to be an important factor.
5. E   See the subsection entitled "Industry and Enterprise Characteristics."
6. A   See the subsection entitled "Personal Characteristics."
7. A   See Exhibit 14.2. Response B is certainly not a bad answer, as the body of empirical research highlights the importance of firm and sectoral characteristics. Response D does not make sense, however, because the legislative framework only varies across jurisdictions and cannot explain why the unionization rate varies within a province or a country.
8. C   Response D is a perceived benefit and thus a demand-side factor. See the section entitled "Factors Influencing Union Growth and Incidence."
9. E   Response E is a demand-side factor. All of the other responses have to do with the costs of setting up and operating a union.
10. B   Response A makes sense, but that is not the reason in this case. Response C is false and is not thought to be a strong factor driving unionization. Response D is true, but irrelevant. Response E is probably not true, but even if it was, response B is much more important.

CHAPTER 15

Chapter Highlights

This chapter deals with the behavioural implications of unionization and collective bargaining. Much of it focuses on the determination of wages and employment.

1. Theory of Union Behaviour

The starting point for any theory of economic behaviour is a treatment of the objective of the primary economic actor. In this chapter, this actor is not the worker or the firm, but rather a worker collective. The ability to describe and characterize union preferences has long been and remains controversial. By union preferences, we typically refer to the trade-off between higher wages and lower levels of employment, or vice versa.

2. Union Objectives

What are the goals of the union? The challenge is to aggregate the preferences of all of the individual members of the union into a common and sole platform to tell management, "Here is what we want." Three factors influence the relationship among the preferences of the members, the union leaders, and those of the union as a whole:

i) The information that is available to the individual members about the available options
ii) The manner in which the union makes its decisions (that is, democratic or not)
iii) The degree of homogeneity of the individual member's preferences

The union's preferences can be expressed analytically by a utility function having wages and employment levels as the two arguments. Geometrically, this translates into downward-sloping indifference curves in wage-employment space. In addition to the variables of wage levels and employment levels, utility may also depend on the alternative (non-union) wage that members could receive in the absence of the union. If the union wage does not exceed this level, there is little reason for a union to engage in collective bargaining.

3. Some Special Cases

These are particular cases for the utility function describing union preferences. Each of them corresponds to a different version of the indifference curves in Figure 15.1. If the indifference curves are horizontal lines, the union seeks to maximize the real wage level and does not care about the level of employment. If the indifference curves are vertical lines, the union seeks to maximize the employment level and does not care about the real wage rate. A fairly realistic objective is to maximize the level of economic rent — the amount by which the union wage exceeds the alternative wage that workers could earn elsewhere. For all of the workers, the level of economic rent is equal to $(W_u - W_a)*E$. These indifference curves are in the form of rectangular hyperbolas (Figure 15.2d).

4. Union Preferences: Some Additional Considerations

Typically, the preferences of individual members are heterogeneous. For instance, senior workers are often more interested in pensions and less interested in current wages than junior members. When layoffs are determined by inverse seniority, and layoffs are threatened, junior workers may be more interested in exercising wage restraint than senior workers. These conflicts in interest must be resolved somehow in order to engage in collective bargaining and arrive at an agreement. Inevitably, the collective agreement is going to favour the interests of some members more than others. This situation is a lot like citizens of a community that must be governed. Another challenge in achieving collective bargaining is a potential disconnect between union leaders and union members. Union leaders have much more information on the financial condition of the firm and the employer's bargaining positions. Union leaders are often accused of not representing the interests of a majority of the members, much like politicians are often accused of favouring the narrow interests of lobbies.

5. Union Constraints

The first constraint that the union faces as it negotiates on behalf of its members is that the firm must remain solvent. In addition, if the firm has the power to choose the level of employment given the union wage, the wage-employment equilibrium will lie on the labour demand curve. The union thus faces a trade-off between wages and employment levels. In this chapter, the isoprofit curves are analogous to those from the chapter on compensating differentials, but they are not the same. In this chapter, they are drawn in wage-employment space and are superimposed with the labour demand curve. Although at each point along the firm's labour demand curve, the firm is maximizing profits given the union wage, ideally it would prefer to pay lower wages and move along the demand curve, as it could reach a lower isoprofit curve reflecting higher levels of profits. The upshot of this subsection is illustrated in Figure 15.4. We can predict that the wage-employment equilibrium will lie somewhere along the labour demand curve between the zero-profit isoprofit curve (higher wages imply negative profits) and the alternative wage level (lower wages imply many workers quit). This is called the bargaining range. Where exactly they locate on this range is determined by the relative bargaining strengths of the partners.

6. Relaxing the Demand Constraint

Even if the wage-employment equilibrium is constrained to be on the labour demand curve, the union can enhance its interests either by bringing about an increase in labour demand or making this labour demand more inelastic.

7. Efficient Wage and Employment Contracts

This is an alternative framework of collective bargaining in which both the wage level and the employment level are subject to negotiation (as opposed to the previous case, in which only the wage level is subject to negotiation). The technical term for this model of negotiations is Pareto–efficient, and it means that the wage-employment equilibrium is off of the demand curve, lying somewhere above and to the right of it. One negotiating partner can be made better off without making the other partner worse off by moving off of the demand curve and negotiating another wage-employment equilibrium. The firm is better off as we move downwards and to the left, while the opposite applies to the union. Given a wage rate, bargaining outcomes will involve the firm hiring more labour than it would if it were free to set the employment level. The firm is not maximizing profits when the equilibrium is off of the demand curve, so this extra employment comes at the expense of firm profits. It is noteworthy that the negative relationship between the wage level and the employment level may not hold in this case. This Pareto–efficient bargaining framework is not thought to apply very often in the real world, but there are some cases.

8.   Empirical Applications

Not many empirical studies exist that deal with union objectives, due to a lack of data on labour contracts. The two questions that are examined are

   i)   Which bargaining model applies: the efficient or the inefficient one?
   ii)   How much importance do unions give to the employment level as they bargain for wages?

The research is based only on the observation of bargaining outcomes, and not on surveys. The results of these studies tend to indicate that both employment and wages are important to unions (with a fairly large weight on the employment level), union preferences are sensitive to the alternative wage, and rent maximization is not often an objective of the union's bargaining strategy.

9.   Theory of Bargaining

The basic idea of this subsection is that the parties involved in collective bargaining engage in strategic behaviour, sort of like a card or chess game. They conjecture about the potential actions and reactions of their collective bargaining partner.

10.   Solutions to the Bargaining Problem

This subsection consists of two more specific theories of how bargaining takes place, that is, what the rules, objectives, and strategies are.

11.   Union Bargaining Power

It was mentioned above that there is typically a range for bargaining outcomes, with maximum and minimum values for wages. One can often predict with a bit more precision the wage level by considering the relative bargaining powers. The more wage inelastic the labour demand, the greater the ability to raise wages without paying a cost in the form of lower employment.

12.   Union Power and Labour Supply

The pressure tactic that the industrial union exercises in order to affect wages (and sometimes employment levels) is the strike. The craft union can also strike, but it can affect labour markets in a way that the industrial unions cannot: It can restrict the supply of labour entering the occupation. Craft unions can exercise some control over hiring. Professional associations operate in a similar fashion, restricting the supply of labour through occupational licensing and certification.

Helpful Hints

- The major diagram for this chapter is Figure 15.1. This graph is in wage-employment space. Both of these variables are goods as far as the union is concerned, so the isoutility curves (the indifference curves) slope downwards. The union wants to move to the north and/or to the east.

- Figure 15.3, which contains the isoprofit curves and the demand curve in wage-employment space, is hard. You should understand why higher isoprofit curves correspond to lower levels of profit, so the firm seeks to reach the lowest isoprofit curve. Note that they slope upwards over low-employment levels and downwards over higher employment levels. It is somewhat difficult to understand why they hit a maximum point at their point of intersection with the labour demand curve. Recall that at all points on the labour demand curve, the firm is maximizing profits given the wage level.
- The diagram of Figure 15.5 consists of the labour demand curve, isoprofit curves, isoutility curves, and the set of Pareto–efficient wage-employment combinations, also called the contract curve. This material is very hard and can be grasped only if you have had a course in intermediate microeconomic theory and have studied the analytical tool of an Edgeworth box. If the wage-employment combination is located on the contract curve, it means that any movement along that curve will make at least one party worse off. It is not possible to make one party better off without making the other party worse off. If the wage-employment combination is off of the contract curve, it is possible to make one party better off without making the other party worse off.
- The subsection relaxing the demand constraint contains information describing union behaviour that we often observe in the real world.
- See the subsection entitled "Efficient versus Inefficient Contracts: A Summary."

Answers to Odd-Numbered End-of-Chapter Questions

1. The objectives of the rank and file may be quite different than those of the leadership. The objectives of union members typically depend on the seniority level, the skill level, and the outside employment opportunity levels of different workers. In practice, the interests of junior workers often conflict with those of more senior workers. If the leaders of a union tend to be of one type, and the majority of the rank and file tend to be of another type, the objectives of these two parties may clash. Furthermore, the leadership can be thought of as politicians, who must stand for re-election in order to have power and publicity. Most of the rank and file are not affected by that motive.

    On a conceptual level, the idea is to elaborate the preferences of many workers into one voice. Since the entire group of workers is to be covered by the wages and working conditions of one collective agreement, one has to somehow aggregate their desires into one platform, much like governments are supposed to choose a solitary course of action in the interests of their citizens. The more heterogeneous the interests of the collective bargaining unit, the less cohesive the union's preferences are, and the more difficult it is for union leaders to reflect those preferences. Besides this heterogeneity-of-preference problem, the other challenge stemming from different objectives that must be overcome in order for the union to have a cohesive strategy is the information that is available to the two parties concerning options that are open to the union. Pages 443–444 talk about the principal agent problem in this union context.

3. *Ceteris paribus,* it reduces the utility of a union in the case that the union's objective is to maximize economic rent. In this situation, no matter where the union is located, its welfare will diminish (Figure 15.2d). If the union has another objective, an increase in the alternative wage may have no immediate impact on the union's welfare, particularly if the going wage is still well above the alternative wage. This would be the case in Figure 15.2c, for example, for which the objective is to maximize the wage bill. The alternative wage will always set a lower bound on

any possible wage outcome, as a union will not accept a wage that is lower than what they would receive in the union's absence.

5. The union would like to move as high as possible on the bargaining range in employment-wage space. Holding employment constant (along a vertical line), it wants the highest wage level possible. It cannot go beyond the zero-profit isoprofit curve, however, as the firm would start to incur losses and, in the long run, would exit the industry. The employer would like to move as low as possible on the bargaining range. Holding employment constant (along a vertical line), it wants the lowest wage level possible. It cannot go below the alternative wage, however, as the firm would no longer be able to employ and hire labour. This is an easy question.

7. Refer to Figure 15.5. The explanation is given in the subsection entitled "Efficient Wage and Employment Contracts." If we are at point A and we move along the isoprofit curve to A", the firm is no worse off and the union is better off because it is now on a higher indifference curve. If, on the other hand, we were to move from point A along the union's indifference curve (to the southeast to the intersection with segment CC'), the union would be no worse off. The firm would be better off, however, as it is on a lower isoprofit curve (not shown on Figure 15.5). Recall that the lower the isoprofit curve, the higher the profit level. In both cases, by moving to the right of the labour demand curve, along either curve going through point A, one party was made better off without hurting the other party. These wage-employment outcomes represent unexploited gains to efficiency that are the subject of bargaining. It is still true that along the segment CC', the union wants the highest point, which corresponds to zero profits, and the firm wants the lowest point, which corresponds to the alternative wage. The two parties will conflict over the outcome that they want along the contract curve, but at least they can agree, through consensual bargaining, to move off of the demand curve and over to some point along the contract curve. What drives the consensual bargaining is the difference in preferences that they have regarding the wage-employment trade-off.

9. The analysis of a craft union is much easier than the analysis of an industrial union. The former can be analysed using conventional supply-and-demand analysis. The key difference is that the union is the gatekeeper for a craft union. It controls the entry of workers into the occupation and thus determines the hiring. For an industrial union, the employer controls the hiring process. (Recall that there are two cases for industrial unions. In the Pareto–inefficient case, the employer is free to hire all of the labour it wants at the wage that the union bargained. The outcome lies on the firm's demand-for-labour curve. In the Pareto–efficient case, both the wage level and the employment level are subjected to bargaining.) In the case of a craft union, there is no need to analyse indifference curves for the union or isoprofit curves for the firm. Most of the union's efforts are focused on strictly limiting the entry of workers into the occupation. This has the effect of shifting the effective supply of labour up and to the left. The artificially restricted supply curve intersects the labour demand curve to generate an equilibrium with a higher wage and a lower employment level than would prevail in a competitive labour market. Although a craft union typically has a contractual wage, most of the economic action is not focused on bargaining activity, but rather on restricting supply. A craft union does have an incentive to negotiate over workloads, however.

11. Professional licensure has a greater impact on restricting the supply of labour into the profession than does professional certification. The goal of excessively strict licensing requirements is to restrict entry into the profession, restricting supply and thus raising the incomes of the incumbent

practitioners. With licensure, no one can legally operate in the trade or profession without holding a license. With certification, no one without the certificate can claim to hold the title of a certified practitioner, but he/she could still practice. Customers and clients are not guaranteed that the non-certified practitioner is fully qualified and has a good reputation, but they can be served be a non-certified practitioner at their own risk. See the very last subsection of the chapter for examples.

Answers to Odd-Numbered End-of-Chapter Problems

1.   The preferences are likely to vary according to age, seniority, family situation, and alternative employment opportunities. Younger workers tend to care less about pension matters than older workers. Due to the last-hired, first-fired convention, they may also be willing to accept lower wages in exchange for more job security, whereas older workers, who already benefit from a fairly high degree of job security, would be less interested in that prospect. Younger workers may be more interested in overtime than older workers are. Those workers with the most attractive outside opportunities would have higher wage aspirations than those who do not.

3.   This statement is true. If the union adopts the latter strategy — agreeing to wage concessions and allowing the firm to choose the level of employment, then the two parties move down and along the demand-for-labour curve. In Figure 15.5, point A to B would be such a move. If the union adopts the former strategy, it would bargain for a wage outcome above and to the right of the demand curve, such as point A". As far as the firm is concerned, this wage-employment outcome is as good as point A, as it lies on the same isoprofit curve. As far as the union is concerned, A" is far superior to point B, as the both the wage level and the employment level are higher. If the union does place a high weight on jobs, then A" is an attractive point, because it represents many more jobs than point A at the cost of only a slightly lower wage.

The basic idea is that if only the wage is subject to negotiation, the outcome will always lie on the labour demand curve. If both the wage level and the employment level are subject to negotiation, the outcome should lie to the northeast of the labour demand, and from the union's point of view, the trade-off between wages and employment becomes more favourable.

5.   The relative bargaining of the two parties determines where they will locate on the contract curve. Yes, they could be prevented from reaching an efficient contract (a bargained wage-employment outcome) that lies on the contract curve, although the reasons are not really tied to that indeterminacy point. The Pareto–efficient contract curve is a neat concept, but in the real world, the task of reaching it is fraught with difficulties. Both sides require much information concerning the other side's preferences. For example, in what fashion, and to what degree, are they willing to trade off wages against employment? It requires that the two sides trust each other to truthfully reveal information about this trade-off. Furthermore, it can be difficult to enforce this contract through all contingencies. It is relatively easy to enforce the agreed-upon wage, but the firm has an incentive to reduce employment (move towards the labour demand curve). It may justify doing so by claiming that market conditions have changed. The firm may say that the product demand or profits have declined, so that it can no longer afford to retain as many workers on payroll. See the section entitled "Efficient Wage and Employment Contracts."

7. This is related to Problem 5. The basic idea is that the direct trade-off between wages and employment levels applies when the outcome is on the labour demand curve. In the situation in which the employer takes the wage as given but is free to set employment levels, concessionary wage bargaining should save jobs (see curve D_L in Figure 15.6). In the situation in which there is a Pareto–efficient contract off of the demand curve and on the contract curve, however, the direct trade-off breaks down, and the locus of wage and employment outcomes may look like CC' in Figure 15.6. A wage cut in this case saves very few jobs. In this case, the trade unionists are correct.

9. This statement is true and is tantamount to saying that a union still has to deal with the force of labour demand, which in turn is driven by the profit-maximizing motive of the firm and is derived from the demand for the product or service, not by the capricious will of the employer.

   a. There are two forms of substitution, one in labour markets and one working through product markets. In both cases, the greater the degree of substitutability, the lower the bargaining power of the union. First, the union must make it nearly impossible to substitute non-union workers for union workers, and difficult to substitute capital for labour. In the real world, witness the reaction of labour unions whenever such a move is threatened. Second, the union will attempt to prevent the sale of products and services made from non-union labour.

   b. The tax that is applied per ton of coal is designed to give an incentive to the union to produce more coal — piece-rate compensation — while at the same time tying employment levels, to some extent, to production levels. Recall that if the two parties do not bargain over both wages and employment, but rather bargain only over wages, then the employer will choose an outcome on the labour demand curve. If the two parties do bargain over both wages and employment levels, the contract is somewhat difficult to enforce as the firm has the incentive to cut back on employment unless business is booming. Under this scheme, the miners can, to a certain extent, create work for themselves by mining coal that the employer is obliged to accept into its inventory and has the right to sell. The objective is to put upward pressure on employment above the level that would exist in the unconstrained (inefficient) case that is depicted in Figure 15.1.

11. One has to distinguish between the effective supply of workers to the occupation and the total, or notional, supply of workers to the occupation. When prevailing wages and working conditions are above the competitive norm, one expects queues of workers who want to enter the occupation to develop. It is a simple case of excess quantity supplied to the occupation. Ways must be found to turn them down in order to prevent them from exerting downward pressures on the wage level. Rationing is a way of removing a certain number of queued workers from the effective supply of labour to the occupation. A minority of the workers who are able and willing to work at the going wage will be fortunate and find work (these are the rationed jobs), while the others remain unemployed. The textbook mentions some of the methods that are used to select the choice applicants, such as apprenticeship programs with unduly restrictive training requirements, discrimination, nepotism, and high initiation fees.

13. The underlying concept is that occupational or professional licensure can be more restrictive than the level that is truly needed to guarantee quality within the profession. The goal of excessively strict licensing requirements is to restrict entry into the profession, restricting supply and thus raising the incomes of the incumbent practitioners. A potential abuse associated with grandfathering practices is that under such a system, the incumbent practitioners have the incentive to set higher and higher standards on people entering the profession without subjecting themselves to these tighter standards. This has the effect of gradually restricting the supply into

Labour Market Economics, Fifth Edition

the profession such that the incumbents bear none of the costs. Meanwhile, the incumbents benefit from higher salaries resulting from the restricted supply. This is discussed in the textbook at the very end of the chapter.

Multiple Choice Questions

For Questions 1 through 5, consider the four graphs that appear in Figure 15.2 of the textbook. Each figure refers to the isoutility curves for a labour union having a certain objective.

1. Which graph corresponds to the isoutility curves for a union that seeks to maximize the wage rate of its members?
   a) A
   b) B
   c) C
   d) D
   e) None of the above

2. Which graph corresponds to the isoutility curves for a union that seeks to maximize the employment level of its members?
   a) A
   b) B
   c) C
   d) D
   e) None of the above

3. Which graph corresponds to the isoutility curves for a union that seeks to maximize the wage bill that its members receive?
   a) A
   b) B
   c) C
   d) D
   e) None of the above

4. Which graph corresponds to the isoutility curves for a union that seeks to maximize the economic rent that its members receive?
   a) A
   b) B
   c) C
   d) D
   e) None of the above

5. Which graph corresponds to the isoutility curves for a union that seeks to maximize the wage level but minimize the employment level of its members?
   a) A
   b) B
   c) C
   d) D
   e) None of the above

6. Which of the following statements is *false*?
   a) The higher the isoprofit curve, the lower the profits.
   b) Isoprofit curves slope downwards.
   c) The demand curve for labour intersects the isoprofit curves at their highest points.
   d) Isoutility curves slope downwards.
   e) The bargaining range for wages lies between the alternative wage and the highest wage associated with the zero-profit constraint.

7. A union would likely support all of the following policies *except* which policy?
   a) Quotas and tariffs
   b) Deregulation and privatization of industries
   c) Unionizing workers of competing firms
   d) Minimum wage and fair wage provisions
   e) Regulations specifying staffing levels at unionized employers

8. A Pareto–efficient contract is:
   a) Off of the labour demand curve, but on the contract curve.
   b) Where the union sets the wage and the employer chooses the employment level.
   c) Located on the labour demand curve.
   d) Any contract that allows the firm to make a profit.
   e) Any contract that transfers all the surplus to the workers so that profits are zero.

9. Which of the following statements about the contract curve is *false*?
   a) It represents a set of efficient contracts.
   b) It represents a set of contracts for which the two parties bargain over wages and employment.
   c) Each party is indifferent as to which of the points is selected as the contract.
   d) Points on the contract curve occur where the slope of the isoutility curve equals the slope of the isoprofit curve.
   e) Along the contract curve, the negative relationship between wages and employment may not hold.

10. Why are unions in the newspaper publishing industry often more powerful than many other unions? All of the following are reasons *except* which one?
    a) The product that they make cannot be stored in advance; production has to occur shortly before consumption.
    b) The product that they produce is indispensable for readers, as there are no substitutes.
    c) A strike has the potential to reduce circulation after the strike ends.
    d) In the event of a strike, advertisers who finance the operation have alternatives.
    e) None of the above.

11. How do craft unions and professional associations promote the interests of their members?
    a) By making the demand for the services of their members inelastic
    b) By bargaining efficient contracts that lie off of the labour demand curve
    c) By setting a contractual wage and allowing the employer to determine the employment level
    d) By restricting the supply of labour before the hiring takes place, thus raising the equilibrium wage
    e) All of the above

12. Which of the following statements about the contract curve is *false* in theory?
   a) It represents the range of the possible equilibria for wages and employment.
   b) It is constructed as the locus of tangency points between the isoprofit curves and the indifference curves.
   c) It may lie off the firm's demand curve for labour.
   d) All other factors held constant, a firm will prefer to move upwards along the contract curve.
   e) The union and the firm will arrive there voluntarily.

13. A good economic explanation as to why some labour unions support practices such as "featherbedding" is that:
   a) Such practices create jobs for the labour market.
   b) Such practices make it difficult for the employer to substitute among inputs, making the demand for labour less elastic.
   c) Such practices make it difficult for the employer to substitute among inputs, making the demand for labour more elastic.
   d) It reinforces the minimum wage law.
   e) It lowers the price elasticity of demand for the product that the firm produces.

14. If the goal of a labour union is to maximize the wage level that its employed members receive, then:
   a) The employer is not maximizing her profits.
   b) The wage-employment equilibrium will be off of the contract curve.
   c) The wage-employment equilibrium will be off of the labour demand curve.
   d) The firm will be on the zero-profit isoprofit curve.
   e) Fewer workers will be hired than is the case with a perfectly competitive labour market.

Answers to Multiple Choice Questions

1. A   These horizontal isoutility, or indifference curves, mean that given a level for the real wage, the union does not care how many workers are employed. See Figure 15.2a.
2. B   These vertical isoutility curves mean that given a level of employment, the union does not care about the wage rate. See Figure 15.2b.
3. C   In this case, there is a trade-off between wages and employment levels. See Figure 15.2c.
4. D   These curves have the same form as the ones in case c, but they have to be entirely above the alternative wage level. See Figure 15.2d.
5. E   This case does not make sense. Since both the wage level and the employment level are goods, indifference curves have to slope downwards. If the employment level were really a "bad," then the indifference curves would slope upwards.
6. B   Isoprofit curves have a positive slope for low levels of employment and a negative slope for high levels of employment.
7. B   For response A, trade restrictions raise the price of the output, thus raising the demand for labour. Responses C and D refer to events that will raise the price of substitute labour, thus lowering the wage elasticity of labour demand and/or raising the demand for their own labour. For response E, these regulations would probably reduce the wage elasticity of labour demand.
8. A   Responses B and C refer to the "right-to-manage" case. Response D is totally wrong; if a contract does not allow a firm to make a profit, it will eventually exit the industry. Response E refers to an efficient contract, but only a very particular case.

9. C   This response is totally false. The union would prefer the contract at the very top of the contract curve, while the firm would prefer the opposite. If the contract is on the contract curve, it means that it is impossible to make one party better off without hurting the other party. See the section entitled "Efficient Wage and Employment Contracts."

10. B   This response is false, as there are substitutes for newspapers. What gives them their power is that there are few substitutes available for the labour services that they provide, so the wage elasticity of labour demand is low. See the section entitled "Empirical Applications."

11. D   Responses A and B are sensible for the case of industrial unions. For response C, this event does not necessarily promote the interests of members. See the section entitled "Union Power and Labour Supply."

12. D   The opposite of this response applies. See the section entitled "Efficient Wage and Employment Contracts."

13. B   The opposite of response C applies, as lesser substitutability is consistent with lower elasticities. Responses D and E have nothing to do with the question. Response A is false because featherbedding will not create jobs in the aggregate.

14. E   If a union cannot deliver a wage that is higher than the competitive level, there is little reason for it to exist. As the wage goes up, however, the quantity demanded goes down (unless they are in the efficient contract bargaining regime). We assume that response A never applies. For responses B and C, in this particular case, the isoutility curves are horizontal and, it turns out, the contract curve coincides with the firm's demand curve. The outcome will lie on the firm's demand curve. For response D, that is only a very particular case, and this does not apply in general.

CHAPTER 16

<u>**Chapter Highlights**</u>

This is the final chapter dealing with labour unions, and it deals with the impact that they have on economic outcomes.

1. Union Wage Impact

The union/non-union wage differential has received the most attention in the research. It consists of the estimated differential between union workers and supposedly comparable non-union workers. In mathematical form, the equation is $(W_u - W_e) / W_e$. There are two fundamental challenges. A major challenge is that the union wage is observed, but the observed non-union wage cannot be observed. It is the counterfactual wage that would exist in the absence of the union that is required, and it must be estimated.

The basic theory of the union wage impact is similar to that underlying the impact of other wage-fixing arrangements such as minimum wage. In particular, there is the crowding effect with the two-sector model depicted in Figure 16.1a. As the union wage is increased, the quantity demanded of labour decreases, and the displaced workers shift the supply of labour in the non-union sector to the right, consequently depressing the equilibrium wage in the non-union sector. The magnitude of the union/non-union wage differential depends on the wage elasticity of demand in each sector, the ability of the union to raise wages in the organized sector, and the elasticity of labour supply.

The threat effect depicted in Figure 16.1b is a competing theory. The basic idea is that non-union employers will pay somewhat higher wages than what would otherwise be the case in order to discourage their employers from unionizing. This would likely cause an excess quantity supplied of labour in the market for non-unionized labour market. Workers in both the unionized sector and the non-unionized sector are likely to be displaced.

The final approach is wait unemployment, which also uses the two-sector approach. In this model, workers who are displaced in the union sector as the union wage is raised do not seek work in the non-union sector, but rather wait for high-paying jobs to open up in the union sector. There is not a great increase in the supply of labour to the non-union sector.

Precise measurement of the union wage impact is complicated by three factors. First, when comparing the wages of union workers to non-union workers, it is necessary to control for other factors that affect wages — factors that are distinct from union status. Second, union status (whether or not the worker is unionized) may be determined by unobservable factors that can also influence the level of wages. This is called the endogeneity, or simultaneity, problem. Third, there is the problem of causality. We seek to measure the impact that unionization has on wages, but to some extent, the level of wages can determine union status. Higher wages are thought to make unionization more likely. In other words, if there is a potential to extract rents from a firm that is presumably profitable, then there is a great incentive for a worker group to organize. When the chain of causality can work in both directions, in practice it is difficult to measure the true effect.

2. Empirical Evidence on Union Wage Impact

Early estimates based on data aggregated by sector for the U.S. labour market were in the range of 10–15%. More recent studies are based on data at the level of the individual or the firm. In the longitudinal studies, workers are followed over time. If a non-unionized worker becomes unionized, or vice-versa, the wage change is observed and correlated to these changes in union status. We would search for a wage increase right after a worker became unionized and for a wage decrease right after he/she became non-unionized. A survey of many more recent studies indicates an average estimate of about 15%, *ceteris paribus,* in both the United States and Canada.

3. Variation in the Union Wage Impact

Much of the information of this section is repeated in the next section. The estimated wage differential varies considerably across firms, industries, and workers. Firm size is positively correlated with both union and non-union wages, but the differential is higher for smaller firms. This means that for small firms, we expect the union/non-union wage differential to be higher than it is for large firms. The union/non-union wage differential is higher for blue-collar workers than it is for white-collar workers, and it is lower for public-sector workers than for private-sector workers. It tends to be higher for unskilled workers than for skilled workers. Overall, union wages are typically found to be less responsive to the attributes of workers than is the case for non-union wages. Workers whose attributes are usually not associated with high wages, such as lower-skilled and lower-educated workers, tend to benefit the most from unionization. Indeed, a primary goal of union activity is to reduce inequalities of wages between workers, as well as to raise the general level of wages paid to workers. The idea is to counteract (at least to a degree) wage premiums and differentials that are generated by supply-and-demand forces in the labour market.

Earlier empirical research suggested that unionization probably has lowered the wages of non-union workers to a slight extent, and that both the threat effect and the crowding effect are at work. Recall that they operate in different directions. More recent research cast doubt on that conclusion, however. Finally, the union/non-union wage differential widens during economic recessions, when union workers are better protected from wage cuts, and narrows during recoveries.

4. Union Wage Impact: Concluding Comments

It is logical to expect that the unionized employers would take advantage of the queue of job applicants in order to select higher-quality workers. For this reason, some researchers believe that a portion of the union/non-union wage differential potentially reflects a higher level of marginal productivity of unionized workers. This higher productivity would not be observable to the researcher.

5. Unions, Wage Dispersion, and the Distribution of Income

There is significantly less wage dispersion among unionized workers than among non-unionized ones, which is due primarily to wage-setting policies. Indeed, one of the deliberate objectives of these wage-setting policies is to reduce wage dispersion. This phenomenon is called wage compression. These policies imply that unions typically raise the wages of those near the bottom of the pay scale by proportionally more than they raise the wages of those near the top.

6. Union Impact on Resource Allocation and Economic Welfare

The effect of union wage setting on allocative efficiency is shown in Figure 16.4. This effect is associated with the two sector-crowding models. As the union wage is raised, the quantity demanded of labour in the union sector falls, leading to a loss of production. The displaced labour then migrates to the non-unionized sector, depressing wages there and leading to an increase in employment. This rise in employment brings about a gain in production, but this gain is less than the loss in the union sector. The discrepancy between the loss in output and the gain — the net loss in output after the reallocation of labour — is called a dead-weight loss. In practice, the magnitude of this loss is probably not very large.

7. Union Impact on Non-Wage Outcomes

In this section, the effect of unionization on a series of variables is discussed. For instance, the empirical evidence indicates that non-wage compensation accounts for a larger share of the total compensation of union workers than is the case for non-union workers. This implies that the estimated union/non-union wage differentials understate the gap in total compensation between unionized and non-unionized workers. Unionized workers definitely exhibit lower rates of turnover than their non-unionized counterparts. They often exhibit very low quit rates, in part due to higher wages, and in part due to contract procedures that give workers recourse other than quitting when they have a grievance regarding working conditions or work assignments. This is called the collective-voice function of the union.

It is often alleged that unions hamper productivity by protecting less competent workers from being fired, as well as through imposing inefficient and restrictive work rules on the employer. On the other hand, they do serve to reduce costly turnover and often to boost labour force morale, which would improve productivity. Furthermore, by improving the lines of communication between workers and management, productivity can be strengthened. Given the increase in labour cost stemming from unionization, one would expect firms to substitute capital for labour, which would render the remaining workers more productive as there is more capital per worker. In summary, there are a number of possible influences that work in both directions. The empirical evidence on the net effect of unionization on productivity is inconclusive, while the effect of unionization on profitability is probably negative, as a portion of the profits are redistributed to the workers.

Helpful Hints

- A key point of this chapter is that unions not only affect the wage levels of their own members but also the wage levels of non-unionized workers.
- There are three competing theories about how unions affect the union/non-union wage differential within a two-sector framework: the threat effect, the crowding effect, and the wait-unemployment, or queuing-unemployment, effect. The first two work in opposing directions, based on fairly straightforward supply-and-demand analysis. You should master this analysis.
- In the empirical analysis of the union/non-union wage differential, the endogeneity, or simultaneity, issue is difficult to understand if you have not studied econometrics. On the other hand, the concept of the problem of reverse causality, or two-way causality, is easier to grasp.
- Read the summary section on the union wage impact carefully.
- To understand the point about the dead-weight loss effect that results from the allocative effects of unions on production, a review of intermediate micro theory would be helpful.

- The subsection on longitudinal studies (especially the reference to fixed-effects models) is difficult to understand if you have not studied econometrics, and it may be beyond the scope of your particular course. It does give you an idea of how modern labour economics research is carried out.
- Figure 16.3 shows the form of the distributions of wages of union and non-union workers. The main point is that the distribution of non-union wages is fatter, which means that their distribution is more dispersed than the distribution of union wages. In statistics, we say that the variance (and the standard deviation) of the distribution of non-union wages is greater than the variance of the distribution of union wages.

Answers to Odd-Numbered End-of-Chapter Questions

1. Unions can influence both the union wage and the non-union wage. By doing so, it can have an impact on some of the wage structures that we have studied thus far, including the private-sector/ public-sector structure, the male-female wage structure, the blue-collar/white-collar structure, the wage structure according to educational attainment and other measures of human capital, the industrial wage structure, and the large-firm/small-firm wage structure. The union wage impact is frequently analysed by a two-sector model of the labour market, in which both sectors have competitive labour markets until the union operates in one of them. The key point to remember is that the union can affect the wage in the non-union sector as well as the sector in which it operates.

3. Because many union jobs pay relatively well, there is typically a queue of applicants waiting for openings. Under these circumstances, employers can be more selective and may be able to hire more motivated and more able workers than what would otherwise be the case. This implies that one may overestimate the true value of the union/non-union wage gap, because part of the wage differential reflects the pure effect of unions on wages, while part of it merely reflects a productivity effect that we cannot observe (other than through educational attainment, for example). On average, *ceteris paribus,* union workers may be somewhat more productive because they are better-quality workers. This explanation is popular among union workers themselves. I have heard well-paid unionized workers say something like, "Sure, we are well paid for what we do; but since we are receiving good pay, we are really dedicated to doing a good job."

   This phenomenon illustrates what is called selection bias. The higher wages that prevail at union firms may draw higher-quality applicants with higher-than-average productivity levels. These higher productivity levels allow higher wages to be paid with or without the union's pressure. According to this scenario, more motivated and more able workers select themselves (or are selected by employers) into the higher-paying union jobs. This creates a two-way causality, which complicates the isolation of a union effect on wages. Everyone agrees that unions cause higher wages, but to a certain extent, the higher wages strengthen the force of unionism. See the subsection entitled "Some Problems in Measuring the Union Wage Impact."

5. This is a broad question that is treated explicitly in the textbook. See the section entitled "Variation in the Union Wage Impact."

7. The effects of unions in this regard are thought to be a two-edged sword. The first function of labour unions is to raise (on average) the wage level of its members to a level that is higher than what would prevail if the labour market were competitive. This has the effect of increasing the

level of inequality *between* union workers and non-union workers compared to the counterfactual case of no unions operating at all. Recall that the union typically raises the wage in the union sector above competitive levels, but often has the effect of slightly reducing the wage in the non-union sector. In effect, a wedge is driven between the wages in the two sectors, which corresponds to the wage differential. This contributes to wage inequality.

Second, they deliberately raise the wages of those at the lower end of the pay scale proportionally more than those at the top end. For philosophical reasons, namely the promotion of equity, they seek to narrow the gap between the highest-paid and the lowest-paid workers within the bargaining unit. This greatly reduces the dispersion of pay *within* the union. The procedures for determining salary in collective bargaining are designed to have this impact. Pay scales typically set entry-level pay and maximum pay levels. The progression up the pay scale is usually determined by a combination of seniority and training/education criteria. The key point is that management cannot determine which workers are more productive and reward them accordingly. That would be tantamount to *individual* bargaining, which is anathema to a union. Raises and demotions can occur only as a result of contractual and formal rules, such as seniority, certain performance evaluations, and so on, which are the product of *collective* bargaining. Equity in pay levels — except for seniority and training differentials — is valued by the union. Wide inequality of pay based on individual performance as judged by the employer — is frowned upon.

9. See the subsection entitled "Unions and Fringe Benefits." Unions typically deliver a much higher level of fringe benefits than those that exist in comparable non-union firms. The interesting question is why that is so. A possible reason is due to the way in which the preferences of the labour force are considered by the firm. In a non-union setting, the employer is probably more responsive to the marginal worker — the one who is indifferent between quitting and staying. In many cases, the marginal worker, who has outside opportunities, is more interested in higher pay than higher benefits. Usually, they are at fairly early stages of their careers and are not close to retirement. In a union setting, the preferences of all members are supposed to be considered by the union and transmitted to the employer. More senior but less-mobile workers who are not at the margin are likely to be interested in fringe benefits, and their preferences will be considered. It is often the case that unionized labour forces are fairly senior and have a long-term attachment to the firm. The deferred-compensation mechanisms that were discussed in a previous chapter often contain fringe benefits as one of their major elements. Essentially, fringe benefits can be interpreted as a "bonding" measure to reduce turnover.

11. This question is open-ended. The role of unions in the social system is well beyond the scope of this book. The pertinent part of the textbook is Exhibit 16.1 and the subsection entitled "Union Impact on Turnover and Mobility." These authors believe that unions are essentially a positive force for several reasons. These reasons have a common theme — the so-called "voice" function of workers. By giving workers a means to express their grievances, their preferences, their ideas, their occupational aspirations, and so on, workers obtain a well-deserved and useful input into the workplace and production process. The impact on productivity is favourable due to some of the reasons that are explained in the subsection entitled "Union Impact on Productivity, Profitability, and Investment." Perhaps the most valuable aspect is the reduction in turnover. These authors feel that the alternative regime that often applies in non-union workplaces — the "exit" regime — is both undemocratic and somewhat unproductive. Rather than tell workers that if they are unhappy, they can quit, the "voice" regime allows them to be heard in a usually constructive fashion such that they can achieve partial satisfaction and remain with the firm.

1a. This is a fine question. The justification for the U variable (the proportion of the labour force that is unionized) is given in the text at the beginning of the subsection entitled "Variation in the Union Wage Impact." Note the discrepancy between CA, which represents the union status of the firm (yes or no), and U, which represents the proportion of the labour force that is unionized within an industry. The justification for the CR variable, representing the concentration of the industry, is similar to the effect posited for firm size and is explained in the subsection entitled "Variation in the Union Wage Impact." The justification for the RLC variable is tied to the elasticity of labour demand.

b. The U variable (the proportion of the labour force in the industry that is unionized) has a positive coefficient. The interpretation is that there is a union advantage (associated with the variable CA, the union status specific to the firm), and it increases in magnitude as U rises. The CR variable, representing the concentration of the industry, is similar to the effect posited for firm size, which is expected to be positive. The interpretation is that there is a union advantage, and it increases in magnitude as CR rises. The RLC variable is expected to have a negative effect due to one of Hicks' laws of the elasticity of labour demand. As the fraction of labour costs among total costs increases, a wage increase becomes more expensive for the firm, and the wage elasticity of labour demand increases. This in turn implies that employers will be more responsive to a wage increase. This should have a negative impact on the wage.

c. All of these variables are interacted with CA. This means that the effect of a worker's own union status (a categorical variable, yes or no) on his/her wage level will vary according to the magnitude of the other three indicators: U, CR, and RLC. In other words, the effect of the variable CA on wages is not constant. If we did not have this interactive structure, but instead specified the equation such that CA appeared separately from the other indicators with its own coefficient, then the effect of CA on W would be linear, with a constant slope, independent of whatever value of U, CR, and RLC.

d. Take the derivative of the endogenous variable with respect to the variable CA. One obtains $0.5 + 0.004*U + 0.003*CR - 0.01*RLC$.

e. By substituting these values into the equation above, one obtains $0.5 + 0.004*40 + 0.003*7 - 0.01*36 = 0.321$.

f. By substituting these values into the equation above, one obtains $0.5 + 0.004*100 + 0.003*7 - 0.01*36 = 0.561$. The effect of union status CA on the wage rate has increased.

g. By substituting these values into the equation above, one obtains $0.5 + 0.004*40 + 0.003*7 - 0.01*20 = 0.481$. The effect of union status CA on the wage rate has increased due to the lower wage elasticity of demand.

h. This indicates that the effect of the worker's union status on his/her wage depends on the values of the other variables as well. In order to estimate the true union wage effect, we have to hold all other relevant factors constant (to the best of our ability) and vary only the union status variable CA. In this particular equation, the variable CA is interacted with the control variables: it enters multiplicatively.

i. One could add terms such that the variables U, CR, and RLC appear by themselves, which would mean that there are seven variables plus the other control variables. It is also possible to estimate a specification in which there are no interactive terms at all. That is the least restrictive form, and it implies that the effect of all of the variables on wages is constant.

3a. This is a good question. The president of the pilots union has much greater bargaining power than the president of the garment makers union because the wage elasticity of demand for the services of airline pilots is less elastic. Nevertheless, the wage elasticity of demand for the services of garment workers is still in the inelastic range. The quantity demanded of pilots would fall by 2%, while the quantity demanded of garment workers would fall by 6%. Just apply the formula for the wage elasticity of labour demand. It is the percentage change in quantity demanded divided by the percentage change in the wage.

b. The pilots would stick with their 10% wage increase, as in Problem 3a. The garment workers would ask for a 3.33% raise. Just apply the formula for the wage elasticity of labour demand.

c. We are told that the wage elasticity of labour demand for pilots has been reduced to -0.1. This is good news for the pilots. If they obtain a 20% raise, they will suffer a 2% reduction in the quantity demanded of labour. In Problem 3b, they could only obtain a 10% raise in exchange for a 2% reduction in the quantity demanded of labour.

d. We are told that the wage elasticity of labour demand for garment workers has been increased to 1.0, which is called a unitary elasticity. This is bad news for the garment workers. A 2% increase in wages will cause a 2% reduction in the quantity demanded of labour, so the total wage bill remains unchanged.

e. As mentioned above, the pilots union will support the merger, and the garment workers union will oppose free trade. The idea is that the union wants the wage elasticity of demand to be as low as possible.

Multiple Choice Questions

1. Given that W_u is the observed union wage, W_{nu} is the observed non-union wage, and W_0 is the competitive wage that would prevail if all the relevant labour markets were perfectly competitive, the *pure* union/non-union wage differential is given by which of the following expressions?
   a) $(W_{nu} - W_u) / W_{nu}$
   b) $(W_u - W_{nu}) / W_0$
   c) $(W_u - W_{nu}) / W_{nu}$
   d) $(W_u - W_{nu}) / W_u$
   e) $(W_u - W_0) / W_0$

2. Given that W_u is the observed union wage, W_{nu} is the observed non-union wage, and W_0 is the competitive wage that would prevail if all the relevant labour markets were perfectly competitive, the *actual* union/non-union wage differential is given by which of the following expressions?
   a) $(W_{nu} - W_u) / W_{nu}$
   b) $(W_u - W_{nu}) / W_0$
   c) $(W_u - W_{nu}) / W_{nu}$
   d) $(W_u - W_{nu}) / W_u$
   e) $(W_u - W_0) / W_0$

3. Consider the two-sector model of the labour market, with a primary sector and a secondary sector. If the primary sector becomes unionized while the secondary sector remains non-union, what impact would we expect for this to have on wages in the two sectors? (This is sometimes called the crowding model.)
   a) Raising the wage in both the union sector and the non-union sector
   b) Raising the wage in the union sector and leaving the non-union sector wage unchanged
   c) Raising the wage in the union sector and depressing the non-union sector wage
   d) Raising the union wage but lowering the union/non-union wage differential
   e) None of the above

4. All of the following conditions would lead one to expect a strong threat effect to operate in labour markets *except* which condition?
   a) When the union wage is relatively high.
   b) When the non-union sector can be organized fairly easily.
   c) When employers have a strong aversion to unionization.
   d) When the union takes an aggressive stance in organizing.
   e) When the demand for labour is wage elastic.

5. Which of the following statements concerning the wait-unemployment, or queue-unemployment, effect is *false*?
   a) Unionization has a relatively lesser impact on the wage in the non-union sector.
   b) It is irrational behaviour because people remain unemployed waiting for jobs to open up in the union sector when they could find jobs elsewhere.
   c) The increase in labour supply to the non-union sector is low, relative to the case of the crowding model.
   d) Unionization has a relatively greater impact on the unemployment level.
   e) All of the above statements are true.

6. In the context of estimating the impact that unions have on the wage level, what is implied by the existence of selection bias? All of the following statements are valid *except* which statement?
   a) Unionized firms may attract higher-quality workers with higher productivity, but these characteristics are unobserved by the researcher and thus excluded from the analysis.
   b) Unionized firms may have workers with more formal education and training, and the researcher cannot exclude this from the analysis.
   c) It is not a problem if unobserved variables have no relationship with the union/non-union status of workers.
   d) The effect of unionization on wages is overestimated.
   e) The union wage premium that one observes actually reflects other factors.

7. Many studies based on North American data have been carried out in efforts to estimate the wage premium between unionized and non-unionized workers. Which of the following figures gives a ballpark estimate for many of the studies?
   a) 16%
   b) 50%
   c) 75%
   d) 65%
   e) 36%

8. Which of the following statements concerning the impact of unionization on wage structures is *false*?
   a) The union impact is larger in the public sector.
   b) Union wages tend to be less responsive to productivity-related individual traits than non-union wages.
   c) Among skilled occupations, the union wage premium can actually be negative.
   d) Lower-skilled workers tend to benefit the most from unionization.
   e) The financial return to education is lower in the unionized sector than it is in the non-unionized sector.

9. What are some of the reasons why the compensation of some workers includes a significant proportion of fringe benefits rather than straight salary? All of the following are reasons *except* which reason?
   a) Workers may have an interest because they are non-taxable.
   b) Large employers may have an interest because they can be administered more cheaply through the firm with group plans.
   c) Employers may have an interest because they reduce turnover.
   d) Governments may encourage the private provision of these benefits as it reduces the pressure on social insurance programs.
   e) None of the above.

10. In the context of a labour market equilibrium in the presence of a union, the threat effect refers to:
    a) Non-union workers receiving a wage above the competitive level.
    b) Workers who are laid off crowding into the non-unionized sector.
    c) The union threatening its employer with violence in order to assert its will.
    d) The union extracting some of the firm's profits, and using this money to increase wages.
    e) Unions restricting entry into an occupation.

Answers to Multiple Choice Questions

1. B See the discussion surrounding Figure 16.1.
2. C See the discussion surrounding Figure 16.1.
3. C For responses A and B, the wage in the non-union sector falls if the crowding model applies. For response D, the only way that this could happen is if the non-union wage increases by more than the union wage.
4. E A central point in this chapter is that an elastic wage elasticity of labour demands weakens the union's power. All of those other responses refer to the threat effect.
5. B The basic idea behind this model is that, given unemployment insurance benefits and a reasonably high probability of being hired, it can be rational to wait for one of the highly prized jobs to open up. Responses A, C, and D are true (see the discussion on wait unemployment).
6. B These traits are observable, so they can be included in the equation that estimates the union/non-union wage differential. All of the other statements are true.
7. A This point is made a number of times in the section entitled "Empirical Evidence on Union Wage Impact."
8. A The opposite is true. See the section entitled "Union Wage Impact: Concluding Comments." Response B is true, and it is one of the crucial points of this chapter.

9. E   See the subsection entitled "Unions and Fringe Benefits." All of the other statements are true.

10. A   Response B refers to the crowding effect. Response C is totally wrong. Response D refers to Pareto–efficient bargaining, while response E refers to the operation of a craft union.

CHAPTER 17

Chapter Highlights

The basic theme of this chapter is that while the aggregate level of unemployment is one of the most important economic variables, as far as society's well being is concerned, there are many complexities involved in measuring it and in analysing its anatomy.

1. Measuring Unemployment

There are three primary data sources that are used to measure the unemployment rate: the labour force survey (LFS), the census, and administrative data for the unemployment insurance program. They do not generate the same values, nor do they capture exactly the same phenomena. The official statistic that is most commonly reported in the media as the official unemployment rate comes from the LFS. In order to be classified as unemployed, one has to be jobless, and available to work, and searching for a job.

A crucial point is that there are at least three major indicators of the performance of the labour market: the unemployment rate, the labour force participation rate, and the employment rate. A thorough analysis of labour market trends should mention all three, as they do not always move together. The values presented in Table 17.1 provide an illustration. There have been times in history when the unemployment rate rose in spite of rising employment because the labour force was growing even faster than employment. Figure 17.1 shows the history of the unemployment rate since 1921. Note a fairly similar pattern in the 1980s and 1990s. The experience of the period of the late 1990s belies the conjecture that there has been an increasing secular trend in unemployment rate since the mid-1970s.

Since the late 1970s, unemployment rates in the U.S. (and to a lesser extent in Canada) have typically been lower than they are in continental Europe. In the 1960s, however, that was not the case. The performance of the labour market in the U.S. during most of the 1990s was phenomenal.

Perhaps the toughest issue in measuring the unemployment rate is the treatment of marginal labour force attachment. These individuals are jobless, but if they are not actively seeking work, then they are considered to be out of the labour force rather than unemployed. Discouraged workers, who are defined as jobless workers who do not actively search for work because they believe that none is available, are an example of marginally attached workers. The key point is the following: To the extent that marginally attached workers are considered to be in the labour force (and thus unemployed), the unemployment rate goes up. To the extent that marginally attached workers are considered to be out of the labour force (and thus not unemployed), the unemployment rate goes down. Fairly recent research has indicated that marginally attached workers should probably not be considered as either unemployed or out of the labour force, but rather as a distinct group. This complicates the classification of individuals, as there would be four states of labour market status: employed, unemployed, out of the labour force, and marginally attached workers.

2. Labour Force Dynamics

Labour force dynamics refer to individuals flowing in and out of various states of labour market activity, such as unemployment, employment, and out of the labour force. Gross flows refer to inflows or outflows from one of these states, while net flows refer to the inflows minus the outflows. In effect, net flows account for two-way traffic, while gross flows measure one-way traffic. Gross flows are typically much larger in magnitude. The main point is that while the unemployment rate, which is the stock of unemployed workers divided by the stock of people that are in the labour force, changes relatively slowly over time, there is usually a high number of individuals transiting between the three states. Except perhaps in the depths of a recession, many of the unemployed workers do transit to employment. There is a great deal of movement among these three states every month.

There are three primary reasons why an individual can end up in the state of unemployment. Job losers comprise the largest group of the stock of unemployed workers, followed by new entrants and re-entrants, and finally, job leavers.

There are two primary elements of unemployment: the incidence rate and the duration. The incidence of unemployment (I) is the proportion of individuals who become unemployed during a certain time period (it is a flow quantity), while the duration of unemployment (D) refers to the length of time spent in the unemployed state before obtaining employment or leaving the labour force. If the incidence rate refers to the labour force, then the unemployment rate can be decomposed according to the following equation, which is an approximation: UR = I * D. This decomposition is illustrated in Table 17.3.

These two variables vary across demographic groups, as illustrated in Table 17.4. Younger workers tend to have relatively high incidence rates but relative low durations of unemployment, while older workers exhibit the opposite traits.

A major point of this section is that the common portrayal of unemployment in the media is that a 10% unemployment rate corresponds to 10% of the population that is jobless and engaged in a long-term and mostly futile search for work. This is the "static" view that prevailed until well into the 1970s. The data on labour dynamics mentioned above refutes that proposition. The "new view" of unemployment, which was popular in the 1970s and part of the 1980s, stressed the role of labour force dynamics and held that, while many individuals may experience a bout of unemployment sooner or later, most unemployment is short-term. That perspective has in turn been displaced somewhat by the "modified new view," which accepts the validity of the "new view" subject to a caveat. Much of the unemployment that does occur is concentrated among a relatively small group of chronically unemployed and disadvantaged workers.

While long-term unemployment is not a common problem in North America (except perhaps during recessions), it is a grave problem in parts of continental Europe.

The unemployment rates in Canada and the U.S. were fairly close to each other until 1983 or so, for reasons that are only partly understood. Since then, the unemployment rate in Canada has far exceeded the rate in the U.S. This economic puzzle has incited many empirical studies. There is doubtless a combination of causes. One factor that can explain part of the "unemployment rate gap" is the way in which non-working time is spent. The fraction of jobless time that is declared as unemployed time rather than out of the labour force time is higher in Canada. A small part of the discrepancy can be attributed to definitional issues such as how incarcerated people are classified. In the 1990s, the macroeconomic performance in Canada was weaker, which may explain a portion of the gap during that period.

3. Unemployment as a Summary Statistic

The unemployment rate is by far the most widely used indicator of labour market performance, aggregate economic performance, and the extent of the economic hardship that is visited on the population. It should be interpreted with care, however, and supplemented by other qualifying information. It is a good measure of unutilized labour supply, but labour supply itself is affected by wage levels. Jobless workers having low labour force attachment may or may not be actively seeking work. If they are waiting for "good jobs" to become available, or are very discouraged in their job searches, they will not be classified as unemployed. The basic idea is that not all jobless workers are necessarily suffering great economic hardship; some may have withdrawn from the labour force for many reasons and are being supported by another wage earner. In order to diagnose how well the labour market is performing, one examines the unemployment rate. In order to understand why the unemployment rate is rising or falling, however, it is important to consider the degree to which employment is rising or falling versus the degree to which people are entering or leaving the labour force.

Helpful Hints

- Some of the material in this chapter has to be memorized, such as a sketch of Canadian labour market history and definitions of various indicators, but much of this information is quite concrete and relevant for real-world labour economics. There is no graphical analysis to master. You should master the chart in Figure 17.2.
- You will probably find Exhibit 17.1 interesting, which compares international unemployment rates. These discrepancies have been the focus of much economic research.
- You should know the difference between a stock and a flow variable. This concept applied to the three primary states of labour market activity is well illustrated in Figure 17.2.
- Do not confuse the three channels for entry into the stock of unemployed workers with the two elements of the stock of unemployed workers. The former includes job losers (layoff victims), job leavers (quitters), and entrants or re-entrants into the labour force. All of the workers can be classified into these three groups. The latter includes the incidence and the duration of unemployment. These are essentially economic variables, rather than types of individuals, that generate the level of unemployment.
- A key concept of this chapter is the state of marginal labour force attachment and its repercussions with the calculation of the official unemployment rate.
- You should be able to explain the evolution of the "static view" of unemployment to the "new view" of unemployment to the "modified new view" of unemployment. You should be able to place the evolution in historical context. These are approaches to analysing the nature of unemployment.

Answers to Odd-Numbered End-of-Chapter Questions

1a. The three measures are drawn from the labour force survey, the population census, and the statistics from the unemployment insurance (renamed employment insurance in 1995) program. Although the data are drawn from different sources, in all cases the underlying concept is the same. The objective is to measure the percentage of the labour force that is able and willing to work, searching for work, but unable to find employment.
  b. Far and away, the most widely used measure is the one drawn from the labour force survey.
  c. The measure drawn from unemployment insurance figures is used to gauge the number of unemployed workers who are actually drawing unemployment insurance benefits. It greatly

understates the number of people unemployed, as a lot of them are ineligible. It also fails to capture some people who are employed. It is not really a very useful measure, except to evaluate the UI program itself. The measure from the census is produced quite infrequently (every five years), and the census is not designed specifically to discern employment or unemployment issues. Furthermore, due to the vast scope of census, it takes a long time to prepare, so the data are typically released long after the workers are actually sampled. On the other hand, the sample is very, very large, and a wealth of information is collected on each worker. The labour force survey is carried out monthly. Its primary focus is on employment and unemployment activity, so it is carefully designed to capture these phenomena. The labour force survey is quite timely, with a lag of only a month or two.

Bear in mind that we can estimate only what the true rate of unemployment actually is. It is a science to do so, and the survey instruments and measurement techniques should be under scrutiny. Although the labour force survey is by far the best measure, it is helpful to have several measures, because if systematic discrepancies between them appear, it can be a signal that the survey methods should be changed.

3a. These are defined on page 509 and listed in Table 17.1. You should know them very well. The labour force participation rate is the labour force divided by the population of working age. The employment rate is the level of employment divided by the population of working age. The unemployment rate is the level of unemployment divided by the labour force.

  b. See pages 509–511. The employment rate is appropriate for assessing job creation and destruction activity. It tells a lot about the trends in labour demand. The labour force participation rate tells a lot about labour supply patterns and is affected by trends. The unemployment rate is affected by both labour demand and labour supply influences and is the most complex measure. It is widely considered to be the most meaningful measure to assess social well being, but changes in the unemployment rate should be analysed and decomposed into supply-side and demand-side influences.

  c. If the economy is in a deep recession, the unemployment rate will rise, but the employment rate and the labour force participation rate will fall. If the economy is in a brisk recovery, the unemployment rate will fall, but the employment rate and the labour force participation rate will rise. In a mild recovery, it is frequently the case that the unemployment rate is resilient or even rising in the face of rising employment, because the increase in the labour force outstrips the increase in the number of jobs (think of the discouraged-worker effect in reverse). In this instance, all three indicators move in the same direction. In the mid-1990s, this was a frustrating problem in Canada.

5. See pages 514–516. The term labour force dynamics is associated with gross flows and net flows. The three primary states are employed, unemployed, and out of the labour force. Gross flows indicate the total number of people who have transited from any of these three states to another (there are six possible transitions), in any direction, given an interval of time. The net flows indicate the sum or difference of these gross flows along any of these channels in the two opposing directions. The gross flow between any two states is always greater than or equal to the net flow. For the net flows, a physics analogy would be the sum of two vectors representing opposing forces. Figure 17.2 provides an excellent illustration.

7. The youngest workers tend to have the highest unemployment rates at any point in time, the highest instability of employment, and the lowest duration of unemployment due to high

Labour Market Economics, Fifth Edition

turnover. They also tend to have the highest incidence of unemployment, which means that over a certain interval, they face the highest probability of being unemployed at least once. See page 518 and Table 17.4.

9a. Generally, one seeks a measure to summarize the degree of economic hardship experienced by the unemployed, or some measure of tightness or looseness of labour markets. See page 524.

b. On pages 524–525, a series of reasons why the official rate may understate economic hardship is given. There is the discouraged-worker effect, which is described above. There is the phenomenon of part-time unemployment, which is also explained above. Unemployment typically contributes to poverty. On pages 524–525, a series of reasons why the official rate may overstate economic hardship is given. Some of the unemployed represent second incomes upon which families don't depend to survive. While this point is controversial, it is true that family incomes are much more diversified than they were 50 years ago, so many families will not become destitute despite the temporary loss of an income through unemployment. Finally, some of the unemployed in Canada receive very extensive unemployment insurance benefits over long periods, which mitigates their losses.

c. See Exhibit 17.1 for a list of the complementary measures of aggregate unemployment, and the top of page 524 for the commentary.

Answers to Odd-Numbered End-of-Chapter Problems

1a. See the subsection entitled "The Divergence of the Canada and U.S. Unemployment Rates." Recall that in order to be classified as unemployed, one has to be jobless and engaged in job search. At issue is the definition of job search. The U.S. has more stringent criteria for what constitutes "active" job search. Certain types of job search activity that are considered to be active job search in Canada would not be considered as such in the U.S. A group of workers meeting the criteria for job search in Canada but not in the U.S. would be considered to be unemployed in Canada but out of the labour force in the U.S. This implies that all other factors held constant, the official rate of unemployment in Canada is higher only due to classification issues.

b. The approach that one may take in order to analyse this empirically is the one outlined in the work by Card and Riddell. It refers back to the point about marginal labour force attachment. To the extent that such groups are classified as unemployed, the official rate of unemployment goes up. To the extent that such groups are classified as out of the labour force, the official rate of unemployment goes down. One compares the population of jobless (not only the unemployed but also all of those who do not have jobs) and classifies them as much as possible according to their degree of labour force attachment, which is tied to how actively they are searching for work. Compare workers across the two countries that appear to have nearly identical degrees of job search, and classify them the same way in both countries. For instance, if they both limited their job search to chatting with friends and networking, then classify both the Canadian worker and the American worker as out of the labour force. Once all workers are classified in the same fashion in both countries, the unemployment rates become more comparable.

3. In order to obtain this graph, you will have to go the university library and dig up this issue of that periodical. The title of the graph basically reveals the punch line, "Discouragement and Unemployment Move Together."

a. The major spikes in the number of discouraged workers (read from the scale on the right side) occurred in 1982, 1983, 1984, and 1993. Apparently, there are no data for the years 1994–1996; in 1997, there are still a fairly high number of discouraged workers. After 1997, note that a different data set is used. So one should exercise caution in comparing the figures from the "Survey of Job Opportunities" to the "Labour Force Survey."

b. That is an interesting observation. One possible response is mentioned in Problem 3a, as the surveys may define and measure worker discouragement differently. It is also possible that there were fundamental changes in labour supply behaviour over this decade. Workers who may have declared themselves out of the labour force in the early 1980s (because they were not actively searching for work), may be (or claim to be) actively searching for work in the 1990s. If they are actively searching for work, they are classified as unemployed and are often eligible for unemployment insurance benefits. In other words, the lure of unemployment insurance benefits, or perhaps some other change in labour supply choices, may have caused some jobless workers from the 1980s period to raise their degree of attachment to the labour force in the 1990s period, implying that they are no longer discouraged workers.

Multiple Choice Questions

1. All of the following are data sources for measuring the extent of unemployment in Canada *except* which?
   a) The labour force survey
   b) The population census files
   c) The survey of consumer finances
   d) The unemployment insurance (now called employment insurance) data files
   e) All of the above contain information on unemployment

2. Which of the following statements is *false*?
   a) There was a trend of growing employment between 1966 and 1981, but the unemployment rate rose nevertheless.
   b) Employment grew rapidly between 1966 and 1982, and the unemployment rate fell.
   c) The rate of employment growth has been low since 1981, relative to many prior periods.
   d) Since World War II, the labour force participation rate rose steadily until about 1990.
   e) Since World War II, the unemployment rate has trended upwards for the most part.

3. Compared to other industrialized countries, Canada's unemployment rate is:
   a) Below average.
   b) About average.
   c) Above average.
   d) Quite variable — sometimes it is relatively high, and other times it is relatively low.
   e) The figures across many countries are not comparable.

4. When one analyses the gross flows of individuals in and out of the three states — employed, not in the labour force, and unemployed — what picture typically emerges?
   a) A static picture in which the unemployed are likely to remain unemployed and the employed are likely to remain employed indefinitely.
   b) A dynamic labour force in which there is a lot of movement in both directions between the three states.
   c) Net flows between states that are greater than the gross flows.
   d) Unemployment that consists largely of new entrants into the labour force.
   e) A dynamic labour force in which there is a lot of movement from employment to unemployment, but not in the other direction.

5. Consider a steady state situation. The rate of unemployment has two components: the average incidence rate as a fraction of the labour force (I) and the average duration (D). What is the relationship between them?
   a) UR = I * D
   b) UR = I / D
   c) UR = D / I
   d) UR = I + D
   e) None of the above

6. Which of the following statements is *false*?
   a) Groups with the highest incidence rates for unemployment have the lowest duration of unemployment.
   b) Youth tend to have higher incidence rates than older workers.
   c) Groups with the highest incidence rates for unemployment have the highest duration of unemployment.
   d) Youth tend to have relatively low unemployment durations.
   e) Older workers suffer a lower incidence of unemployment than younger workers.

7. The "new view" of unemployment in the labour market, attributed to famous economist Martin Feldstein in the 1970s, held that:
   a) A 10% unemployment rate generally meant that the same 10% of the labour force was stuck in unemployment.
   b) Unemployment can be lowered by stimulative fiscal and monetary policies.
   c) Unemployment tends to be concentrated among certain disadvantaged segments of the labour force who suffer from long-term unemployment.
   d) Unemployment tends to be associated with rapid turnover and instability.
   e) None of the above.

8. One reason that researchers have discovered about the phenomenon of an unemployment rate in Canada that is nearly twice as high as the official rate in the United States is:
   a) Canada's unemployment insurance system is much more generous.
   b) The two economies have different industrial structures.
   c) In Canada, time spent not working is more likely to be reported as time spent unemployed rather than time spent out of the labour force, so some of the discrepancy is a matter of semantics.
   d) The incidence of unemployment in the United States is higher than it is in Canada.
   e) The duration of unemployment in Canada is longer.

9. Which of the following variables would be considered part of the labour force dynamics?
   a) The flow of workers into the state of unemployment
   b) The rate of change of wages
   c) The level of unemployment
   d) The average level of human capital in the labour force
   e) The number of people who are out of the labour force at a given point in time

10. What is the most common avenue for workers entering the state of unemployment?
    a) Workers leaving their jobs
    b) Workers losing their jobs
    c) People entering or re-entering the labour force
    d) Workers retiring from the labour force
    e) None of the above

11. Which of the following statements regarding the group of males and females 15–24 years of age is *true*?
    a) They tend to have the highest average duration of unemployment as well as the highest average incidence rate of unemployment.
    b) They tend to have the lowest average duration of unemployment as well as the lowest average incidence rate of unemployment.
    c) They tend to have the highest average duration of unemployment and the lowest average incidence rate of unemployment.
    d) They tend to have the lowest average duration of unemployment and the highest average incidence rate of unemployment.
    e) The steady state condition always holds for this particular demographic group.

12. Which of the following statements is *true*?
    a) The incidence and duration of male and female unemployment is very similar, as is their overall unemployment rate.
    b) Older workers tend to have relatively short durations of unemployment.
    c) Women have higher rates of labour force participation than men.
    d) Older workers tend to have a relatively high incidence rate for unemployment.
    e) The rate of long-term unemployment, often defined as longer than six months, is particularly high among middle-aged men.

13. The "modified new view" of unemployment that developed over the 1980s holds that:
    a) Most unemployment is short term in nature.
    b) Policies aimed at reducing turnover and employment instability may be more successful in achieving lower levels of unemployment than policies aimed at increasing the number of jobs.
    c) While much unemployment is short term in nature, a significant share of the total length of time spent unemployed is experienced by a significant minority of workers.
    d) All unemployment is structural in nature.
    e) The official unemployment rate is based on the number of workers who are experiencing long-term joblessness.

Answers to Multiple Choice Questions

1. C   This is made explicit in the textbook in the section called "Measuring Unemployment."
2. B   There was a recession in the mid-1970s and in the early 1980s during which unemployment rose considerably. All of the other statements are true. See the subsection entitled "The Canadian Experience."
3. B   See Exhibit 17.1.
4. B   The opposite of response A applies. For response C, it is the gross flows that are larger than the net flows. For response D, the most common transition into unemployment is via layoff. For response E, workers do flow from unemployment to employment.

5. A   See Equation 17.1 and the discussion surrounding it.
6. C   Since response A is true, response C cannot be valid. See Table 17.4.
7. D   Response A refers to the discredited "static view." Response C is the "modified new view." Response B is true under certain circumstances, but it has nothing to do with the "new view."
8. C   See the subsection entitled "The Divergence of the Canada and U.S. Unemployment Rates" Responses A, D, and E are sensible, but do not address the heart of the matter.
9. A   Responses C and E refer to stocks, not flows. Responses B and D have nothing to do with labour force dynamics.
10. B   See Table 17.2 and note how the proportions for the job leavers are the largest.
11. D   See Table 17.4 and compare the figures for the incidence and the durations across age groups.
12. A   See Table 17.4 and compare the figures for the incidence and the durations across age groups.
13. C   Response A is untrue according to this view, as there is a core of structurally unemployed workers. Response E is totally wrong. For response D, this views holds that only some unemployment is structural. Response B refers to the "new view."

CHAPTER 18

Chapter Highlights

This is an extremely long chapter that deals with several alternative views of the nature of unemployment. At the broadest level, the material is divided into three headings: the types (that is, the definitions of the categories) of unemployment, the explanations (the theoretical models) for unemployment, and the role of Canada's unemployment insurance system. This chapter deals essentially with the microeconomic foundations of the macroeconomic phenomenon of unemployment. The fundamental question is why the transactions wage rate fails to reach an equilibrium level at which there is no excess quantity supplied of labour.

Types of Unemployment

1. Frictional Unemployment

Frictional unemployment is associated with the normal turnover of the firm's labour force. The process by which firms are matched with suitable employees and vice versa is a costly, time-consuming process. Much information is required, and searching for jobs while unemployed can be economically useful, provided that the unemployment does not have a long duration. Often, the benefits of job search and the acquisition of information by employers and job seekers will exceed the costs incurred by the spell of frictional unemployment.

2. Structural Unemployment

Structural unemployment is associated with a mismatch between the job vacancies and the job qualifications that unemployed workers have. It is typically considered to be either regional or occupational in nature. This is the most pernicious type of unemployment, as it can generate very long-term unemployment. The remedies include substantial job training to raise human capital levels or encourage job mobility. The adjustment that the affected worker has to make is often very costly.

3. Demand-Deficient Unemployment

Demand-deficient unemployment is the same thing as cyclical unemployment. There is an insufficient level of aggregate demand throughout the economy, which results in a global shortage of available jobs.

4. Seasonal Unemployment

Seasonal unemployment is associated with insufficient demand for labour on a seasonally recurring basis. It resembles demand-deficient unemployment, except that the shortage of jobs is restricted to a certain season of the year. It also has an aspect of structural unemployment in the sense that some seasonally unemployed workers tend to exhibit low regional and occupational mobility, making it difficult for them to qualify for jobs that are available during the off-season.

5. Involuntary Unemployment/Wage Rigidity

This is not a type of unemployment that is an alternative to the other four types mentioned above. Instead, there is an opposition to voluntary versus involuntary unemployment. One is involuntarily unemployed if one is willing to work at the going wage but unable to find employment. One is voluntarily unemployed if one is unwilling to work at the going wage in the face of job openings.

Explanations of Unemployment

These five different approaches to modelling unemployment (job search, implicit contracts, efficiency wages, insider-outsider, and sectoral shifts) go beyond the simple, classical model of supply and demand. A common theme is that involuntary unemployment can persist without putting much downward pressure on the wage. This phenomenon is called wage rigidity in the face of unemployment. These approaches are not totally disjoint, meaning that if one approach applies to a certain situation involving unemployment, it is not the case that none of the others apply. A situation may involve elements of two or more of these approaches. Nevertheless, these five different approaches stress the role of different variables in generating unemployment.

6. Job Search Unemployment

It is a model of the matching process, and can be thought of in terms of a dating game. The key element for this model is imperfect information regarding the availability of job vacancies, the availability of qualified workers, and wages on both sides of the market. The basic idea is that it takes time (and sometimes errors are made) for suitable job matches to occur. The key actor is the jobless worker, who weighs the costs of searching for a job against the benefits in an environment of uncertainty. They are assumed to conduct their search in an optimizing fashion, ending their search and accepting an offer when the marginal expected benefit equals the marginal expected cost. At that point, the worker's reservation wage is equal to or lower than the offered wage. An important implication is that the labour market takes a while to clear, which means that wages do not adjust quickly to equilibrate the quantity of labour supplied and the quantity of labour demanded. This approach can be used to explain why younger workers tend to have shorter durations of both unemployment and employment than older workers: They are sampling the labour market for a suitable match. This approach can be used to explain why quit rates and re-entry rates into the labour market differ across age groups and/or genders, and why they are cyclical. Unemployment insurance is thought to have a major effect of reducing the marginal cost of job search while unemployed, which would raise jobless durations. The quantity and quality of information about the labour market is thought to have a major effect of reducing the marginal benefit of job search while unemployed, which would shorten jobless durations.

7. Implicit Contracts

This is a totally different approach to modelling unemployment. It is a model of existing, long-term employment relationships between firms and workers, and the key element is the risk to these relationships caused by variations in product demand. The unemployment in this model is caused by layoffs. The principal actors are the firms and the groups of workers. The key results are that wages can often be quite rigid, even in the face of variations in product demand, as a result of an agreed-upon risk-sharing arrangement (the implicit contract) between the two parties. The basic idea is that workers purchase a certain degree of job security in the face of lower product demand in exchange for lower wages. In bad times, wages are higher and layoffs are lower than what would be the case in an unfettered labour market. In good times, wages are lower than what would be the case in an unfettered labour market. In that sense, they have purchased some insurance coverage against the risk of layoff.

8. Efficiency Wages

This is a totally different approach to modelling unemployment that was treated in Chapter 10. It is a model of existing, long-term employment relationships between firms and workers, and the key element is the effect of wages on incentives and worker productivity. The unemployment in this model is caused by wages that are substantially above market-clearing levels. The principal actors are the firms and the groups of workers. The key results are that wages can often be quite rigid even in the face of a long queue of job applicants. The basic idea is that firms may prefer to pay above-market wages because doing so enhances worker productivity. It is difficult to test the empirical validity of this approach, in part because according to the theory of marginal revenue product, it is the marginal productivity that determines the wage. According to the efficiency wage theory, it is the wage that determines in part the marginal productivity. It is hard to disentangle these effects.

9. Insider-Outsider

This is another totally different approach to modelling unemployment. It is a model of existing, long-term employment relationships between firms and workers, and the key element is the wage-setting mechanism between the incumbent employees (the "insiders") and the firm. The unemployment in this model is caused by wages that are substantially above market-clearing levels. The principal actors are the firms and two groups of workers: "insiders" and "outsiders." The key results are that wages can often be quite rigid even in the face of a long queue of job applicants. The basic idea is that firms and insiders set wages without any regard for the interests of the outsiders. It is costly for the firm to replace all or some of its existing workforce with new workers recruited from among the ranks of the unemployed. These high turnover costs give incumbent workers bargaining power that they use to raise their wages higher than what would otherwise be the case.

10. Sectoral Shifts and Unemployment

This is again a totally different approach to modelling unemployment. The key element is the shifts in the sectoral composition of demand (by region, industry, or occupation). The costs of adjustment are high, which slows adjustment to these shifts, which generates structural unemployment. Although periods of high dispersion of employment growth across industries are associated with high aggregate unemployment, the empirical evidence in favour of this approach is inconclusive. In Canada, this approach is sometimes applied to the high regional imbalances of unemployment.

Unemployment Insurance and Unemployment

11. Canada's UI System

Compared to most other industrialized countries, the federal unemployment insurance program plays a very important role in the labour market. It is somewhat unique in that seasonal workers qualify for generous benefits on a recurring basis based on short working periods. This subsection consists of the institutional details and various changes that have been made in recent years.

12. Economic Effects of UI

Unemployment insurance (UI) has at least three supply-side effects on labour market behaviour. First, as mentioned above, if an unemployed worker is searching for employment and is covered by UI, the unemployment duration is likely to be prolonged. Second, the provision of UI can also have the effect of raising employment by inducing certain individuals who would otherwise not participate in the labour market to accept jobs that will eventually give rise to entitlement for UI benefits if they are laid off. Third, if one is employed, the cost of being unemployed diminishes in the presence of UI, which may bring about an increase in the incidence of unemployment. Those two effects have opposing influences on labour supply. As far as firm behaviour is concerned, it is argued that the provision of UI increases the incidence of layoffs. As far as interregional mobility is concerned, there is little doubt that it dampens migration from areas of high unemployment.

Helpful Hints

- You should memorize the types of unemployment. This matter is definitional and should thus not pose a great challenge. You can review this material in any textbook of introductory macroeconomics.
- It is quite difficult to grasp the five competing theories of unemployment (search unemployment, implicit contracts, efficiency wages, insider-outsider, and sectoral shifts) and keep them straight. I would suggest trying to focus on the basic ideas that underlie each one and avoid getting bogged down in technical details. Perhaps the key is to remember which variables in each approach play the greatest role in generating unemployment.
- For the job-search approach, the lower diagram in Figure 18.1 is probably easier to understand, although it is economically equivalent to the upper diagram. You should be able to explain why the marginal benefit curve is decreasing and why the marginal cost curve is increasing.
- The technical details of the implicit-contract model, which involve the economics of insurance, are difficult, and the treatment in the textbook is very thorough and involved. You may want to ask the instructor what his/her expectations are. If you are really interested in the economics of insurance markets, intermediate microeconomic textbooks typically treat that topic.
- For the section on efficiency wages, you may want to reread the material contained in Chapter 10 on efficiency wages.

Answers to Odd-Numbered End-of-Chapter Questions

1a. Frictional unemployment occurs as workers and firms take time to find appropriate matches. When workers are on temporary layoff from a firm, this is often considered to be a form of frictional unemployment. The government role in this case is generally thought to be to improve the transmission of information between employers (what jobs they offer) and workers (what skills and abilities they offer).

b. Structural unemployment occurs when there is a mismatch between the jobs that employers have to offer and the skills and abilities that workers can bring. Unlike the previous case, it is not a question of incomplete information. The unemployed workers typically lack the necessary skills, or they are not located in the geographical areas where jobs are available. It is very difficult for governments to deal with structural unemployment. Government policies include retraining and geographical-mobility benefits, as well as regional development policies.

c. Demand-deficient or cyclical unemployment occurs when there is a general shortage of jobs throughout the economy. This occurs only during recessions and depressions. Unlike the previous case of structural unemployment, in which some jobs are available but are going begging, the unemployment cannot be traced to a mismatch of skills or geographical location. The joblessness is pretty pervasive throughout the economy. The government policy response is stimulative demand-management policies.

d. Seasonal unemployment defines itself, but it is a combination of frictional unemployment (because of its temporary nature) and cyclical unemployment (because of a fairly generalized shortfall in jobs during the off-season). Many would argue that the government should not intervene in this case. In Canada, seasonally unemployed workers are typically eligible for generous unemployment benefits.

3. Younger workers typically face a lower degree of dispersion of their wage offers, so the payoff to search is lower. If they are searching for work, they have less to gain by holding out for a better offer, because there is less of a chance that one job offer (just around the corner) is a lot better than the others. We thus expect for them to experience shorter durations of unemployment as they search. On the other hand, one may expect for them to be jobless and thus in the process of searching more frequently than is the case with older workers. They typically try out a number of jobs (this practice is called "job shopping") with a number of different employers, before settling into a longer-term position. The fact that there is not a lot of dispersion in their job offers also means that they have more of an incentive to quit if they are employed, as well as less of an incentive to prolong search for a new job. Note that this question illustrates an important concept: The greater the dispersion of wage offers, the greater the benefits to job search as workers try to find the "dream job."

5. The implicit-contract framework implies a fair degree of wage rigidity over the business cycle. Wages are not renegotiated over the course of the implicit contract. Wages are sensitive to the business cycle at the time of negotiation, however. During recessions, one can expect the contractual wage to be lower than what would otherwise be the case. During expansions, one may expect the opposite. The wage is much more stable than it is in the situation depicted in Figure 18.3a, which involves a spot market (also called the "Walrasian auction market") for labour where wages are renegotiated continuously between individual workers and employers in order to clear the market instantaneously. That type of pay mechanism yields productive efficiency, as wages are always equal to the marginal revenue product. The implicit-contract framework also implies that firms will hoard labour during downturns in demand. This means that they will retain workers whose marginal revenue product is below the wage level. To compensate for the loss incurred over those periods, they will pay their employees less than their marginal revenue product during good times. One of the reasons why one sometimes sees layoffs rather than wage reductions is due to the reservation wage. If the reservation wage were very low, the optimal contract would have a rigid wage and a fixed level of employment (no layoffs). Given a positive reservation wage, the factor of risk sharing, and the factor of productive efficiency, a optimal contract will have a provision for layoffs, but not for wage reductions.

7. There are basically four parameters of any unemployment insurance program that affect the benefit levels and structure and have an impact on the behaviour of recipients as well as firms. They are the following:
i) The replacement ratio (the ratio of benefits to prior earnings, which are subject to a ceiling of maximum-insurable earnings)

ii) The eligibility requirements in terms of employment (for how long a period of time one must contribute in order to draw benefits)

iii) The coverage of the regime (there are a few sectors, such as agriculture, in which workers do not contribute and they have no chance of drawing benefits)

iv) The maximum duration of time during which benefits may be drawn

These four facets make unemployment insurance a very rich and substantive topic with several applications to labour market analysis.

The first effect of unemployment insurance (UI) on labour market behaviour concerns job search behaviour. According to this approach, one would expect the provision of UI benefits to raise the durations of unemployment, because UI subsidizes job search by lowering its cost. Note that within limits, this is thought to be economically efficient as it can lead to more appropriate job matches between workers and employers. Nevertheless, the fact that much research has indicated that a substantial portion of unemployed workers exit unemployment very near the point in time in which their benefits are exhausted indicates that this function of UI is abused somewhat, and that extending the duration of benefits for long time periods is probably undesirable. The empirical research on this point is conclusive: UI serves to prolong unemployment durations.

UI also has important effects on the behaviour of firms. The basic idea is that because UI makes layoffs less costly for the workers, it indirectly lowers the labour cost of the employer. If layoffs and employment instability are a significant risk involved with the job, the employer may be forced to make compensation of some kind to the workforce in order to accept that disamenity (like a compensating differential). With the provision of UI benefits, however, some of this cost is borne by the UI system, so the employer is under less pressure to pay either higher wages or her own unemployment compensation to her workers. This can be expected to increase the incidence of layoffs compared to a situation with no public UI program. One would expect larger variations in employment in response to cyclical and seasonal fluctuations in demand.

Another economic effect of UI is related to the qualification or entry effect. Those with strong labour force attachment are more likely to reduce the amount of time that they work, as was analysed in the chapter on labour supply. This does not mean that they quit their job, but that they may work fewer weeks per year. On the other hand, workers with low labour force attachment are likely to supply more labour to the market — especially by entering seasonal occupations — in order to qualify for UI benefits in the future. Total employment may increase or decrease, but labour force participation is expected to increase, as is unemployment. The textbook discusses some studies that are very particular to Canada's UI system. The basic idea is that in regions where the duration of benefits is extended to 36 weeks, and the eligibility requirements are limited to 12 weeks of qualifying employment experience, employers and employees have adjusted the employment patterns to take maximum advantage of the UI program. This means that there are many very short-term jobs that are rotated among a pool of workers. When they qualify for UI benefits, the job ends, and they collect UI benefits during the lengthy off-season period.

The final effect of UI is on interregional mobility. Most analysts agree that the structure of UI benefits in Canada has retarded interregional mobility and discouraged workers from leaving areas with depressed economies.

Answers to Odd-Numbered End-of-Chapter Problems

1. Frictional unemployment is described near the beginning of the chapter. The basic idea is that matching the right person for the right job yields productivity benefits that are usually worth incurring a cost in the form of frictional unemployment. Provided that it is not too long, job search can be a very productive activity. Temporary layoffs can also be efficient in the sense that production and productivity are enhanced by the worker enduring a spell of unemployment rather than leaving the firm permanently. In the latter case, the worker would relocate to another job and have to be retrained, and her replacement would have to be retrained. It is quite possible that both workers were well matched to their previous jobs before the temporary layoff occurred.

3. One may expect for the landless labourer to be paid an hourly wage. Since this worker has no other source of subsistence, the employer has an incentive to pay a wage that is high enough to allow the worker to obtain a proper diet. This nutritional efficiency wage raises the worker's productivity, and hence, this wage supplement pays for itself as far as the employer is concerned. One may expect a fairly steep Q = g(W,L) function. This wage, however, is above the competitive level and may generate some unemployment. The worker who has his/her own farm probably has an adequate source of nutrition, and so the employer need not worry about designing a compensation scheme that takes account of that factor. The employer is more likely to compensate directly according to marginal revenue product. This may involve a piece-rate compensation scheme. This piece rate is likely to be set by supply-and-demand forces without many constraints. Unemployment of these types of workers is likely to be lower.

5a. The range of this function is from 0 to 30. It is a constant function with a value of 0 for wages between $0 and $8. For wages between $8 and $30, it is an increasing function of the wage in the form of a parabola that has a concave, downward shape. The slope is 3 - W /10 (see Problem 5b), which means that at $8, the slope is 2.2, and at $30, the slope is 0. This production function hits its maximum value at W = $30. For wages higher than that, production remains fixed at 30. This implies that increases in the wage above $30 will not raise productivity. In the middle segment, increases in the wage rate do elicit greater levels of effort, but at a slower and slower rate of increase as the wage increases.

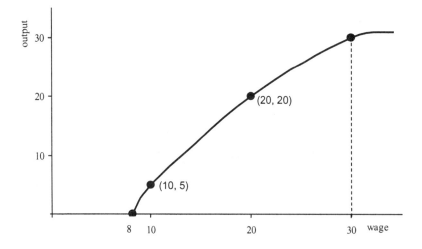

b. Apply the profit-maximization condition that (delta Q / delta W) = Q / W. The change in Q divided by the change in W is given: 3 - W / 10. Substitute the three potential values for W into that equation for the equilibrium. When W = $10, we have a value of 2 for the slope, and a value of 1 / 2 for the ratio because Q = -20 + 30 - 100 / 20 = 5. Since there is an inequality, $10 cannot be the profit-maximizing value for the wage. When W = $30, we have a value of 0 for the slope (we already established that result), and a value of 5 / 6 for the ratio because Q = -20 + 90 - 900 / 20 = 25. Since there is an inequality, $30 cannot be the profit-maximizing value for the wage. When W = $20, we have a value of 1 for the slope, and a value of 1 for the ratio because Q = -20 + 60 - 400 / 20 = 20. Since there is equality, $20 is the profit-maximizing value for the wage. This means that if wages are changed to any other value, profits will decrease. For instance, if they are lowered, the labour costs fall, but the productivity falls by even more.

7a. Any factor that improves the flow of information regarding the availability of jobs will probably raise the marginal benefit of job search, given by a and b. When labour market conditions are favourable (unfavourable), the benefits to job search increase (decrease). As the dispersion in the wage/job offers rises, the benefits to job search rise.

b. The provision of unemployment insurance lowers the marginal cost of job search, which is denoted by c and d. The provision of portable pensions also lowers the marginal cost of job search. See the subsection in the textbook labelled "Factors Determining Optimal Search."

c. Setting the marginal benefit of job search equal to the marginal cost, substituting in the given values, and solving the equation yields a value of 15 weeks.

d. Solving the equation algebraically yields W* = (a - c) / (d - b). If d increases, W* falls, and the optimal search period becomes shorter. If b increases, W* rises, and the optimal search period becomes longer. If either the marginal cost increases, through the d parameter, or the marginal benefit decreases, through the b parameter multiplied by -1, it does not pay to search for as long as what was previously the case.

9. The basic question is whether the baker prefers to have a stable wage that is somewhat lower than the average, or the expected value of the wage, that he/she would earn given that the wage is contingent on the weather. In order to answer this question, we have to compare the utility of the average wage to the average utility that is obtained when the worker can expect to receive the high wage during good times and the low wage during bad times. For the first case, the baker is guaranteed a wage of $9.50 at all times, so the value of the utility function is the square root of 9.5, or 3.1. For the second case, when times are good, the wage is $16, which gives a value for the utility function of 4. When times are bad, the wage is $4, which gives a value for the utility function of 2. Since both of these outcomes are equally likely, with a probability of 0.5 each, on average the utility value is (4 + 2) / 2 = 3. Compare the value of 3 to 3.1, and we conclude that the baker is better off receiving a wage of $ 9.50 with no risk than he/she is receiving a wage that averages out to $10, but involves an element of risk. That risk involves the fact that in the short run, there could well be a long spell of bad times for which he/she is paid $4.

Multiple Choice Questions

1. Which of the following types of unemployment is probably the most difficult for governments to resolve?
   a) Frictional unemployment
   b) Structural unemployment
   c) Demand-deficient unemployment
   d) Seasonal unemployment
   e) Voluntary unemployment

2. Which of the following statements is *false*?
   a) Frictional unemployment can take the form of temporary layoffs.
   b) It is always desirable to lower frictional unemployment.
   c) In instances of structural unemployment, it is difficult to ascertain whether a downturn is permanent or temporary.
   d) Seasonal unemployment is sometimes considered to be a type of frictional unemployment.
   e) Individuals are involuntarily unemployed if they are willing to work at the going wage rate but cannot find work.

3. Which of the following statements is *false*?
   a) In the search unemployment model, both employers and employees operate in a climate of imperfect information.
   b) Job search is a microeconomic decision.
   c) Individuals search in optimal fashion weighing the costs of continuing search against the benefits of continuing search.
   d) In the job-search model, aggregate demand is always insufficient to provide enough jobs.
   e) The search for jobs and the acquisition of information consumes time and economic resources.

4. Which of the following statements is *false*?
   a) The job-search framework illustrates structural unemployment.
   b) Given imperfect information in the labour market, it does not clear very fast, so there can be involuntary unemployment.
   c) Given imperfect information in the labour market, some workers may temporarily opt to be unemployed.
   d) Given imperfect information in the labour market, wage rates will vary even if the workers and their jobs are very similar.
   e) Employers may possess, under imperfect information, some monopsony power to set wages in the short run even if the market is competitive.

5. Which of the following factors will *not* affect the optimal job-search behaviour?
   a) The dispersion of wage offers
   b) The expected duration of new jobs
   c) The overall state of the market
   d) The dissemination of information about wages and job opportunities
   e) The sunk cost of job search that the worker has already incurred

6. Which of the following groups of workers is not likely to engage in job search while already holding a job?
    a) Full-time workers
    b) Women
    c) Less-educated workers
    d) Those in managerial, professional, and service occupations
    e) None of the above

7. Which of the following statements is *false*?
    a) Implicit-contract theory seeks to explain why firms often resort to layoffs rather than wage cuts given adverse conditions in the product market.
    b) Implicit-contract theory applies to situations in which there is a long-run attachment between firms and workers.
    c) Implicit-contract theory seeks to explain why workers may quit jobs or remain unemployed rather than take the first job that is offered.
    d) In implicit-contract theory, wages are rigid because otherwise the workers would find the risk of fluctuating wages too great.
    e) In implicit-contract theory, the average wage paid over the long term is somewhat lower than the average level that would be paid in a competitive labour market.

8. Which of the following statements is *false*?
    a) Efficiency wages can be used to explain wage rigidity when there is market pressure for a wage cut.
    b) There is unemployment at the efficiency wage.
    c) Wages are higher than the competitive level, but they pay for themselves by raising productivity.
    d) In the efficiency wage model, wage setting is determined by bargaining between the employer and the employees with little regard for the welfare of unemployed workers.
    e) In markets where there is a higher unemployment rate, wages are lower because the penalty for shirking — dismissal — is already high.

9. Which of the following statements is *true*?
    a) In the efficiency wage model, the firm selects the employment level taking the wage as given.
    b) In the efficiency wage model, the firm selects the wage level taking the employment level as given.
    c) In the efficiency wage model, the firm selects the employment level and the wage level simultaneously.
    d) In the efficiency wage model, the firm negotiates the wage level with a group of its current workers, without regard for the welfare of laid-off workers.
    e) In the efficiency wage model, the firm is able to exploit monopsony power so that it pays a wage below the competitive level.

10. Which of the following statements regarding unemployment is *true*?
    a) Only inefficient labour markets are characterized by unemployment.
    b) Unemployment can typically be rectified by a downward wage adjustment because there is an excess quantity supplied of labour.
    c) While there are several different types of unemployment, after all economic factors have been taken into account, only one type really matters.
    d) If the labour market is competitive, unemployment will disappear in the long run.
    e) Even if the labour market is competitive, and the labour supply is approximately in balance with labour demand, there will be jobless workers.

11. According to the sectoral-shift hypothesis, which of the following statements is *true*?
    a) Unemployment can be generated by changes in the composition of demand among sectors, occupations, or regions.
    b) Unemployment can be generated by shifts in labour supply patterns, such as immigration, the baby boom, and retirement trends.
    c) Unemployment can be generated by rigid wages that are systematically above the competitive level.
    d) Unemployment can be generated by risk-averse workers acting in a climate of imperfect information.
    e) None of the above.

12. What is one of the more unique features of Canada's unemployment insurance system?
    a) It pays indemnities to workers who are laid off during recessions.
    b) The benefits paid are taxable.
    c) Workers who are seasonally unemployed on a recurring basis are entitled to benefits.
    d) It is the most generous system in the industrialized world.
    e) The overall generosity was reduced over the 1990s.

13. Unemployment insurance can affect unemployment in all of the following ways <u>except</u> which?
    a) Prolonging the jobless durations of unemployed workers
    b) Inducing some employed workers to become unemployed in order to search for a better job
    c) Reducing the incentive of workers in high-unemployment regions to migrate to lower-unemployment regions
    d) Encouraging workers who would otherwise be out of the labour force to enter the labour force in order to gain eligibility for UI benefits
    e) Reducing the incentive for employers having variable product-demand conditions from laying off workers

14. Which of the following factors is thought to play the greatest role in explaining the U.S.-Canada unemployment gap?
    a) The employment protection regulations
    b) The unemployment insurance system
    c) The minimum wage levels
    d) The degree of unionization
    e) None of the above

15. All of the following are important parameters of the Canada's UI system <u>except</u> which?
    a) The experience rating
    b) The replacement ratio
    c) The entry requirements regarding prior employment
    d) The maximum duration of benefits payable
    e) The contribution rate

Answers to Multiple Choice Questions

1. B   See the "Chapter Highlights" section above. Often, substantial job retraining or long-distance geographical mobility is required. The affected workers are often low skilled.
2. B   Some level of frictional unemployment is desirable in order to obtain suitable job matches between firms and workers. Statements B, C, and D are true and are made explicit in the textbook. Response E is true by definition.
3. D   Response D applies to demand-deficient unemployment, which does not necessarily apply to a jobless worker who is searching. The key variable is imperfect information.
4. A   A worker engaged in job search could be seasonally, structurally, cyclically, or frictionally unemployed. Statements B, C, D, and E are made explicit in the textbook in the subsection on job-search theory.
5. E   There may be a sunk cost of job search, but it is the marginal cost and the marginal benefit of job search that matter. All of the other statements are true.
6. D   For these occupations, the type of contacts and information that are required in order to find a suitable new job is probably more available while they are employed in the profession or occupation.
7. C   Response C pertains to the job-search approach. The other responses are made explicit in the textbook in the subsection on implicit-contract theory.
8. D   This statement applies to the insider-outsider theory. The other responses are made explicit in the textbook in the subsection on the efficiency wage theory.
9. C   Response D refers to the insider-outsider approach. For response E, monopsony implies a lower than competitive wage, while the efficiency wage theory implies a higher than competitive wage.
10. E   This point is made explicit in the textbook near the beginning of the chapter. Response B is incorrect in many situations for which the equilibrium wage is above the competitive level wage. All of the other statements are false.
11. A   Response B is totally incorrect. Response C applies to a number of other theories, such as the efficiency wage approach. Response D mixes implicit-contract theory with job-search theory.
12. C   Response D is false, while responses A, B, and E apply to the UI regimes of many nations, including Canada's.
13. E   UI increases the incentive for employers to lay off workers when demand conditions are seasonal or cyclical.
14. B   The point is made in the textbook subsection on labour supply.
15. A   See the subsection entitled "Canada's UI System." The premiums are never experience rated.

CHAPTER 19

Chapter Highlights

This chapter deals with the interface between the aggregate labour market and the macro economy, and has a strong macroeconomic flavour. The central thrust is the relationship between aggregate wage inflation, aggregate price inflation, and the unemployment rate.

1.   Canadian Experience

This section consists of a sketch of post-war macroeconomic history in Canada. A major turning point was the stagflationary period of the early 1970s, during which high unemployment coincided with high inflation. This phase resulted in part from the first oil price shock in 1973. Until that period, it was thought that there was typically a trade-off between inflation and the unemployment rate. At the end of the 1970s, inflation was high, and inflationary expectations were quite entrenched. These expectations had an impact on economic behaviour. The restrictive monetary policy of the early 1980s and early 1990s was designed to reduce inflation, but it helped bring on steep recessions during which unemployment rose to very high levels. The nature of the fundamental relationship between inflation and unemployment is somewhat unknown and has been a dominant policy concern for the past four decades.

2.   Determinants of Wage Changes

The analysis commences with the well-known Phillips curve, which specifies a negative relationship between wage inflation and the unemployment rate. It has micro foundations that are oriented around supply-and-demand analysis of the labour market. The unemployment rate is considered to be a measure of the overall excess demand or supply in the aggregate labour market; excess demand is associated with low unemployment rates, while excess supply corresponds to high unemployment rates. There is thus an inverse relationship between the excess demand for labour and the unemployment rate, as indicated in Equation 19.6. Equation 19.7 is the simplest case of the Phillips curve. When the level of excess demand or excess supply in the labour market is zero, there is no pressure on wages, and the rate of wage inflation therefore is zero. In this situation, the rate of unemployment is the natural rate denoted by U^* in the textbook, and the aggregate labour market is in equilibrium. Note, however, that individual labour markets (pertaining to a certain region, industry, or occupation) need not be in equilibrium.

U^* is considered to be a long-run equilibrium for the rate of unemployment, which is obtained when aggregate supply equals aggregate demand in the product market. Unless U^* is constant at all times, which is certainly not the case, the most appropriate measure of aggregate excess demand for labour is not simply the actual unemployment rate U. Instead, it is the difference between the observed and the natural rates of unemployment, with $U > U^*$ implying excess supply of labour (followed by lower wage inflation), and $U^* > U$ implying excess demand for labour (followed by higher wage inflation). The first modification from the simplest case of the Phillips curve appears in Equation 19.8. An increase in U^* shifts the Phillips curve upward, while a decrease shifts it downward.

For the second modification of the Phillips curve, the expected rate of inflation is taken into account. If both employers and employees expect prices to increase, they will adjust wage changes upward by the amount of expected inflation in order to achieve the desired change in real wages. The equation for the expectations-augmented Phillips curve is presented in Equation 19.9. Increases in expected inflation shift the Phillips curve vertically upward because both the labour demand and the labour supply functions shift upward by the anticipated increase in the price level. The basic idea is that at a given unemployment level, there is now a higher rate of wage inflation as nominal wages rise to cover the higher expected inflation. Nominal wages eventually adjust to generate constant real wages. In essence, these shifts of the short-run Phillips curve will trace out a vertical long-run Phillips curve situated at the natural rate of unemployment U*. There is a short-run trade-off between the rate of wage inflation and the unemployment rate, as one moves along a short-run Phillips curve. This short-run Phillips curve will shift upwards, however, if there is an increase in the expected rate of price inflation. There is no long-run trade-off between inflation and unemployment.

The expectations-augmented Phillips curve reflects many possible influences on the rate of wage inflation that are not specified in the equation. The only variables that are specified in the equation are the state of excess demand in the labour market (U - U*) and the anticipated rate of output price inflation. Productivity growth is an important variable and, in the long run, is the primary driver of real wages. If the rate of growth in real wages is out of sync with the rate of productivity growth, then there is a change in the share of national income received by capital and labour.

3.   Empirical Evidence

There are a number of difficulties involved in using the aggregate rate of wage inflation as a measure of the excess demand in the labour market. There are thus many studies that use less aggregated data on labour contracts (at the firm or industry level) rather than data for the entire labour market. Many studies involve estimation of the expectations-augmented Phillips curve. The results generally suggest that the short-run Phillips curve is fairly flat for high levels of unemployment, meaning that a lower wage-inflation rate is associated with a significant rise in unemployment. The curve is non-linear, which means that the trade-off is not constant. The expected rate of inflation is found to play an important role, which lends support to the view that, in the long run, the trade-off between wage inflation and the unemployment rate is weak.

4.   Price Inflation and Unemployment

This section explains the link between the standard Phillips curve, which specifies the relationship between wage inflation and the unemployment rate, and a derived Phillips curve, which specifies the relationship between price inflation and the unemployment rate. To derive this curve, it is necessary to consider the interface between the labour market and the goods-and-services market. The long-run Phillips curve in price-inflation/unemployment space is vertical at the natural rate of unemployment. In order to arrive at this equilibrium (that is, where the actual rate of unemployment = the natural rate of unemployment), the actual rate of price inflation must equal the expected rate of price inflation. U* is sometimes called the NAIRU, or the non-accelerating inflation rate of unemployment.

5.   Challenges to the Natural-Rate Hypothesis

In the mid-1970s, the "natural-rate" approach of the Phillips curve was widely accepted. The macroeconomic performance in much of Western Europe during the 1980s led many analysts to question this natural-rate paradigm, however. Even in the face of economic growth, unemployment rates remained stubbornly high. Inflation was approximately stable over this period, yet there was a trend toward rising unemployment. In other words, a higher and higher rate of unemployment was associated with a stable inflation rate. This scenario is inconsistent with the prediction of the natural-rate paradigm that unemployment should have been roughly stable. According to this persistence of unemployment approach, the natural rate of unemployment was rising, and this might have been caused by a rising actual rate of unemployment. In the natural-rate paradigm, U^* can change due to factors such as demography or labour market policy. In the persistence paradigm, changes in U can cause changes in U^*. In other words, if some external shock causes the actual rate of unemployment to rise, some of this effect is translated into a permanent shock that becomes embedded in the natural rate of unemployment U^*. If this persistence mechanism applies, this finding has very negative implications for macroeconomic stabilization policy, because the cost of a reduction in inflation (through tight monetary policy, for example) is no longer a temporary rise in the unemployment rate (as the conventional Phillips-curve analysis would predict), but rather a permanent rise in it.

The empirical evidence on the validity of this persistence, or hysteresis, approach is mixed. The evidence in favour is fairly strong for Europe in the 1980s, which might be associated with the rise in long-term unemployment. Canadian studies almost uniformly reject this persistence approach.

6. Anti-Inflation Policy

The fundamental challenge of stabilization policy or demand-management policy is to bring about as low an unemployment rate as possible without triggering much of a rise in the inflation rate. According to the natural-rate paradigm, there is a trade-off between inflation and unemployment in the short run but not in the long run. If this applies, then attempting to reach lower levels of unemployment in exchange for higher rates of inflation is not a feasible option in the long run. The empirical evidence seems to support the conjecture that the natural-rate paradigm applies to the labour market in the U.S. By definition, if the demand-management policy reduces the actual unemployment rate U below U^*, we expect the inflation rate to accelerate. If the natural rate, or the NAIRU (non-accelerating inflation rate of unemployment), is fairly high, this implies that the labour market is essentially stuck with a high long-run equilibrium unemployment rate. It is in this context that policies designed to reduce structural unemployment, such as social insurance reform, job retraining, improving labour market information, and mobility assistance, may be considered.

Recent macroeconomic experience in Canada suggests that the trade-off between inflation and unemployment is very unfavourable at low rates of inflation. For example, the cost of reducing the inflation from 3% to 1% is much higher in terms of increased unemployment than the cost of reducing unemployment from 8% to 6%.

The term "incomes policies" refers to a wide range of programs that intervene in the wage-setting activities in order to reduce the rate of inflation that corresponds to a given rate of unemployment. If they are successful, it may be possible to lower the unemployment rate without triggering more inflation. In contemporary North America, they currently do not figure in the macroeconomic policy debate.

Disinflation via demand restraint (either restrictive monetary or fiscal policies) is a very costly policy to pursue because of the persistence of inflation and inflationary expectations. Wringing inflation out of the macro economy through leftward shifts in aggregate demand often exacts a high price in the form of unemployment because nominal wages are very inflexible, and often, real wages are fairly inflexible. If wages and prices were more responsive to downward shifts in product demand and labour demand, inflation could be reduced without massive increases in unemployment. Some analysts have recommended that the institutional features of wage determination could be reformed in order to bring about greater wage flexibility in the face of negative shocks, which would have positive impact on employment.

Helpful Hints

- The outline of macroeconomic history near the beginning of the chapter is fascinating and informative. It illustrates the major principles of basic macroeconomics in a way that most people can relate to.
- A review of a topic of intermediate macroeconomic theory — the functioning of the aggregate labour market — would be useful for this chapter. In an intermediate macro textbook, search for a chapter treating the labour market.
- There are essentially two versions of the Phillips curve that are laid out in this chapter. The simplest case has either U or U - U* as the variables on the right side of the equation. There is no long-run Phillips curve in this case. The other case is the expectations-augmented Phillips curve, which has the expected rate of price inflation appended as an additive term. That is the equation that is associated with the "natural-rate" view of the Phillips curve, and that is the case that generates the short-run and the long-run versions of Phillips curves. No Phillips-curve-type equation was presented for the persistence, or hysteresis, approach.
- The derivation of the simplest the version of the Phillips curve in Equations 19.2 to 19.7 is not that hard, and is intuitive. This is a good illustration of the micro foundations to macro.
- The derivation of the expectations-augmented Phillips curve is a bit difficult, but the end result is straightforward and intuitive.
- The derivation of the Phillips curve specifying the relationship between price inflation and the unemployment rate is difficult.
- The natural rate of unemployment U* is also called the NAIRU. This is the long-term equilibrium for the unemployment rate, and the level of unemployment that exists at the long-run aggregate supply curve. This is the rate of unemployment that exists when the inflation rate is stable and in line with expectations. It is not the case that inflation = 0.
- The subsection on the U.S. economic performance in the 1990s is very interesting and relevant. It explains a very recent period of economic history that had a strong and positive effect on the Canadian economy.
- A good essay-type question would involve an explanation of the evolution of demand-management policy since the 1960s. According to the simple Phillips-curve analysis, the best way to lower unemployment is to stimulate the economy. A small price must be paid in the form of higher price inflation. This view was jettisoned in favour of the natural-rate hypothesis, which posits that there is no long-run trade-off to be had. The lowest rate of unemployment that was attainable was U*. Once this weakness of conventional demand-management policies became apparent, the name of the game was to develop new policies designed to reduce U*. If they are successful, then demand-management policies can be used to stabilize that actual unemployment rate U to U*, thus obtaining price stability. The basic concept is that by lowering U*, the trade-off between inflation and unemployment becomes more favourable.

Answers to Odd-Numbered End-of-Chapter Questions

1. The rate of increase for aggregate wages is the weighted average of the rate of increase (or decrease) for wages in many thousands of labour markets throughout the economy. One expects

most labour markets to be in a state of disequilibrium, in which the number of vacancies is not matched by the number of qualified candidates seeking employment in each market. Wages are therefore fluctuating. Wages may be increasing in some markets where there is excess demand for labour, while decreasing in others where there is excess supply of labour. The unemployment rate is an aggregation — a summary statistic like an average — for the overall state of excess demand — either positive or negative — throughout the economy. Given this interpretation, one applies the simple law of demand to derive the Phillips curve. This law states that there is an inverse relation between the degree of excess quantity demanded for any good/service and its price (in this case, the wage rate).

This theory is attributed to Lipsey's classic work, and is explained on pages 578 and 579.

3. This is also a good question. If one expected the Phillips curve to be a straight line, the U variable would appear in linear form with a negative coefficient. Graphically, the reciprocal form $1 / U$ has a hyperbolic shape and becomes flatter as the unemployment rate increases. The slope is not constant, as the trade-off varies according to the level of unemployment. Economically, this means that to reduce inflation to very low levels requires a very large increase in unemployment. To reduce unemployment to very low levels requires a tremendous increase in the inflation rate. As one moves from left to right, the trade-off of higher unemployment in exchange for lower inflation becomes less and less favourable. Why may this be the case? The basic idea is that there is an asymmetry about the equilibrium wage. If there is an excess demand for labour, wages and inflation will rise, but if there is an excess supply of labour, wages (and prices) will not adjust much. In order to achieve a wage reduction to eliminate the excess supply of labour, one requires very adverse labour market conditions.

    A positive sign to the variable indicates an inverse relationship. The derivative of $1 / U$ is $-1 / U^* * 2$, which is always a negative quantity. Without appealing to calculus, as the denominator of a quotient increases, the quotient itself decreases.

5. Non-competitive forces, such as monopolies in product markets and unions in labour markets, can lead to wage and price inflation, but normally we would expect for them to cause product prices and/or wages to be at a higher *level* than they would be if the product and labour markets were perfectly competitive. In other words, we would expect to see unduly high but stable prices for goods and services and unduly high but stable wages.

    We would expect these factors to have an impact on price and wage inflation if there is a major *change* in the structure and functioning of labour markets that occurs. If the trade-off between wage inflation and unemployment became less favourable during the 1970s and the 1980s, one possible reason would lie in an increase in the rate of unionization and/or an increase in the concentration of product markets. We are searching for ways in which the relationship between the excess demand and/or excess supply of labour — which is measured in the aggregate unemployment rate — and wage inflation changed over this period. While imperfections and monopolies in output markets and input markets may make the *level* of unemployment higher than what would otherwise be the case, it does not explain how the relationship mentioned above might have been modified over this period. The only way in which these forces can worsen inflation is if the degree of market power is intensified.

1a.

$$Q'(L) = bAL^{b-1} K^{1-b} = bA(L^{-1} L) L^{b-1} K^{1-b} = bL^{-1} AL^b K^{1-b} = \frac{(bQ)}{L}$$

b. When the labour market is in equilibrium, and both the product market and the labour markets are in equilibrium, $W = VMP = MP_L * P = b (Q / L) * P$, where W denotes the wage, VMP denotes the value of the marginal product of labour, P denotes the product price, and MP_L denotes the marginal product of labour. Now multiply both sides by L in order to obtain $W*L = b*Q*P$. Labour's remuneration is $W*L$, and the value of the total product (and the value of aggregate income) is $Q*P$, so b represents the share of total income received by labour. This result only occurs if the technology of production is characterized by constant returns to scale, which is the case this time, as the exponents of b and 1 - b sum to unity.

c. This question as it appears is incorrect. The expression should read: (dW/dt) / W - (dP/dt) / P = (dA/dt) / A + (db/dt) / b. In words, the growth rate for wages - the growth rate for b = the growth rate for A minus the growth rate for b.

First set the wage equal to the VMP. Then take logarithms of both sides of the equation.

$$W = \frac{bQP}{L} = \frac{bAL^b K^{1-b} P}{L} = bAL^{b-1} K^{1-b} P$$
$$\log W = \log b + \log A + (b-1) \log L + (1-b) \log K + \log P$$

The final step is to differentiate that expression with respect to time. Due to the optimization process in a long-run equilibrium process, we can treat the level of labour input and capital input as fixed values, so the derivatives of those two terms are zero. The derivatives of log W, log b, log A, and log P are W-hat, b-hat, A-hat, and P-hat, respectively. Subtract b-hat from both sides of that equation in order to obtain the desired result. What this equation means is that the rate of growth in real wages (on the left side of the equation) has to be aligned with the rate of growth of the productivity of labour, which is determined by the parameters b and A. The rate of growth in real wages is equal to the rate of growth of nominal wages minus the rate of growth of prices.

d. Given these constant returns to scale technology, if productivity increases, labour's share will remain the same, at b. The gains to productivity will always be divided into a share of b accruing to labour and a share of 1 - b accruing to capital.

3. See pages 584–585. An increase in labour demand causes an increase in the price level, which causes a leftward shift in labour supply as workers seek to maintain real wages, which causes an increase in the wage rate and an upward shift in the Phillips curve. At first, the initial increase in aggregate demand causes the price level to increase, which causes the demand for labour to increase in many individual labour markets. The number of vacancies relative to the number of job seekers increases, and unemployment should fall in the short run. So far, this is the Keynesian scenario. Workers do not remain content for long, however, and as soon as they ask for higher wages to compensate them for the increased cost of living, this initial positive effect on employment is nullified. They demand higher nominal reservation wages, which shifts the labour supply curve to the left. The Phillips curve shifts upward. At each and every possible unemployment rate, there is a higher rate of wage increase than was previously the case. Workers

almost always ask for wage increases to compensate them for inflation, and asking wages are often affected by wage norms elsewhere in the economy. In other words, what matters to employees and employers are relative wages and real wages, and nominal wages matter only in the short run.

5. As lambda approaches unity, asking wages rise in perfect tandem with expected price inflation. In order to maintain a stable unemployment rate over the long term, wages have to rise by the same percentage as prices do. Once the Phillips curve shifts upward, it is possible that one could temporarily move up the new short-run Phillips curve and lower unemployment by accepting higher wage inflation. If lambda is equal to one half, then the asking wage increases by only half as much as the expected inflation rate. In this case, the Phillips curve does shift upward from the case where lambda is zero, but only by half as much as the previous case. The same rate of unemployment can be achieved at a higher wage inflation rate than in the case in which lambda is zero, but at a lower wage inflation rate than the case where lambda is unity.

7a. Insert these values into the Phillips curve equation. One obtains 2.5 + 9 - 1.5 = 10%.
  b. Insert these values into the Phillips curve equation. One obtains 2.5 + 9 - 2.5 = 9%. Compared to the prior case, a much higher unemployment rate yields a slightly lower wage-inflation rate.
  c. Insert these values into the Phillips curve equation. One obtains 2.5 + 4.5 - 1.5 = 5.5%. Most of the decrease in inflationary expectations is translated into a lower wage-inflation rate compared to case a.
  d. The coefficient of 0.9 implies that the asking wage of workers increases by almost as much as their expectations for inflation. Apparently, they are willing to accept slightly lower real wages in the event of inflation — slightly less than full escalation of wages.
  e. It is negative, as one would expect. This means that it has a negative slope. The economic intuition is that a higher (lower) unemployment rate is associated with many (few) job seekers relative to vacancies, which generates negative (positive) pressure on wages.
  f. See Figure 19.3. An increase in inflationary expectations should shift the Phillips curve upward, which means to each possible unemployment rate now corresponds a higher wage inflation rate.
  g. Substituting the short-run aggregate-price equation into the short-run Phillips curve equation gives

$$\widetilde{W} = 2.5 + 0.9 \, [2 - 0.25 \, U + 1.1 \, \widetilde{W}] - 0.25 \, U$$

The wage terms cancel (approximately), and by solving for U, one obtains a natural unemployment rate of about 9%. The long-run Phillips curve is vertical at this rate of unemployment.

Multiple Choice Questions

1. Which of the following gives the basis (the foundation) for the Phillips curve?
    a) A positive relationship between the wage change and the excess of job vacancies over unemployment
    b) A positive relationship between price inflation and wage inflation
    c) A gap between the natural rate of unemployment and the actual rate of unemployment
    d) A positive relationship between unemployment and job vacancies
    e) A negative relationship between aggregate excess demand and unemployment

Labour Market Economics, Fifth Edition

2. Which of the following statements is *false*?
   a) The aggregate labour market is in equilibrium when the unemployment rate is equal to the job vacancy rate.
   b) Wages can often fall less rapidly in response to excess supply of labour than they rise in response to excess demand of labour.
   c) The natural unemployment rate depends on the job-search behaviour of workers and the efficiency of the employer-employee matching process.
   d) In the Phillips-curve model, the natural rate of unemployment depends on the stage of the business cycle.
   e) The rate of wage change is a function of the excess demand for labour.

3. All of the following are elements of the Phillips curve *except* which element?
   a) The relationship between wage changes and excess demand for labour
   b) The relationship between excess demand and unemployment
   c) The relationship between wage inflation and price inflation
   d) The relationship between unemployment and job vacancies
   e) None of the above

4. The heyday for the Phillips-curve theory was the 1960s, but it has lost favour in more recent times. All of the following are reasons *except* which reason?
   a) It could not account for the simultaneous upward drift of prices, wages, and unemployment during the 1970s.
   b) It could not account for a decline in the natural rate of unemployment.
   c) Major demographic and structural changes occurred in labour markets.
   d) The Phillips-curve theory did not properly account for inflationary expectations.
   e) It could not account for the phenomenon of stagflation.

5. Which of the following statements concerning the expectations-augmented Phillips curve is *false*?
   a) There is no long-run trade-off between wage inflation and unemployment.
   b) When inflationary expectations are realized over a long period, the equilibrium occurs at the natural rate of unemployment.
   c) When inflationary expectations change, the Phillips curve shifts upward.
   d) When wage inflation occurs, the Phillips curve shifts upward.
   e) The long-run Phillips curve is vertical.

6. The version of the Phillips-curve model that features the natural rate of unemployment holds that:
   a) There is no long-run trade-off between either wage inflation or price inflation and unemployment.
   b) The natural rate of unemployment is fixed and thus cannot change over time.
   c) There is no trade-off, even in the short run, between wage inflation and unemployment.
   d) There is no business cycle, as the economy is always near the natural rate of unemployment.
   e) All of the above.

7. Why has the expectations-augmented Phillips curve featuring the natural rate of unemployment lost favour?
   a) It fails to account for the phenomenon of persistently high unemployment coupled with low inflation and price stability.
   b) The macro economy is reverting back to the natural rate of unemployment.
   c) New evidence supports the view that the natural rate of unemployment has no relationship with the actual rate of unemployment.
   d) Evidence that inflationary expectations do not matter.
   e) Evidence that wages are becoming more downwardly flexible and are thus adjusted to take account of adverse market conditions.

8. The idea of hysteresis in unemployment means that adverse shocks to labour demand become permanent instead of eventually reverting back toward the original labour market equilibrium. All of the following are microeconomic mechanisms that are thought to contribute to this phenomenon *except* which?
   a) A decay in the human capital of unemployed workers
   b) A wage-determination mechanism dominated by the insider parties of incumbent employees and employers
   c) Strong wage growth for incumbent employees
   d) Very flexible wage-employment contracts that allow employers to adjust wages and employment levels in response to changes in market conditions
   e) Generous unemployment insurance payments that are paid for long durations of joblessness

9. Why was the Phillips curve model so popular with policy makers in the 1960s?
   a) It was thought that by using stimulative fiscal and monetary policies, one could permanently reduce the unemployment rate at virtually no economic cost.
   b) It was thought that by using stimulative fiscal and monetary policies, one could permanently reduce the unemployment rate in exchange for higher wage inflation.
   c) It was thought that by restructuring labour markets, one could permanently reduce the unemployment rate.
   d) It was thought that by increasing the unemployment rate, one could guarantee long-run price stability.
   e) None of the above.

10. Incomes policies refer to which of the following types of interventions?
   a) Policies designed to restrict aggregate supply
   b) Monetary policy designed to reduce the recessionary gap
   c) Policies designed to encourage wage and price flexibility
   d) Fiscal policy designed to reduce an inflationary gap
   e) None of the above

Answers to Multiple Choice Questions

1. A   Responses B and E make sense, but they are not the essence of the Phillips curve. Response C is a variable in the Phillips curve, but that says nothing about another key variable, the rate of wage inflation. Response D is illogical.

2. D   The natural rate of unemployment is independent of the stage of the business cycle and depends on factors such as the structure of labour markets, labour market policy, and demographics. All of the other statements are true and are made explicit in the textbook.

3. E   All of the other responses are elements that are mentioned in the textbook in the development of the Phillips-curve model.

4. B   The natural rate of unemployment increased over the period, which posed a challenge to the Phillips-curve approach. All of the other statements are true, and responses D and A are very similar.

5. D   This event corresponds to a movement along the short-run Phillips curve. All of the other statements are true and are made explicit in the textbook.

6. A   Statement B is totally false. For response C, there is often a short-run trade-off between wage inflation and unemployment, but it is ephemeral. Response D is nonsensical, as the economy is rarely at the natural rate of unemployment.

7. A   For response B, the opposite is true. The opposite of response C is the essence of the theory of hysteresis. Responses D and E are totally false.

8. D   The opposite of response D applies, as the hysteresis is thought to be associated with wage inflexibility.

9. B   For response A, it was never believed that there would be no economic cost, only a low economic cost. Response C refers to an idea that arrived in the 1980s and 1990s. For response D, long-run price stability was not an important policy objective, as the goal was to reduce unemployment.

10. C   The opposite applies for response A. Both responses B and D correspond to restrictive demand-management policies.